Phonics Bug

Teaching and Assessment Guide

Interactive synthetic phonics for reading and spelling

Key Stage 1 (P2-P3)

Joyce Watson & Rhona Johnston

Contents

Welcome to *Phonics Bug* 3

Teaching synthetic phonics using *Phonics Bug* 4

Teaching syllables 11

Phonics Bug Teaching Software navigation and controls 14

Guided independent work 20

Phonics Bug decodable readers 24

Phonics Bug eBooks and *Bug Club* 25

Phonics Bug components 26

Bug Club components 28

Assessing progress 30
- Before starting 30
- Assessment and catch-up work in preparation for Key Stage 1 32
- Assessment 35
- Assessment sheets 37

Guide to teaching Sessions 43

Daily lesson plans 45

Alphabetic overlay 120

Welcome to Phonics Bug

Overview

Teach
Teach whole-class phonics using the *Phonics Bug* teaching software and lesson plans for each Unit. Make use of the opportunities that whole-class teaching provides for ongoing observational assessment.

Practise
Consolidate pupils' understanding using the *Phonics Bug* PCMs and games, which can be found in the *Phonics Bug* teaching software.

Apply
Allocate the decodable readers and eBooks, matched to each Unit, to help pupils practise reading, ensuring that they approach any unfamiliar words by using their knowledge of phonics to decode the word. Extra breadth and variety is provided by the *Bug Club* books and eBooks.

Assess
Assess children's knowledge and understanding using the assessments in the *Phonics Bug Teaching and Assessment Guides* and the online tools. Keep children in the whole-class teaching programme, and provide extra catch-up for slower learners. Use the *Phonics Bug Prepare and Assess Handbook* and online resources to prepare children for the Phonics Screening Check in Year 1.

Phonics Bug is the dedicated phonics strand of *Bug Club*, a core reading programme that can be used for independent and guided reading from Reception (Primary 1) to Year 6 (Primary 7). Together, *Phonics Bug* and *Bug Club* provide a complete solution to helping you teach children to read in Reception (P1) and Key Stage 1 (P2 and 3).

This Teaching and Assessment Guide focuses on *Phonics Bug*. The programme is a balanced approach to the teaching of reading using synthetic phonics (see page 4 for details). It simultaneously teaches the segmentation of words for spelling, and develops phonemic awareness skills. The programme is the product of seven years' research in Clackmannanshire, Scotland, which produced remarkable gains in reading and spelling among those children who followed the programme (the full research details are available within the software).

This interactive edition of the programme unites the proven pedagogy of the original programme with the most engaging and motivating delivery methods. This edition comprises:

- Teaching and Assessment Guides for Reception (P1) and Key Stage 1 (P2 and 3)
- Flashcards
- Photocopy Masters
- 134 decodable readers
- 134 eBooks and activities, available on www.bugclub.co.uk
- Teaching software and pupil games, available on www.bugclub.co.uk

Phonics Bug Quick Start

1) Go to **Before starting the programme** (page 30) and check that your children are ready to begin the programme.
2) Open the software and read **Software navigation and controls** (page 14).
3) Read the **Guide to teaching Sessions** (page 43).
4) Start using the programme!

Essential tips

- The basic Revision and Lesson elements of the Teaching Sessions are essential and should be carried out at a brisk pace. This may not be possible to begin with but, as you and your children get used to the format, the pace will quicken. The independent work provided by the PCMs and games can then be tailored to meet the needs of individuals or groups.
- Units 13–30 need not be run on consecutive days. Teaching of these units is intended to continue through Years 1 and 2 (Primary 2 and 3), with the majority being taught in Year 1 (Primary 2).
- You will need an interactive whiteboard, but if you do not have access to one, simply use the Flashcards and make sure you have a large magnetic letter board and letters for modelling. (The Flashcards are available as printed items and are also downloadable from the software. They include picture stimuli, letters, words and sentences.)
- Your class may need small magnetic letter boards and letters for individual use or to share between two, as your professional judgement dictates. However, many of your children will now be using pencil and paper.

Teaching synthetic phonics using *Phonics Bug*

What is synthetic phonics?

In synthetic phonics the graphemes and corresponding phonemes are taught just before the introduction of words that contain these letters. To read these words, children are taught to pronounce the individual phonemes (sounds) associated with the graphemes (letters) they see, and then to blend them together (synthesise) to form the word. (In this programme, we use slashes / / to denote phonemes and inverted commas ' ' to denote graphemes.) The process is as follows:

- Children *see* a word, e.g. "cat"; it is not pronounced for them.
- They break it down into its individual letters (graphemes) and pronounce the corresponding sounds (phonemes) for each letter in turn: /c/ /a/ /t/
- Then they blend the separate phonemes together to form the word.

This process is known as **blending**. (See page 46 in the Reception Teaching Guide for more details.)

Synthetic phonics teaches letter sounds very rapidly, explicitly showing children how to build up words with letters from the start, and always includes blending with printed words.

Synthetic phonics does not normally teach spelling, but *Phonics Bug* does teach spelling by reversing the reading process described above, i.e.

- Children *hear* a word, e.g. "cat" and say it.
- They say the first phoneme: /c/
- They write the corresponding grapheme: 'c'.
- They say the word again and say the next phoneme: /a/
- They write the corresponding grapheme: 'a', and so on.

This process is known as **segmenting**, and is followed by the children reading the word they have produced by sounding and blending.

In our approach, both blending for reading and segmenting for spelling are fully scaffolded. We model for the children how to sound and blend words for reading, but in each lesson children must attempt to sound and blend words for themselves to find out how they are pronounced. We also model for the children how to segment for spelling and continue to scaffold the children through the process with each word they spell. This ensures that they identify each phoneme and choose the appropriate grapheme in turn, until the word is spelt.

Synthetic phonics differs from analytic phonics in that in analytic phonics children are shown word families. For example, they may be introduced to the letter sound 'c', and then be shown a list of words all starting with the same letter sound, e.g. 'cat, cake, cut, cup'. Sounding and blending starts when all the letters of the alphabet have been taught in the beginning, middle and final positions of words, whereas in synthetic phonics this process starts after the first few letter sounds have been taught.

Programme rationale

Pace and order of teaching

Phonics Bug teaches a new grapheme and related phoneme, or alternative spellings to previously-taught phonemes, in every Phoneme Session. This fast pace, backed up by daily revision of past teaching, has proved the most effective and successful method of phonic training. This means that the basic 40+ phonemes (Units 1–12), and then the alternative spellings of these phonemes (Units 13–30), are acquired quickly, and early reading skills develop rapidly. Decodable readers are introduced after just 10 days' teaching at the end of Unit 2. This enables children to apply the taught strategies and enjoy contextualised reading early on.

The order of grapheme introduction (see page 7) ensures that children start reading and spelling a wide range of words at the earliest possible stage.

Introduction of graphemes and phonemes

In *Phonics Bug* children are taught graphemes and phonemes at the same time. The research study showed that children progressed quickly if they learnt about phonemes in the context of letters and print right from the start of the phonics teaching.

Blending and segmenting

In *Phonics Bug* blending for reading and segmenting for spelling are given equal prominence, and taught to be reversible, though blending is always taught first in a Session.

Introduction of letter names

The names of letters can be taught first, via the Alphabet song and magnetic letters. During the seven or so years over which the programme has been in use, children have not had any difficulties learning both letter names and sounds early on. One of the benefits of this is that any child who misses a Session will know the names of the letters they have missed. In many cases the letter names give a good guide to the letter sounds. Other benefits include assisting with the language of instruction and oral spelling. However, the teaching of letter names is optional in this programme.

Multi-sensory learning

Bringing a multi-sensory element to the teaching of phonics is widely recognised to be hugely beneficial to its effectiveness. *Phonics Bug* recommends the use of magnetic letters and boards to consolidate children's blending and segmenting abilities. Mini-magnetic boards are to be used by pairs (or individuals) during and after the Whole Class Teaching Sessions. The interactive whiteboard acts as an electronic magnetic letter board for teacher demonstration.

Additionally, teaching the formation of the letters at the same time as the sounds helps to consolidate the letters in memory. By KS1, many children will be able to write the letters and can dispense with the individual boards.

Teaching synthetic phonics using *Phonics Bug*

Handwriting

Phonics Bug does not necessarily seek to replace your normal handwriting programme, but it does work on the premise that letter formation is a helpful kinaesthetic consolidation of grapheme acquisition and spelling. Therefore, the teaching of letter formation accompanies the introduction of every grapheme and the talking-through element of such teaching also supports the children's cognitive processes.

Note: The letter formation is non-cursive, so if you teach cursive handwriting, you may wish to omit this feature from your *Phonics Bug* lessons and deal with the handwriting separately.

Less common grapheme–phoneme correspondences

Based on experience of the hundreds of children who have been through the programme over the last ten or so years, *Phonics Bug* takes the view that children are best served by learning the basic 40+ grapheme–phoneme correspondences in the first year at school. The less frequent pronunciations, particularly for vowels, are taught when the children are secure in the basic principles, normally in the second year of school, although the teaching of common vowel digraphs and trigraphs too can be started in the first year at school.

Very minor variations in pronunciation are not taught separately, and this has been found to pose no difficulties for the children. We do, however, provide notes within daily lesson plans, which outline areas where you may want to adopt your own regional pronunciation.

High-frequency (common) words and irregular words

High-frequency decodable common words are included for reading and spelling throughout *Phonics Bug*. For Units 1–12, these are listed in the chart on page 5 of the *Reception Assessment and Teaching Guide* under 'Decodable words' and are always taught by sounding and blending. On page 7 of this Key Stage 1 Guide, there is also a list of 'Not fully decodable (irregular) words' covered in Units 1–12; the term used in *Letters and Sounds* is 'tricky words'. Table 2 on page 7 lists those Irregular or High-frequency words covered in Units 13–30. Many of these words have spellings that have irregular pronunciations; these words are always deemed 'tricky', e.g. 'one'. However, some of the words in the list have regular pronunciations and become fully decodable later on as the phonics teaching progresses; for example, 'like' becomes completely decodable when split digraphs are taught. Children are encouraged to use their phonic knowledge to help them decode these words as far as possible; you can point out and talk through the irregular aspects to help them read the words. (See page 52 in the *Reception Assessment and Teaching Guide* for more details of how to do this). You may want to introduce additional irregular words as deemed necessary by the content of your particular reading schemes. You may also want to practise the irregular words throughout the school day. However, these words, and the high-frequency decodable words, are never taught as 'sight' words using flash cards.

For a chart showing the *Phonics Bug* progression in irregular and high-frequency words at Key Stage 1 (Primary 2 & 3), see Table 2 on page 7 of this guide.

Language Sessions

Language Sessions occur at the end of each Unit. These Sessions combine the teaching of irregular and/or high-frequency words with using words in the context of captions and sentences. The acquisition of skills for reading single words is only part of the reading process. To read with fluency and comprehension, children need to apply and develop the skills taught during the synthetic phonics teaching element of the programme. The Language Sessions serve to consolidate the teaching of reading and spelling in the Phoneme Sessions, and promote early comprehension skills.

Comprehension is not an end product. It is a process that occurs during active interaction between the reader and the text. In the *Phonics Bug* Language Sessions, a progressive programme of text-related directed activities has been assembled to enable children to progress from single-word reading to reading intelligently to grasp meaning from the text.

Guided independent work

Although *Phonics Bug* is delivered through teacher-modelling and rehearsal with the whole class, there are also resources for guided independent work. These can be tailored to meet the needs of an individual or groups and to give you a chance to work with children who may need more help to consolidate their learning. The resources consist of one photocopy master (PCM) for each Session, plus five categories of pupil games per Unit: Sounds, Names, Reading, Spelling and Language.

Introduction of graded readers

Phonics Bug is supported by decodable readers which match the order of phoneme introduction. When the children have completed Unit 2 of *Phonics Bug*, they will have acquired a sufficient number of grapheme-phoneme correspondences to start reading their own books. This should be a motivating and enjoyable experience for them.

There are books to match each Unit of the teaching programme. These will help children to practise and consolidate their learning at each stage.

Before, during, and after the introduction of the *Phonics Bug* readers, children should be exposed constantly to a rich and varied diet of book experiences to ensure their enthusiasm for reading is nurtured, their comprehension skills are being developed, and their speaking and listening skills are extended.

Speaking and listening skills

The *Phonics Bug* strategy of teacher-modelling and rehearsal for teaching reading and spelling provides opportunities for pupils to be both spectators and participants. As spectators, they listen to words and structures; as participants, they try them out. While sharing pupil magnetic boards, working in pairs or small groups, pupils respond to each other, learning to adjust the language to suit the situation and the response of partners. Using graded readers, the teacher can encourage pupils to express opinions and explore, develop and sustain ideas through talk and discussion.

Teaching synthetic phonics using *Phonics Bug*

Teaching sequence

Phonics Bug is structured with Phoneme Sessions and Language Sessions (see pages 7–9 for the breakdown of the 'Teaching Elements' in both these Session types). This structure fully supports the daily phonic teaching sequence recommended by the Primary National Strategy in the renewed Framework. The following diagram illustrates the alignment of the *Phonics Bug* lesson structure to this teaching sequence.

Recommended Teaching Sequence	*Phonics Bug* Lesson Structure
Introduce ▼	Learning intentions and outcomes for the day are discussed at the start of the lesson. The daily lesson plans in this guide provide an overview of these learning intentions/outcomes.
Revisit and Review ▼	Every Phoneme Session begins with Revision to review previous learning. In Reception (P1) the Revision is not just of the previous day's target grapheme-phoneme correspondence, but also of blending for reading and segmenting for spelling of the relevant words. In Key Stage 1 (P2&3) the Revision is sometimes a review of previous learning which links with the planned teaching for that day.
Teach ▼	Every Phoneme and Language Session is composed of Teaching Elements (e.g. Sounds, Reading, Spelling etc) which are easily navigated to structure the new phonic teaching. The teaching of grapheme-phoneme correspondences and high-frequency (common) words is covered.
Practise ▼	Practise opportunities are available in the following areas: • 'Follow-up' parts of the lessons • Unit-linked pupil games • Unit-linked photocopy masters • 'Free-teaching' within the software's Magnetic Board
Apply ▼	Language Sessions provide opportunities to apply developing phonic skills to reading, spelling and writing captions and sentences. This application also covers Irregular (not fully decodable) common words. In addition, phonic skills can be applied when using the linked decodable readers, starting as early as Unit 2 of *Phonics Bug*.
Assess Learning	Assessment guidance and materials provided within this guide and in the software enable ongoing formative assessment during the daily lessons and summative assessment at regular periods through the programme. The *Phonics Bug Prepare and Assess Handbook* and online resources can be used to prepare children for the Phonics Screening Check in Year 1.

Teaching synthetic phonics using *Phonics Bug*

Programme structure

Unit structure

The following tables show what is covered in each of the Units of *Phonics Bug*, and relate the content to the 'Phases' of progression recommended by the *Primary National Strategy in Guidance for practitioners and teachers on progression and pace in the teaching of phonics* (September 2006). (See also the section '*Phonics Bug* and the Phases of Progression' on page 9.)

For reference purposes, Table 1 (covering Units 1–12) shows what will have already been taught in Reception (Primary 1).

Table 1 Units 1–12 of *Phonics Bug Reception (Primary 1)*

Phase	Unit	Focus	Not fully decodable words (Irregular words)
2	1	s a t p	
	2	i n m d	
	3	g o c k	to
	4	ck e u r	the, no, go
	5	h b f, ff l, ll ss	I, into
3	6	j v w x	me, be
	7	y z, zz qu	he, my, by
	8	ch sh th ng	they, she
	9	ai ee igh oa oo (long) oo (short)	we, are
	10	ar or ur ow oi	you, her
	11	ear air ure er	all, was
4	12	Adjacent consonants (cvcc, ccvc, ccvcc, cccvc, cccvcc)	said, have, like, so, do, some, come, were, there, little, one, when, out, what

The following table (Table 2) shows what is covered in each of Units 13–30, the Key Stage 1 (Primary 2 & 3) part of the programme.

Table 2 Units 13–30 of *Phonics Bug Key Stage 1 (Primary 2 & 3)*

Phase	Unit	Focus	Irregular/High-frequency words
5	13	zh wh ph	oh their
	14	ay a–e eigh/ey/ei (long a)	Mr Mrs
	15	ea e–e ie/ey/y (long e)	looked called asked
	16	ie i–e y i (long i)	water where
	17	ow o–e o/oe (long o)	who again
	18	ew ue u–e (long u) u/oul (short oo)	thought through
	19	aw au al	work laughed because
	20	ir er ear	Thursday Saturday thirteen thirty
	21	ou oy	different any many
	22	ere/eer are/ear	eyes friends
	23	c k ck ch	two once
	24	ce/ci/cy sc/stl se	great clothes
	25	ge/gi/gy dge	It's I'm I'll I've
	26	le mb kn/gn wr	don't can't didn't
	27	tch sh ea (w)a o	first second third
6	28	suffix morphemes ing ed	clearing gleaming rained mailed
	29	plural morphemes s es	men mice feet teeth sheep
	30	prefix morphemes re un prefix+root+suffix	vowel consonant prefix suffix syllable

Session structure

The following table illustrates the breakdown of Teaching Elements in Phoneme and Language Sessions.

- Every Phoneme and Language Session is composed of the same Teaching Elements.
- Each Phoneme Session starts with Revision to review previous learning. This covers new graphemes, and blending for reading and segmenting for spelling.
- Each Lesson within the Phoneme Session starts with introducing the new grapheme-phoneme correspondence for the day, sometimes using a fun video clip. Children examine Asset bank words in order to highlight the new grapheme in beginning, middle or end positions. Some Asset bank words are beyond the decodable experience of the children at this point and so are not intended for blending and reading; those that are will appear for blending in the Reading part of the Lesson.

Teaching synthetic phonics using *Phonics Bug*

Phoneme Session

Teaching Element	Description
Alphabet song	Sing the Alphabet song
Revision	
Letters and Sounds	Quick-fire practice of previously taught grapheme-phoneme correspondences
Reading	Children practise reading words composed of previously taught grapheme-phoneme correspondences
Writing and Spelling	Children practise spelling and letter formation using previously taught graphemes and words
Lesson	
Introduction	Discuss learning intentions and outcomes for the day
Sounds	Children are introduced to new grapheme with corresponding phoneme, highlighting its position in words from the Asset bank
Reading	Children blend phonemes for reading words
Spelling	Children segment words for spelling
Writing	Children form letters to cement letter-sound correspondences
Follow-up	Children are introduced to guided independent work, consolidating any teaching from Lesson
Plenary	Discuss learning outcomes
Alphabet song	Sing the Alphabet song

Language Session

Teaching Element	Description
Alphabet song	Sing the Alphabet song
Introduction	Discuss learning intentions and outcomes for the day
Irregular/High-frequency words	
Reading	Children read irregular/high-frequency word(s)
Spelling	Children spell irregular/high-frequency word(s)
Lesson	
Reading	Children read captions and sentences
Spelling/Writing	Children write captions and sentences
Follow-up	Basic comprehension and introduction of guided independent work
Plenary	Discuss learning outcomes
Alphabet song	Sing the Alphabet song

Description of the blending process

We recommend a smooth articulation of the sounds for blending.

- Pupils *see* the word but are *not told* what it is, e.g. 'whip' (see the electronic version of Unit 13, target phoneme /wh/ under the Lesson Reading tab).
- Pupils sound out each separate phoneme in the word: /wh/ /i/ /p/.
- They repeat each phoneme slowly and smoothly, stretching each sound out into its adjoining sound without a pause, and giving the same emphasis to each sound, blending the sounds together to achieve the single sound of the complete word. This is known as 'co-articulation'. In the electronic version, one child physically carries out the blending process of the letters by pushing along the green arrow, while the rest of the children blend the sounds together to read the word.
- Children read the word as one complete sound.
- Note: By clicking the Blend button, children can hear and see the automatic blending of the first few words. By clicking on Undo, the children can repeat the modelled process for themselves.

Procedure for spelling words of one syllable using the *Phonics Bug* whole-class teaching software

This example is from KS1 Unit 15 (/ee/ written as 'ea'). Children *do not* see the word first. Click Lesson. Click the Spelling tab and then select the Words tab on the Spelling screen. Click Say to hear the word "beach". Say the word. You may wish to put it into a sentence to ensure that children understand its meaning. The children (or child, where appropriate):

- Say the word "beach", say the first phoneme /b/, drag up the lowercase letter (grapheme) 'b' and place it in the leftmost empty box shown on the Work area.
- Say the word "beach" again, say the second phoneme sounding /ee/, drag up the graphemes 'e' and 'a' and place the digraph 'ea' in the empty double space next to the 'b' on the Work area.
- Say the word "beach" again, say the last phoneme /ch/, drag up the graphemes 'c' and 'h' and place the digraph 'ch' in the empty double box next to the 'ea' on the Work area.
- Push the letters together by clicking on the green arrow symbol and moving it along to the right while all the children blend the sounds together out loud to say "beach".
- Spell the word "beach" orally using the letter names b e a c h, "beach".
- Click Undo if you want to repeat the blending procedure.

Procedure for spelling using pupil magnetic boards

This example is from KS1 Unit 14 (/ai/ written as 'ay'). Children *do not see* the word first. Click Lesson. Click Spelling and select the Pictures tab. Scroll for the picture of a tray and click Show. The children:

- Say the word "tray", say the first phoneme /t/, find the magnetic letter 't' and place it on the left side of their magnetic boards.
- Say "tray" again, say the next phoneme /r/, find the magnetic letter 'r' and place it next to the letter 't'.
- Say "tray" again, say the last phoneme /ai/, find the magnetic letters 'a' and 'y' and place the digraph 'ay' next to the 'r'.

Teaching synthetic phonics using *Phonics Bug*

Now you can use the interactive whiteboard to help the children check their spelling. With your support, ask a child to:

- Go to the Work area, select the Pictures tab and scroll for the picture of a tray.
- Click Show, hear and say the word "tray" and drag up the letters placing them in the boxes provided on the Work area.
- Click on the green arrow, moving it along to the right as all the children blend the sounds together to say "t-r-ay" and push their letters together on their magnetic boards blending the sound together to make "tray".
- Spell the word "tray" orally using the letter names t r a y, "tray".

Phonics Bug and the Phases of Progression

Phase 5

Units 13–27 of *Phonics Bug* offer coverage of Phase 5 phonic progression, but also match the recommended teaching and learning in *Letters and Sounds* (DfES, 2007). The following tables illustrate how the *Phonics Bug* daily lesson plans ensure complete coverage of the *Letters and Sounds* Phase 5 recommendations, as well as offering a structured route through the recommended teaching and learning.

Note: Alternative pronunciations of known graphemes for reading are covered within the *Phonics Bug* programme at the point of teaching the alternative spellings. For instance, the pronunciation of the known grapheme 'c' in the word 'cent' is taught in Unit 24, when all the spelling alternatives for the /s/ phoneme are taught.

Table 1 *Graphemes for Reading within Phonics Bug Key Stage 1*

Letters and Sounds Phase 5 Teaching: new grapheme-phoneme correspondences for reading	*Phonics Bug* Unit
s for /zh/	Unit 13
wh	Unit 13
ph	Unit 13
ay	Unit 14
a-e	Unit 14
ea	Unit 15
e-e	Unit 15
ie	Unit 16
i-e	Unit 16
oe	Unit 17
o-e	Unit 17
ew	Unit 18
ue	Unit 18
u-e	Unit 18
aw	Unit 19
au	Unit 19
ir	Unit 20
ou	Unit 21
oy	Unit 21
ear/ere/eer	Unit 22
air/are/ear	Unit 22

NB: Subsequent sessions could be said to be phonic rules, not new graphemes.

Table 2 Alternative spellings within *Phonics Bug Key Stage 1*

Letters and Sounds Phase 5 Teaching: Alternative spellings for each phoneme	*Phonics Bug* Unit
w / wh	Unit 13
f / ph	Unit 13
ai / ay / a-e / eigh / ey / ei	Unit 14
ee / ea / e-e / ie / y / ey / eo	Unit 15
igh / ie / i-e / y / i / ey	Unit 16
oa / ow / o-e / oe / o	Unit 17
oo / ew / ue / u-e /ui / ou	Unit 18
oo / u / oul	Unit 18
or / aw / au / al	Unit 19
ur / ir / er / ear	Unit 20
ow / ou	Unit 21
oi / oy	Unit 21
ear / ere / eer	Unit 22
air / are / ear	Unit 22
c / k / ck / qu / x / ch	Unit 23
s / c / sc	Unit 24
j / g / dge	Unit 25
m / mb	Unit 26
n / kn / gn	Unit 26
r / wr	Unit 26
ch / tch	Unit 27
sh / ch / t / ss / s / c	Unit 27
e / ea	Unit 27
o /(w)a	Unit 27
u / o	Unit 27

So, *Phonics Bug Key Stage 1 (Primary 2 & 3)* starts with the Phase 5 skills of learning new graphemes for reading and then moves through the alternative pronunciations and spellings of all graphemes.

This programme provides inbuilt formative and summative assessment that follows closely the phonic phases of progression: Assessments 8 and 9 examine the children's ability to spell using these new graphemes and spelling alternatives. Assessments 10 and 11 then examine reading skills. Suggestions for catch-up work are made after each assessment.

Phase 6

Phonics Bug supports learning in Phase 6 by introducing more complex, multi-syllabic words and morphemes such as prefixes and suffixes. This teaching occurs in the Phoneme and Language Sessions and in Guided independent work, with the children also covering less-common grapheme–phoneme correspondences and phonic irregularities, and applying their phonic skills in a wide range of reading and spelling settings.

Teaching synthetic phonics using *Phonics Bug*

The children will become increasingly fluent in sounding and blending unfamiliar words, and will develop more automatic recognition of familiar ones based on a sound foundation of phonic skills, so you will be able to devote more and more time to developing their reading comprehension. Phase 6 skills are assessed in Assessments 12 and 13. Suggestions for catch-up work are also provided.

Delivery method

Phonics Bug has been developed for use on an interactive whiteboard.

However, if you do not have access to an interactive whiteboard you can still deliver *Phonics Bug*. You can use non-interactive data projection facilities, and use the mouse to control the elements on the screen. For activities that require free-writing, you will have to use a conventional whiteboard or a flip chart.

If you do not have access to any kind of data projection facilities, the resources you will need are available on the software (page 19), all clearly referenced to their relevant Units, ready for printing off and making into cards (these include picture stimuli, letters, words and sentences). You will also need a large magnetic board and upper- and lowercase magnetic letters, plus a whiteboard or flip chart for writing on.

How to run the programme
Duration of programme

Units 1–12 of *Phonics Bug* can take as little as 16 weeks to complete, while a little more time can be taken with Units 13–30, the teaching being intended to continue through Years 1 and 2 (Primary 2 and 3). As a general rule, you should aim to complete of Units 13–27 within Year 1 (Primary 2), enabling Year 2 (Primary 3) to be an opportunity to consolidate the word recognition skills from the first two years of schooling. To prepare the children adequately for the Year 1 Phonics Screening Check, Units 13–27 should be completed by half term of the summer term. You should therefore try to maintain a fairly brisk pace with Units 13–27, whereas Units 28–30 can be taken at a slower pace. However, you should, of course, use your professional judgement to moderate the pace in accordance with the needs of the class. You may, for example, decide to take a day or two after each Unit to consolidate your teaching.

While reading will become more fluent and automatic in Year 2, learning about word structure and spelling will then continue in Key Stage 2 (Primary 4–7).

The Sessions for Units 13–30 do not need to be delivered on consecutive days, but you should try to maintain the brisk pace of lesson delivery as far as possible in order to achieve maximum benefits from the programme.

Daily time allocation

The time it takes to deliver the Whole-Class Sessions will depend on your familiarity with the programme and how you choose to use the more flexible elements such as the video clips, alphabet song and so on. The independent work provided by the PCMs does not necessarily have to be done immediately after the Whole-Class Session, but it should be completed before the next Session if possible. The games can be used as consolidation work at any point in the day, and are ideal for slower learners if appropriate to their learning needs.

Classroom organisation

It is recommended that the children are kept together for the Daily Sessions in spite of different ability levels. This has been shown to foster a sense of social inclusion and boost the performance of the children who are progressing more slowly. However, you will need to differentiate your questioning within the lesson to ensure that all children are fully engaged. Some of the follow-up activities are provided at different levels of ability to support differentiation.

Children usually sit together on the floor in front of the interactive whiteboard at the start of the daily Teaching Sessions for the Introduction, Revision, Lesson Sounds, Lesson Visual Search and Lesson Reading elements. The children return to their seats when the Spelling element is reached.

Classroom management of the magnetic letters

During Key Stage 1, you may find that, even early on, the class no longer needs to use their individual magnetic boards for spelling and letter formation with the relevant interactive whiteboard teaching elements. However, if you feel your children still need them, they can be provided with small magnetic letter boards and sets of magnetic letters. One board between two is ideal. Paired work is useful because it enables the children to explain what they are doing and hear explanations from others, and in so doing consolidate the learning. (Additional magnetic letters will be required when double letters are being practised.)

The boards can be available on the children's tables, and the children can return to their seats when the Spelling Teaching Element is reached during the Daily Phoneme Session to build the target words themselves on their boards. As children become more advanced they will begin to spell using pencil and paper instead of magnetic letters.

Experienced practitioners of the programme have found it useful to place the photocopiable alphabetic overlay (see page 120) on top of each of the boards.

The magnetic letters should be placed in their correct positions on the overlay at the end of each Session, thereby consolidating knowledge of the alphabet and making it easier to see if any letters are missing.

If you feel your Year 1 and 2 (Primary 2 and 3) children are ready to exchange their magnetic boards and letters for paper and pencils, then of course you can do this.

Teaching syllables

Recognition of syllables is a critical word-attack skill for both reading and spelling. Breaking words into syllables is a strategy that should be taught for both reading and spelling. A syllable is a word or part of a word that can be spoken independently – e.g. the word "alphabet" has 3 syllables, al/pha/bet. Children need to know that:

- all words have at least one syllable
- each syllable has one vowel sound
- long words are made up of short syllables
- syllables can be one letter or a group of letters, one of which must be a vowel sound (including 'y' used as a vowel).

Prior to teaching about syllables, children need to have mastered the basic vowel and consonant sounds.

What is a 'syllable'?

Use the following procedure to help children understand what a syllable is:

1. Write the word "fluff" on the board. Ask the children to say the word "fluff".
2. Clap your hands once saying "fluff". Ask the children to clap their hands once, saying "fluff".
3. Explain that the word "fluff" has one beat – i.e. one syllable.
4. Write the word "fluffy" on the board. Ask the children to say the word "fluffy".
5. Clap your hands twice saying "fluffy". Ask the children: How many beats does the word "fluffy" have? How many syllables does the word "fluffy" have?
6. Do one or two more examples on the board – e.g. sun/sunny, fun/funny.

Number of syllables equals number of 'beats'

Use the following procedure to help children understand that you can tell the number of syllables in a word by the number of 'beats' in the word.

1. Use your class children's names. Chant each name, clapping hands for each syllable as each name is pronounced. For example, chant and clap "Kate". Repeat, chanting and clapping "Kate".
2. Ask the children: How many beats does "Kate" have? How many syllables does "Kate" have? Ensure they understand that "Kate" has one beat and one syllable.
3. Repeat the chanting and clapping activity with two-syllable names (e.g. "Samir", "Alice"), three-syllable names (e.g. "Samantha", "Benjamin"), and so on.
4. Prepare and give to each child a sheet with 3 columns (see below).

5. Write the children's names on the board, one at a time, asking the children to pronounce the name and write it in the column for one, two or three syllables. Do an example on the board:

Kate (Kate)   Samir (Sa/mir)   Samantha(Sa/man/tha)

Number of syllables		
1	2	3
Kate	Samir	Samantha

Each syllable has one vowel sound

Vowel digraphs count as one vowel.

1. Draw three columns on the board (see below).
2. Select your own words as appropriate for each column to be completed, writing each on the board, one at a time and separated from the table on the board.
3. Ask the children to pronounce each word and say which column to write it in – one, two, three syllables – e.g. "school", "a/cross", "ba/na/na".
4. Do two or three more examples, including words with a vowel digraph, e.g. "train", "boat/ing", "ap/point/ment".
5. Reinforce the idea that each syllable has one vowel sound, and that vowel digraphs count as one vowel.

Number of syllables		
1	2	3
school	across	banana
train	boating	appointment

6. Draw four columns on the board (see below).
7. Write examples on the board separate from the table before, e.g. "lamp", "basket", "Saturday", "sail".
8. Demonstrate with each word how to complete the table. For example, write "lamp" in column 1. Ask the children: How many vowels? Write the answer in column 2. Ask the children: How many vowel sounds? Write the answer in column 3. Ask the children: How many syllables? Write the answer in column 4.
9. Repeat for each of the other examples. Note in particular the word "sail" – a vowel digraph counts as one vowel sound in a syllable.

Syllables			
Word	Number of vowels	Number of vowel sounds	Number of syllables
lamp	1	1	1
basket	2	2	2
Saturday	3	3	3
sail	2	1	1

Teaching syllables

Syllable categories

The following table outlines basic rules for syllabification, and is provided as background information for teachers.

Category rules	Examples
1. A vowel digraph counts as one vowel sound in a syllable.	pearl count [both one syllable]
2. Compound words are split between each part of the compound.	milk/man foot/ball
3. Silent 'e' does not count as a vowel sound in a syllable.	star stare [both one syllable]
4. When two consonants are between two vowels, the division of syllables is usually between the two consonants.	rabbit rab/bit sister sis/ter
5. When a vowel is followed by a single consonant, the consonant usually starts the second syllable.	before be/fore vacant va/cant
6. When a word ends in 'le' and a consonant precedes it, the consonant goes with the 'le' syllable.	table ta/ble candle can/dle
7. If a word contains a prefix, the division comes between the prefix and the root word.	return re/turn explain ex/plain
8. If a word has a suffix, the division comes between the suffix and the root word.	likely like/ly smiling smil/ing

Strategies for reading and spelling syllables

Reading words of more than one syllable

In reading activities, children will be breaking down words into syllables visually. The children SEE the printed word and will need to be able to:

1. Separate the target printed word into syllables.	pumpkin pump/kin
2. Sound and blend successive letters of each syllable.	p-u-m-p pump k-i-n kin
3. Sound and blend successive syllables to read.	/pump/ /kin/ pumpkin
4. Read the whole two-syllable word.	pumpkin

Sometimes the first sub-unit will end with a consonant, and the second sub-unit will start with the same consonant, e.g. "applaud", "ap/plaud". We recommend sounding the /p/ twice when saying the syllables separately, but, when it comes to blending the two syllables together, both /p/ sounds should taper into one sound. This is demonstrated in the software for the lesson.

Spelling words of more than one syllable

In spelling activities, children will be dividing words into syllables by auditory segmentation. The children HEAR the target word and will need to be able to:

1. Pronounce the target spelling word.	pumpkin
2. Break the word into syllables, pronouncing each syllable.	pump/ /kin/
3. Segment and spell the successive letters of each syllable.	p-u-m-p pump k-i-n kin
4. Sound and blend the successive syllables to say the word.	/pump/ /kin/ pumpkin
5. Spell the word orally using the letter names.	p u m p k i n pumpkin

Procedure for spelling words of more than one syllable using the *Phonics Bug* whole-class teaching software

This example is from Unit 13 (/f/ written as 'ph'). Children *do not see* the word first. Click Lesson. Click Spelling. Select the Pictures tab. Scroll for the picture of a dolphin. Click Show. With your support, the children (or a child, where appropriate):

- Say the word "dolphin" and say the two syllables **dol** and **phin** as indicated on the Work area by the two sets of empty boxes. (Note: If the word has three syllables this will be so indicated by three sets of empty boxes on the Work area.)
- Say the first syllable **dol**, say the successive phonemes /d/ /o/ /l/, drag up the successive graphemes 'd', 'o', 'l' to the first syllable boxes on the Work area and say the first syllable again: **dol**.
- Say the second syllable **fin**, say the successive phonemes /f/, /i/, /n/, drag up successive graphemes 'p' and 'h' (for the 'ph' /f/ digraph), 'i' and 'n' to the second syllable boxes on the Work area and say the second syllable again: **fin**. Push the letters together for each syllable by clicking on the green arrow symbol, moving it along to the right as before while the children blend the sounds together for the first syllable **dol** and for the second syllable **phin**.
- Sound and blend the successive syllables to say the word "dolphin".
- Spell the word "dolphin" orally using the letters names d o l p h i n, "dolphin".

Teaching syllables

Procedure for dictation

Note: In *Phonics Bug Key Stage 1 (Primary 2 & 3)* sentences for dictation have been designed to provide examples for dividing words into syllables according to different categories (see above, under 'Syllable categories').

1. Revise any particular point being stressed within the sentence being dictated, e.g. digraph combination(s), the inclusion of a word of more than one syllable and so on.
2. Slowly and distinctly dictate the sentence to be written.
3. Ask the class to repeat the sentence together.
4. Dictate the sentence again and ask the children to write it.
5. Ask some of the children to assist with the production of the sentence on the screen/board (with teacher writing the sentence, not the children).
6. Ask a child to read the sentence.
7. Children can then compare their sentence with that on the screen/board, writing corrections above any errors (for discussion with the teacher as soon as possible).
8. Repeat with the next sentence.

Dictation example

- The sentence you have in mind might be: *The teacher is in the school.*
- Write on the screen/board the syllable word *"teacher"*.
- Ask the children where the syllable breaks should be: *2 beats, 2 syllables, 2 vowels.*
- Ask a child to come out and put in the syllable break: *teach/er.*
- Remove from the board and remind the children to use the strategy for helping them to spell such words, breaking them into small parts, into syllables.
- Dictate the sentence *"The teacher is in the school."*

Understanding morphemes

In *Phonics Bug Reception (Primary 1)*, our beginning readers and spellers will have been using a phonemic approach based on letter–sound correspondences. In *Phonics Bug Key Stage 1 (Primary 2 and 3)*, this phonemic approach of connecting letters to sounds provides the children with a method for connecting letters to syllables which, in turn, will lead children to thinking about the relationship between letters and meaning, namely 'morphemes'.

'Morphemes' are the smallest units of meaning in language. A morpheme can be as small as a single letter, e.g. the words "a" and "I", or the letter 's' when added to a noun to make it plural as in "horses". A word can consist of only one morpheme (e.g. "horse"), two morphemes (e.g. "horse/s") or three or more morphemes (e.g "horse/back/rid/ing"). Understanding morphemes helps children to break down an unfamiliar word into meaningful parts, and to add morphemes to already known root words to make new words, thus extending their vocabulary.

Prefixes and suffixes are morphemes. A 'prefix' is a morpheme added to the beginning of a word to change its meaning, e.g. 'un' is the prefix in 'unlucky'. A 'suffix' is a morpheme added to the end of a word to change its tense (e.g. work/worked), number (house/houses) or word class (swim – verb; swimmer – noun). A 'root word' is a word to which prefixes and suffixes can be added to make other words, e.g. 'load' is the root word in 'unloading'.

In Units 28–29 of *Phonics Bug Key Stage 1 (Primary 2 & 3)*, children are introduced to suffixes with which they are already familiar – e.g. 'ing', 'ed', 's' and 'es', but now focusing on the morpheme meaning element. For example:

- 's' can be a morpheme added on to a word to make it plural (more than one) as in "dog/dogs";
- 'es' is another small plural morpheme used with words ending in 's', 'ss', 'x', 'sh' and 'ch' as in "bus/buses", "dress/dresses", "fox/foxes", "wish/wishes" and "arch/arches";
- 'ed' means something happening 'in the past' as in "work/worked";
- 'ing' means something happening now, 'in the present' as in "work/working".

In all the above examples, a single morpheme word becomes a two-morpheme word with the addition of a suffix morpheme.

In Unit 30, children are introduced to prefixes, focusing on the morpheme meaning element of the prefixes 're' and 'un'.

- 're' is a prefix morpheme and can mean "again" or "back" as in "turn/return";
- 'un' is a prefix morpheme and can mean "not" as in "clear/unclear" and "tidy/untidy".

Note that the word "untidy" has two morphemes (un/tidy) but three syllables (un/ti/dy).

In Unit 30, children are also introduced to the concept of root words having both a prefix morpheme and a suffix morpheme, for example:

Prefix	Root	Suffix	New word
re	print	ing	reprinting

Phonics Bug Teaching Software navigation and controls

The *Phonics Bug* teaching software is accessed from www.bugclub.co.uk. Simply go to the website, enter your personal log-in details and click on the Phonics Software tab. From here you will be able to launch the software for display on your whiteboard. (You can also access the eBooks from this website, see page 25 for more details.)

Main Menu

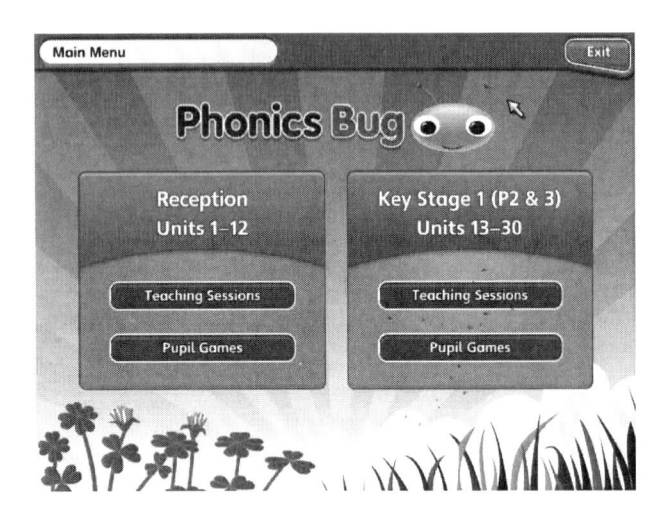

On starting the software you will be presented with the Main Menu, as shown above left. Choose which part of the programme (Units 1–12 or Units 13–30) you wish to enter from this Main Menu.

You will now be presented with a screen containing the Unit and Session Select Menu, as shown above right. The function of this menu is described below. The Navigation bar at the top of this screen contains four buttons. Clicking 'Tour' will begin a demonstration of the software. Clicking 'Help' will take you to the relevant help areas. Clicking 'Back' will take you back to the Main Menu, and clicking 'Exit' will enable you to leave the software. At the bottom of the screen are some Additional features. These provide links to the 'Pupil Games', 'Print Material' and 'Magnetic Board'. These features are described in more detail later on.

Unit and Session Select Menu

When you select a Unit from the Unit Select menu, the Session Select menu will become populated. There are two kinds of Sessions within each Unit: Phoneme Sessions and Language Sessions.

If you select a Phoneme Session, the Revision and Lesson buttons will appear, as shown below left.

If you select a Language Session, the Irregular (or High-frequency Words) and Lesson buttons will appear, as seen below right. Clicking on any of these buttons will take you into the main body of the software.

Phonics Bug Teaching Software navigation and controls

Controls

Labels on screenshot: Teaching Element Tabs, Toolbar, Alphabet panel, Navigation bar, Work area, Guide character

On reaching the main body of the software, you will be presented with a similar screen to the one shown above. There are a number of controls on this screen that are important for getting the most out of your software.

When you enter the screen for the first time, a pop-up will appear, describing how to use the controls on the screen. Clicking 'Do not show this again' will ensure that this guide will not reappear. You can, however, access it at any time by clicking on the Guide button on the Navigation bar.

Work area

The light blue area in the middle of the screen is called the Work area. This is where the Session takes place.

Guide character

The Guide character has been programmed to give the children encouragement and feedback. Clicking directly on the Guide character will pause the animation; clicking again will resume playback.

Teaching Elements

Each Session is broken down into a number of Teaching Elements. These are accessed by clicking on the Tabs at the top left of the screen:

| Sounds | Reading | Spelling | Writing | Follow-up |

Navigation bar

Phonics Bug | Unit 13 ph: Lesson | Guide | Back | Exit

The Navigation bar contains three buttons as shown above. Clicking 'Back' will return you to the Unit and Session Select Menu, and clicking 'Exit' will enable you to leave the software. Clicking 'Guide' will open a dialog box that contains the teaching points for the Teaching Element that you are currently on.

Phonics Bug Teaching Software navigation and controls

Toolbar

The Toolbar sits down the left-hand side of the screen.

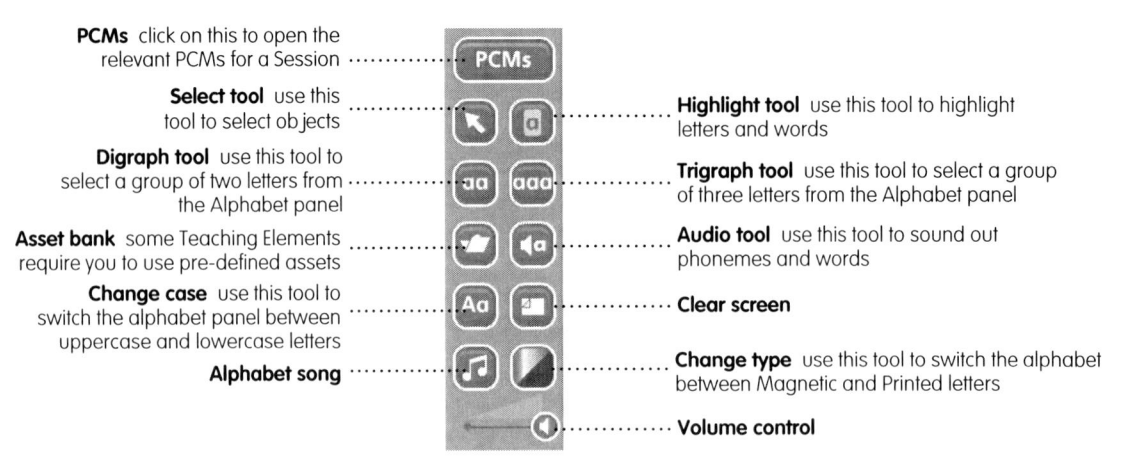

PCMs click on this to open the relevant PCMs for a Session

Select tool use this tool to select objects

Digraph tool use this tool to select a group of two letters from the Alphabet panel

Asset bank some Teaching Elements require you to use pre-defined assets

Change case use this tool to switch the alphabet panel between uppercase and lowercase letters

Alphabet song

Highlight tool use this tool to highlight letters and words

Trigraph tool use this tool to select a group of three letters from the Alphabet panel

Audio tool use this tool to sound out phonemes and words

Clear screen

Change type use this tool to switch the alphabet between Magnetic and Printed letters

Volume control

Alphabet song

The Alphabet song has three buttons, sitting at the top right of the screen.

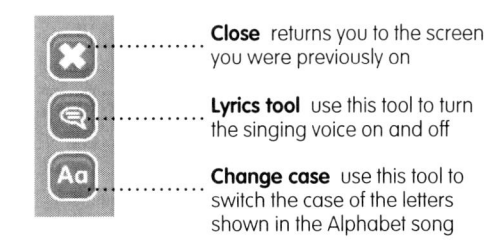

Close returns you to the screen you were previously on

Lyrics tool use this tool to turn the singing voice on and off

Change case use this tool to switch the case of the letters shown in the Alphabet song

Alphabet panel

Bin

a b c d e f g h i j k l m n o p q r s t u v w x y z

At the bottom of the screen is the Alphabet panel. This has been positioned specifically so that it is within reach of the children. Letters from the Alphabet panel can be moved onto the Work area either by clicking and dragging them, or simply by clicking once. The Teaching Element that you are currently on determines where the letters can be dropped onto the Work area. Letters can be removed from the Work area by dragging them into the Bin (see above) or by clicking the Clear screen button on the Toolbar (see top of this page).

Control panel

Scroll through content

Control buttons

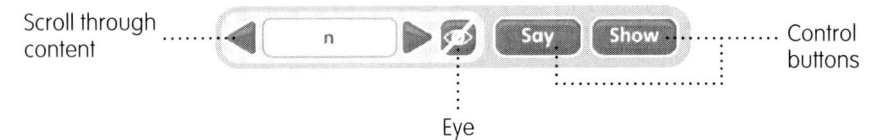

Eye

Some Teaching Elements are managed by a Control panel that sits at the top right of the Work area. This Control panel is tailored to the Teaching Element that you are currently on, and the Control buttons on the right-hand side will alter accordingly.

Clicking on the arrows will allow you to scroll through the pre-defined content for the current Teaching Element. Clicking on the Eye will allow you to preview the content.

Phonics Bug Teaching Software navigation and controls

Video

Some Teaching Elements contain a video clip. The tools from the Toolbar are still available for you to use during the playing of the video.

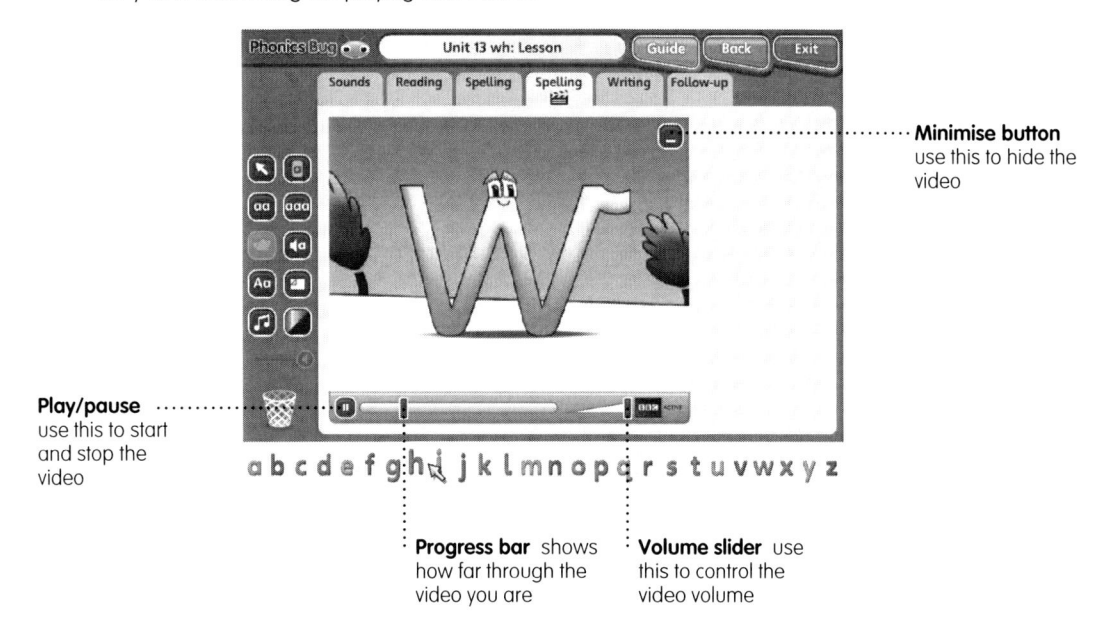

Minimise button use this to hide the video

Play/pause use this to start and stop the video

Progress bar shows how far through the video you are

Volume slider use this to control the video volume

Phonics Bug Teaching Software navigation and controls

Pupil Games

Unit and Game Select menu

Clicking on 'Pupil Games' from the Unit and Session Select Menu will bring you to the screen above. There are five different games for the pupils to play: Sounds, Letters, Reading, Spelling and Language. There is a version of each game for every Unit. On entering this screen you will be presented with the Unit and Game Select Menu. This operates in the same manner as the Unit and Session Select Menu. To begin a game, simply click 'Start'.

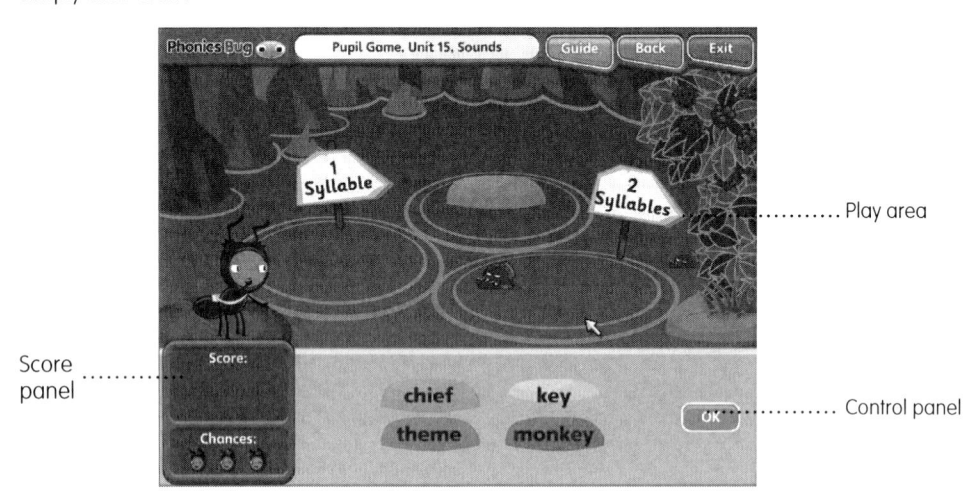

Play area

Score panel

Control panel

Each Pupil Game has a similar interface. The Pupil Games are very easy to use and the instructions are explained before the game starts. The instructions can also be accessed by clicking 'Guide' on the Navigation bar or found on pages 22–23 of this Teaching Guide.

Each game has a Play area where the action happens, a Score panel and a Control panel.

Phonics Bug Teaching Software navigation and controls

Print Material

Clicking on 'Print Material' on the Unit and Session Select Menu will bring you to the first screen above. There are two different kinds of print material specific to each Unit and Session: the PCMs and the Resources, both supplied as PDFs. The PCMs are copies of those printed in the *Phonics Bug Photocopy Masters* book and the Resources can be printed out and made into cards.

In addition to the print material specific to each Unit and Session, you will find PDF print material specific to each assessment activity for Units 13–30 (Flashcard Resources).

At the bottom of the screen there are three additional features. Clicking 'Teaching Guide' will open a PDF of this document and clicking 'Graphemes' will open a document, again, which can be printed out and made into cards.

Phonics Bug also contains additional resources allowing you to create your own PCMs for independent use. These consist of PCM Templates in the form of Word documents and a selection of clipart, which can be accessed by clicking on 'PCM Templates' at the bottom of the screen. A Zip file will be downloaded to a location specified by you. This Zip file can be extracted by double-clicking on it and following the on-screen instructions. In order to use the clipart simply open one of the Templates in Microsoft Word and select 'Insert', 'Picture' and 'From file' from the menu at the top of the screen and then point to the location of the extracted clipart.

Magnetic Board

The Magnetic Board is the final feature accessible from the Unit and Session Select Menu. This is a blank screen that can be used to continue your teaching of phonics, outside of the *Phonics Bug* lesson structure. Furthermore, the Asset bank accessible from this screen allows you access to all the assets (pictures, words and sentences) from the whole programme.

Note: The multi-coloured magnetic letters of the alphabet can be switched to printed letters of the same colour by clicking the 'Change type' button. Clicking on the 'Change case' button switches the alphabet between lowercase and uppercase letters.

Guided independent work

Photocopy masters (PCMs)

Over 70 PCMs have been specifically written for independent consolidation work, to be completed once you have modelled and rehearsed the Teaching Elements in the Whole Class Session. They don't necessarily need to be completed immediately after the Whole Class Session but should be done before the next Session. There are two types of PCM provided to accompany the teaching of *Phonics Bug*.

1) Phoneme Session PCM

To be completed after each Phoneme Session, each of these PCMs provides three activities, consolidating work covered in the Lesson. The tasks form a progression through the Units (see the table below) offering pupils a variety of ways to demonstrate their learning. In the assisted-cloze procedure tasks (sentences, texts and word puzzle clues) deletions have been selected to provide forward-acting cues (The postman brings the _____.), backward-acting cues (_____ are we waiting?) and forward/backward-acting cues (Hang your _____ on the peg.). The alphabetic order tasks build upon the alphabetic teaching in *Phonics Bug Reception (Primary 1)* and are included as preparation for dictionary skills.

Phonics PCM task progression

Task / Units	13	14	15	16	17	18	19	20	21	22	23	24	25	26	27	28	29	30
Making semantic decisions	●																	
Matching words to pictures	●	●	●	●	●	●	●	●	●	●	●	●	●	●	●	●		
Assisted-cloze procedure word puzzles **D**	●	●	●	●	●	●	●											
Assisted-cloze procedure sentences **D**		●	●	●	●	●												
Meaning clues for crosswords **D**								●	●									
Assisted-cloze procedure text **D**							●	●	●	●	●	●	●	●	●			
Alphabetic order letters											●	●	●	●	●			
Alphabetic order words **D**														●	●	●		
Adding suffix morphemes																●	●	●
Adding plural morphemes																	●	
Adding prefix morphemes																		●
Matching meanings to prefix words																		●
Forming words from prefix+root word+suffix																		●
Identifying syllables in words																		●

D indicates activities where opportunities for differentiation can be made (see 'Differentiation', page 21).

2) Language Session PCM

To be completed after each Language Session, each of these PCMs comprises two tasks, which aim to consolidate the children's comprehension skills. You will find that some of these tasks mirror the software's Language Session Follow-up Teaching Elements. The table on the following page charts the progression of tasks covered in the Language Session PCMs.

Guided independent work

Language PCM task progression

Task / Units	13	14	15	16	17	18	19	20	21	22	23	24	25	26	27	28	29	30
Assisted-cloze procedure with picture clues **D**	●																	
Sentence reading and modelling	●	●	●															
Dialogue to promote discussion and stimulate thinking skills		●	●															
Reading sentences – semantic choice		●	●															
Completing story – writing ending		●																
Completing story – writing begining			●															
Matching meaning clues and words				●	●	●												
Constructing story from title/picture				●	●													
Reading and illustrating sentences						●	●	●	●	●	●	●						
Matching words to meaning clues							●	●	●	●	●	●						
Sequencing related sentences													●	●	●	●	●	●
Illustrating specific sentences													●	●	●	●	●	●
Choosing a title for sentences																●	●	●

D indicates activities where opportunities for differentiation can be made (see 'Differentiation', below).

Instructional text

Each task is preceded by a printed instruction. You may read this with the whole class, and perhaps draw attention to certain phrases such as 'Put a ring round …', 'Write in the best word …', 'Read the clues …' and 'Tick the box …'. Please bear in mind that the children are by no means expected to read these instructions at the beginning stage of the programme, but it is hoped that, with time, they will become familiar with these words, understand their meanings and begin to read the instructions themselves.

Differentiation

Although the PCMs are not specifically differentiated, there are a number of ways they can be differentiated for different ability groups. For example:

- In sentences and text tasks where children are required to choose best-fit words, they can either write them in the deletion space or put a ring around or highlight the best word.
- In word puzzle tasks, pupils can complete the word grid as normal using the clue words, or the first letter of each word can be placed in the word grid to give support.
- In assisted-cloze procedure tasks where children are given picture clues only, a choice of words for the missing word could be provided in a box below the activity.
- Some of the activities lend themselves to paired or group work – e.g. matching tasks could be enlarged when photocopied, and then cut up for paired or group game playing.

Self-assessment

At the bottom of each PCM you will see 'happy', 'neutral' and 'sad' faces. In order to encourage children to consider their own performance, they should tick one of the faces in accordance with how confident they felt about the tasks. The inclusion of a 'neutral' face enables the children to think about the finer distinctions between being simply satisfied or dissatisfied with their performances. For example, they may select the 'neutral' face if they feel that they have performed particularly well in one task but not the other.

Create your own PCMs

A number of Templates (including a clipart bank) have been provided on the software, allowing you to create your own PCMs to match the requirements of your class (see page 19).

Pupil Games

There are five Pupil Games in each Unit, each game consolidating one of the five areas that the children have been working on in the Lessons:

- Sounds
- Letters
- Reading
- Spelling
- Language

Guided independent work

Sounds

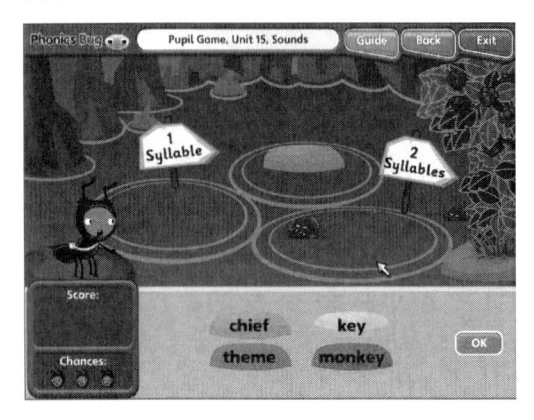

What is tested
This game tests the children's ability to hear and distinguish the different number of 'beats' (syllables) in a word.

How to play
The children will see a collection of pebbles (2, 4, 6 or 8 depending on the level), each containing a word. As they click on each word, they will hear the word being read out. They then have to decide how many syllables the word has and drag the word to the correct 'zone' – 1 syllable, 2 syllables or 3 syllables. By dragging and dropping the pebbles into the correct waterpool, the children can make stepping-stones across the piranha-infested water. Once they are happy with their sorting, they click 'OK'. If they have sorted correctly, they will see a reward animation of the character skipping across the stepping stones to grab a berry from the bush. Children can have a re-try at the sorting before the software demonstrates the correct answer.

Score
There is a maximum of 5 points to be scored.

Letters

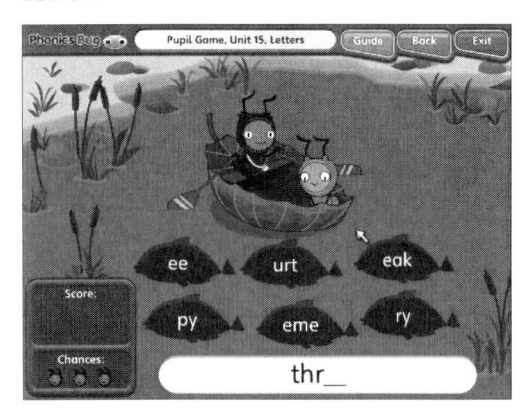

What is tested
This game tests the children's knowledge of the letter combinations that make up the consonant blends, vowel digraphs and trigraphs, prefixes, suffixes and spelling rules targeted in the Units.

How to play
The children will see part of a word and have to select, from several fish containing options, the letter combination that completes the word. If they select correctly, they see a reward animation of the fish splashing up and out of the water. Children can have a re-try at the choosing before the software demonstrates the correct answer.

Score
There is a maximum of 5 points to be scored.

Reading

What is tested
This game tests the children's knowledge of the pronunciation of words and their ability to find the consecutive letters that make up that word.

How to play
The children will hear a word being read out, and they have to find the correct word within a simple wordsearch grid. They highlight the word by clicking each letter. If they select correctly, they will see a reward animation of the character doing stunts on a wake-board. The number of 'goes' increases (5, 8 and 10) as the Units advance, as does the size and complexity of the search grid. Children can have a re-try at the wordsearch before the software demonstrates the correct answer.

Score
There is a maximum of 5, 8 or 10 points to be scored, depending on the level.

Guided independent work

Spelling

What is tested

This game tests the children's ability to spell words of one, two and three syllables.

How to play

The children will hear a word being read out, and they have to select the correct letters to spell the word by scrolling through a list of letters, using the up and down arrows. Once the children have spelt the word, they click 'OK'. If the word is spelt correctly, the children will see a reward animation of the character travelling across a spiderweb tightrope. Children can have a re-try at the spelling before the software demonstrates the correct answer.

Score

There is a maximum of 5 points to be scored.

Language

What is tested

This game tests the children's comprehension skills, by testing their ability to change a sentence from nonsense to sense by choosing the correct word.

How to play

The children are given a nonsense sentence with the nonsense word highlighted. They then have to choose, from a number of options, the word that will make the sentence sensible and drag the word into the highlighted position in the sentence. The new word will now replace the nonsense word in the sentence. The children then read the sentence and, when they are happy with their choice, they click 'OK'. If their choice is correct, the children will see a reward animation of bugs flying by. The position of the nonsense word in the sentence is varied and the number of 'goes' increases (5, 8 and 10) as the Units advance. Children can have a re-try at the choosing before the software demonstrates the correct answer.

Score

There is a maximum of 5, 8 or 10 points to be scored, depending on the level.

Phonics Bug decodable readers

The *Phonics Bug* readers have been designed to fully support the teaching sessions in the *Phonics Bug* software and daily lesson plans. The books have been written to match the order in which grapheme-phoneme correspondences are introduced in *Phonics Bug* (and in *Letters and Sounds*). The books begin at Phase 2 and continue through to Phase 5.

Each Unit of *Phonics Bug* links with a series of decodable texts. These are designed to give children the opportunity to practise their blending skills and to consolidate their knowledge of grapheme-phoneme correspondences, in the context of engaging texts, in addition to the sentence level work on the Language Sessions.

Using the books

We are aware that the *Phonics Bug* readers may be used for a variety of purposes, such as Independent Reading, assessment, take-home reading and guided reading. Therefore, we have tried to make the teaching support (printed inside the covers of the books) as flexible as possible.

Decodability

The books have been designed to support children as they gain in confidence and become fluent and automatic decoders. The books do not contain any grapheme-phoneme correspondence until it has been taught in the main teaching programme, with the exception of a few common irregular words needed to make the text meaningful. The points at which these are introduced match to the Phases in which they are introduced in the teaching plans, although the Phase 3 books do contain a few words with adjacent consonants. Children should sound and blend unfamiliar words until they have sight recognition of them; they should not guess from context or use picture cues.

In Phase 5, we have followed the introduction of graphemes according to the order set out in the teaching software. However, in some instances, we have introduced additional graphemes (i.e. 'u' for long /oo/ in Set 18 and 'our' for /or/ in Set 19). Furthermore, there is one instance where we have introduced a grapheme slightly earlier than in the teaching plans. We have introduced the grapheme 'le' for /l/ in Set 24 to enable us to cover the 'st' grapheme for /s/ in this Set (for example, in words such as 'castle' and 'whistle').

Some books contain environmental print which is often above the reading level of the child. The adult can decide whether or not to draw attention to this text as appropriate.

Polysyllabic words

Simple polysyllabic words (words with two syllables or more) are introduced from Set 5. These words are pulled out and given special attention in the teaching notes when they occur. Children sometimes have problems with polysyllabic words as they have to break down the word into its component syllables, before blending each one and then combining to read the whole word.

Plurals and 3rd person verbs

Simple plurals and 's' forms of verbs are used from the start as they are extremely common and research indicates that they do not pose problems for most children. These word forms are not referred to as adjacent consonants.

Sentence level progression

In addition to the cumulative coverage of grapheme-phoneme correspondences, *Phonics Bug* readers also develop their level of challenge in other ways. They gradually move from captions in the earliest books, through to simple sentences and more complex sentence structures in the later ones. There is also a carefully planned gradual increase in the number of words and the number of different words at each level. The stories themselves also become generally more sophisticated at later levels, while maintaining their appropriateness for the age group.

Book Bands

We have not attempted to place the *Phonics Bug* readers in Book Bands, as we recognise that the Book Band levelling system is designed for texts constructed on a very different basis from phonic readers. However, to help teachers organise their resources, a very rough correlation can be made:

Letters and Sounds Phase	Book Band
Phase 2	Pink
Phase 3	Red–Yellow
Phase 4	Yellow
Phase 5	Blue–Orange

Phonics Bug eBooks and Bug Club website

Using Phonics Bug and Bug Club readers together

The *Phonics Bug* readers are designed to support children in practising and consolidating the knowledge they acquire during the whole-class teaching sessions. They also allow children to experience the pleasure of reading their own books. In addition, children need to access a rich variety of books, so that they develop enthusiasm for reading. The books available in *Bug Club* are the perfect complement to *Phonics Bug*. They are aligned to the Phases of *Letters and Sounds*, and the chart on pages 28–29 shows the phonic progression within them. The books contain a small number of words that are classed as 'tricky' for a particular phonics level. This is so that the stories can be richer and more meaningful – and so that they can help children develop the vital skill of comprehension.

Teachers vary in their approach to organising resources. You might find it helpful to keep the decodable readers in a separate box, and use them specifically for consolidating phonics work. You could then use the *Bug Club* books for further consolidation and application of decoding skills, as well as comprehension. The *Phonics Bug* and *Bug Club* books are finely levelled to ensure that children feel that they are making progress. It is not necessary for every child to read every book, as some will progress faster than others, but the two series provide plenty of breadth and choice at each level, to help make sure that all children get the reading experiences they need to progress.

Phonics Bug eBooks and the Bug Club website

Once a child has read a *Phonics Bug* book, they can practise reading that text again, using the *Phonics Bug* eBooks which are accessed through a child's personalised online reading world. The eBooks have three main features for the child:

- **Phoneme pronunciation guide:** A child (and parent) can hear audio recordings of the sounds that each book is designed to practise, so that they can listen out for them during their reading.
- **Read to Me:** A child can also hear a model reading of the text. We recommend that you do not use the 'Read to Me' feature before a child has read the printed books for the first time, as the aim of synthetic phonics teaching is to enable pupils to work out the pronunciation of unfamiliar words for themselves. This feature can be used subsequently as a model of fluent reading, to help them give expression to their reading, and to develop a sense of how stories work.
- **Quiz question**: A child can read the text again onscreen, but this time, access an interactive quiz question embedded within the book pages. Each question is designed to reinforce phonic skills, and attempted questions feed back information to teachers.

Bug Club's online reading world

Bug Club's online reading world helps children improve core reading skills at school or home with exciting texts and fun rewards. It also enables teachers to monitor every child's progress, providing valuable evidence of their reading for Assessment Focus 1 in Assessing Pupils' Progress (APP). *Bug Club* contains 305 *Bug Club* books, as well as the 134 *Phonics Bug* books. *Bug Club* books have a greater range of quiz questions, designed to reinforce comprehension skills and provide information across the full range of Assessment Focuses.

Child experience

Bug Club facilitates independent practice at school, home, or any computer that has an internet connection. With easy-to-remember logins (which you can also personalise) a child can log in to their personalised reading homepage and access eBooks for further reading practice.

My Books: Five eBooks can be allocated to a child at one time. Children can also re-read the last 10 eBooks again, and see how many eBooks they have read in total.

Bug Points and Rewards: A child can collect Bug Points by completing quiz questions within eBooks and then exchange these points for rewards.

My Pictures: A child can personalise their avatar and side-panel design.

Parent's Help: Handy hints and tips for a parent reading with their child, customised to their child's reading level.

Teacher experience

For you, the teacher, *Bug Club* provides a quick and easy way of allocating reading practice to every child in your class, as well as at-a-glance reports on their attainment. With personalised logins, you can log in to your own personalised teacher homepage and access all the planning and assessment tools you need for *Bug Club*.

Book search: You can search by reading level (Book Band, Phonic Phase or Reading Recovery level). Alternatively, you can use *Quick Search* to find books by a keyword search.

Search results: You can see basic eBook information in your results, or choose to see more details about the book.

Open or allocate: From your search results, you can either open eBooks and use these in your planning or teaching in school, or allocate through to children's bookshelves.

Phonics Bug Books and eBooks

Teaching Support

- Flashcards for every Phase
- Fantastic teaching tools
- Lesson plans and assessment support

100% decodable readers with an example eBook for every title

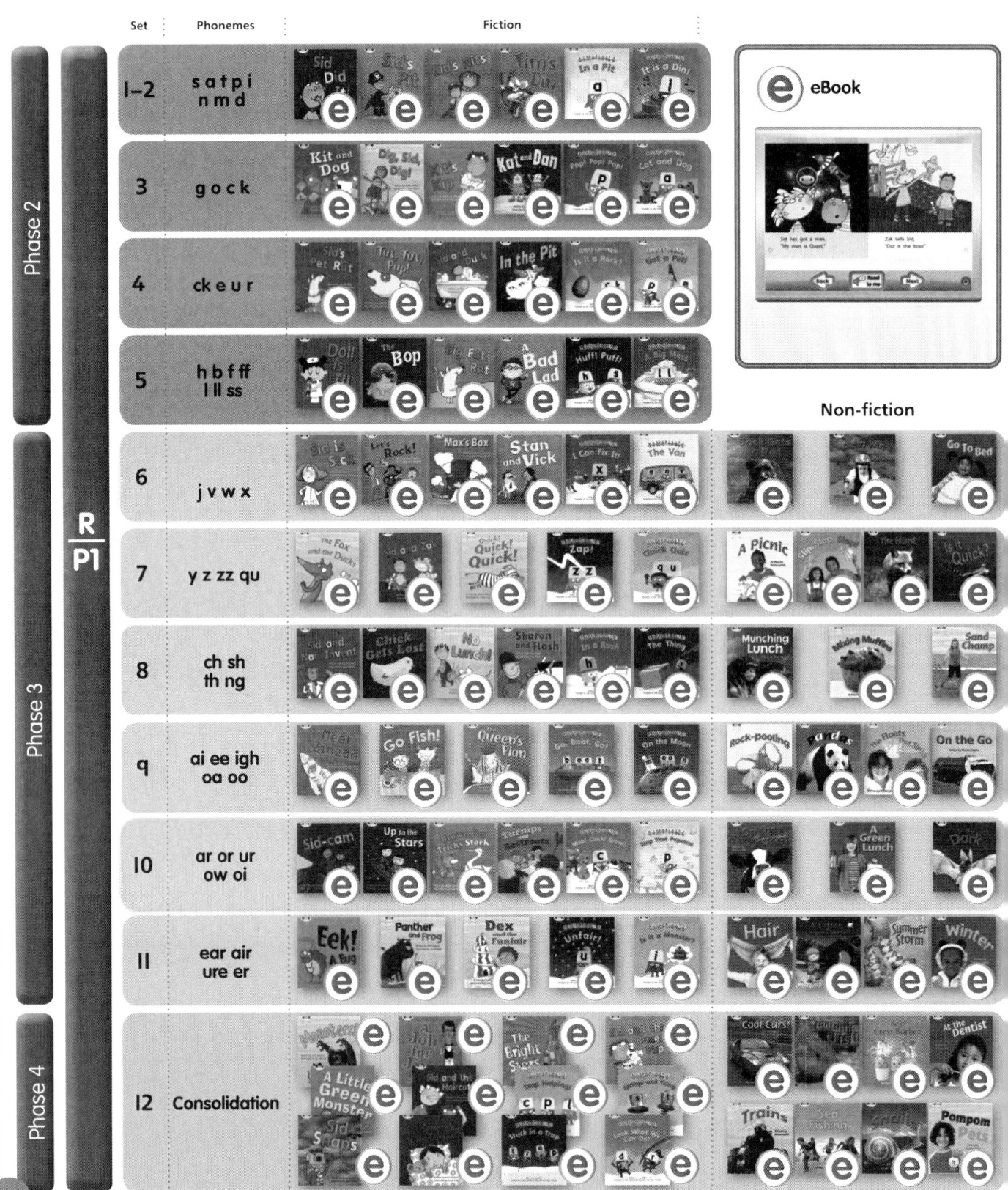

Phase	Set	Phonemes
Phase 2	1–2	s a t p i n m d
Phase 2	3	g o c k
Phase 2	4	ck e u r
Phase 2	5	h b f ff l ll ss
R/P1	6	j v w x
R/P1	7	y z zz qu
Phase 3	8	ch sh th ng
Phase 3	9	ai ee igh oa oo
Phase 3	10	ar or ur ow oi
Phase 3	11	ear air ure er
Phase 4	12	Consolidation

eBook

Non-fiction

26

Some books above were originally published in print form as part of the Rigby Star Phonics series

Phase 5 | 1/P2

Set	Phonemes	Fiction		Non-fiction
13	wh ph	e	e	e
14	ay a–e eigh ey ei (long a)	e	e	e
15	ea e–e ie ey y (long e)	e	e	e
16	ie i–e y i (long i)	e	e	e
17	ow o–e o oe (long o)	e	e	e
18	ew ue u–e (long u) u oul (short oo)	e	e	e
19	aw au al our	e		e
20	ir er ear	e		e
21	ou oy	e		e
22	eer ere are ear	e		e
23	k ck ch	e		e
24	ce c sc st se	e		e
25	ge g dge	e		e
26	le mb kn gn wr	e		e
27	tch sh alternatives ea (w)a o	e		e

Bug Club Books and eBooks

Phase	Band	Book Band Level	Fiction	Non-fiction	Comics/Graphic Novels	Phonics Comics
Phase 2	R/P1	Lilac				
Phase 2	R/P1	Pink A — RR1				
Phase 2	R/P1	Pink B — RR2				
Phase 3	R/P1	Red A — RR3				
Phase 3	R/P1	Red B — RR4				
Phase 3	R/P1	Red C — RR5				
Phase 4	1/P2	Yellow A — RR6				
Phase 4	1/P2	Yellow B — RR7				
Phase 4	1/P2	Yellow C — RR8				
Phase 5	1/P2	Blue A — RR9				
Phase 5	1/P2	Blue B — RR10				
Phase 5	1/P2	Blue C — RR11				
Phase 5	1/P2	Green A — RR12				
Phase 5	1/P2	Green B — RR13				
Phase 5	1/P2	Green C — RR14				

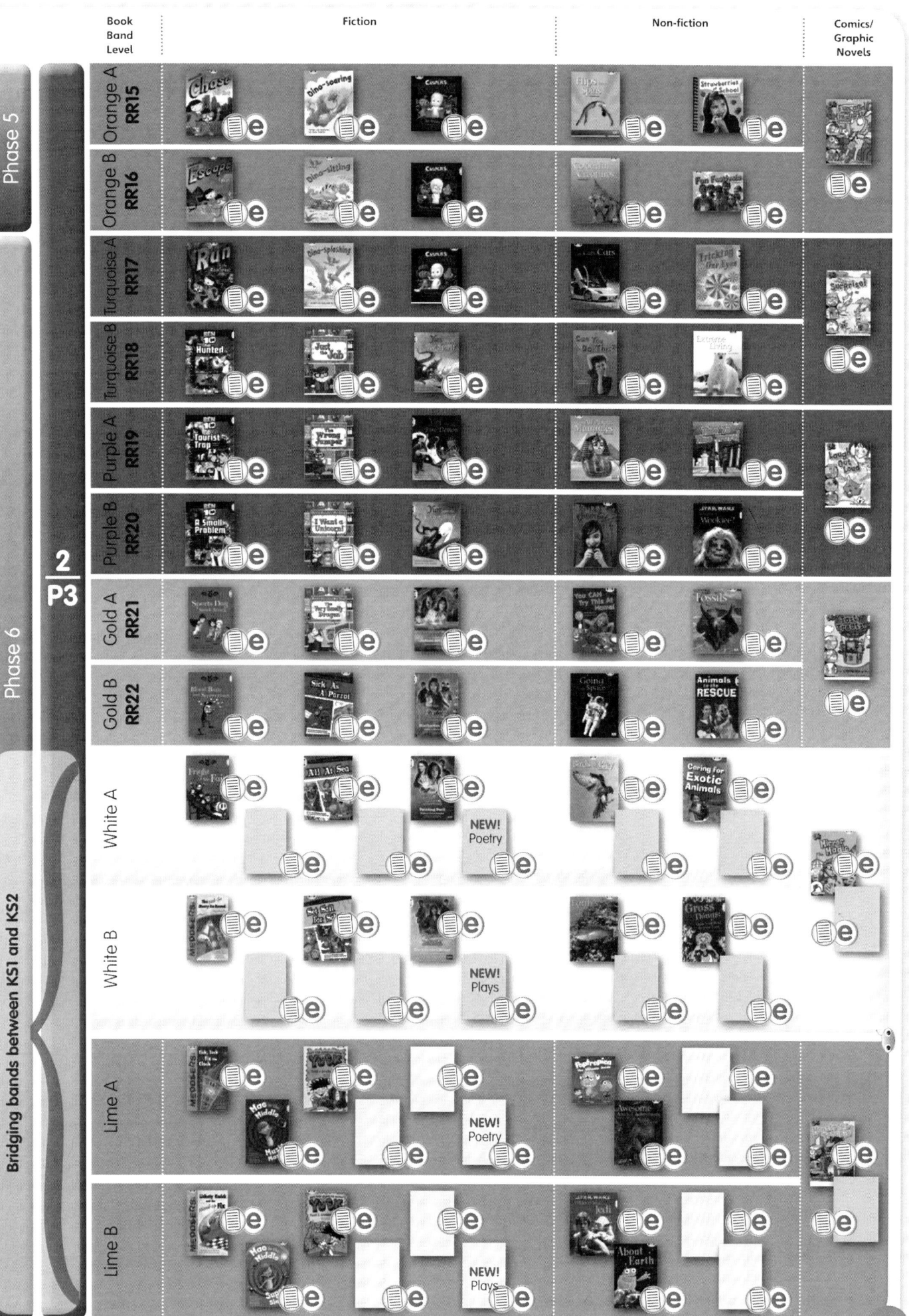

Comes with a Planning and Assessment Guide for each year

Key printed book   e eBook   new title, coming Spring 2012

Bug Club

Phase		Book Band Level		Fiction			Non-fiction		Comics/Graphic Novels
Phase 5	2/P3	Orange A	**RR15**						
		Orange B	**RR16**						
		Turquoise A	**RR17**						
		Turquoise B	**RR18**						
		Purple A	**RR19**						
		Purple B	**RR20**						
Phase 6		Gold A	**RR21**						
		Gold B	**RR22**						
Bridging bands between KS1 and KS2		White A				NEW! Poetry			
		White B				NEW! Plays			
		Lime A				NEW! Poetry			
		Lime B				NEW! Plays			

29

Assessing progress – Before starting

Before beginning *Phonics Bug Key Stage 1 (Primary 2 and 3)*, the children will have completed the twelve Units of the *Phonics Bug Reception (Primary 1)* programme. Working with individual letters, children have already learned to sound and blend successive letters to read words, and to segment spoken words for spelling. They will also have started learning some vowel digraphs and trigraphs. Now the children will be introduced to syllabification, moving forward from blending letter sounds to blending syllables.

Before embarking on Units 13–30, children should:

Competence	Teaching suggestions
Know that the vowels **a**, **e**, **i**, **o**, **u** can have both a short and a long sound.	Use the Alphabet song to demonstrate that the long vowel sound is the same as the letter name, e.g. be, he, me, we.
	For the short vowel sound, remind the children of the relevant phoneme lessons: "The letter 'a' sounds ?" (/a/ as in cat) "The letter 'e' sounds ?" (/e/ as in egg) Repeat for 'i', 'o', 'u'.
Be able to clap/tap the number of beats in one- and two-syllable words.	Use names of children in the class with one and two syllables. Demonstrate how to clap the beats for them. Ask children to say the name, clap the beat(s) and say the number of syllables. Children can clap their hands, clap their chins, tap on the table, nod their heads to the beat, etc. (See also page 11 'Teaching syllables'.)
Be able to follow the procedure for spelling words, selecting or writing the letters for each sound and blending them together to be able to say and read the word.	Say the target word, embed it in a sentence and repeat the word again for the children to spell.
	Children look at a picture, say the picture word, repeat it and spell the word.
Know that: (i) a sentence is a group of words. (ii) a sentence begins with a capital letter. (iii) a sentence ends with a full stop.	Remind the children of these points using a question-and-answer technique.
	Demonstrate on the board using children to model, e.g. It is hot and sunny. The first day of the week is Sunday.
Be able to help the teacher write sentences from dictation, leading to being able to write sentences independently from dictation.	Dictate a given sentence slowly and clearly. Ask one of the children to repeat the sentence. Dictate the sentence again. Invite children to tell you how to write each sentence on the board. Any errors can be used as a teaching opportunity for revision and discussion. Such an opportunity is also valuable for identifying individual problems.

Assessing progress – Before starting

Competence	Teaching suggestions
Be able to follow the procedure for completing a sentence with a deleted word, by choosing from given words one which will make sense.	Write a sentence with a deleted word on the board, together with the words from which children make a choice to complete the sentence (assisted cloze procedure), e.g. We had ham and _____ for tea. (end egg)
	Remind the children to: (i) read the two parts of the sentence. (ii) read the words in brackets. (iii) read and choose the best word. (iv) write in the word or circle the word. (v) read the sentence to see if it makes sense.
Be able to follow the assisted cloze procedure technique to complete simple word grids and crossword puzzles.	Model the completion of the Across clues by doing one or two examples on the board with a simple grid, mirroring what the children are asked to do.
	Use and explain the word **Across**. The clue might be: The sun is very _____ today. (wet hot icy)
	There are three empty boxes going across. Therefore the word will need three letters. Which one will make sense?
	Ask a child to write 'hot', one letter in each box.
	Follow the same procedure for **Down** clues.
	Follow the same procedure for **Across** and **Down** clues.

Assessment and catch-up work in preparation for Key Stage 1

Catch-up work for learning letter sounds and letter formation

This procedure can be done at any point in the programme, but we have outlined here a scenario for early detection and support for slower learners.

Around 2 months into the programme, Unit 7 has been completed with the whole class, and all 26 letters of the alphabet have been introduced. The teacher has decided to carry out a test of the children's knowledge of the sounds of the letters of the alphabet (Assessment 1), and the writing of those sounds to dictation (Assessment 3).

As she knows from the whole-class sessions that she has a small group of children who only know a few letter sounds, the teacher now has to decide whether to continue to keep these children together with the whole class or to form ability groups. As previously taught letter sounds are reinforced on a daily basis with the whole class, the teacher thinks that if she forms, within the classroom, a nurture/needs group for the three or four slower learning children to target their specific learning needs, they may be able to keep up with their class mates, which will boost their self-esteem and give them a feeling of social inclusion. Four is generally considered to be the optimum size for such a nurture/needs group, to allow for individual efforts and co-operative learning.

Although the teacher knows that, ultimately, these children may need 1:1 individually tailored support programmes, Assessments 1 and 3 indicate that the 4 children are all needing to do extra work on the letter d. That is, they are not sure of the letter sound and are having difficulty in forming the letter. She also feels that it would be useful for them to consolidate their learning of all the letter sounds in Unit 2.

Revisiting the sound for 'd'

The teacher can set aside an area in the classroom for the group of four children with a table and four chairs. They will need:

- facilities for operating the programme on the interactive whiteboard or a laptop computer
- access to materials which will be needed, e.g. magnetic boards, magnetic letters, individual pupil whiteboards, black marker pens, a tray of damp sand, soft modelling clay
- a new PCM for /d/ for each pupil.

At the start of the session, to let the children know their learning target, the teacher selects the Sounds tab for the children to see the "This is 'd'" video clip from Unit 2 (Phase 2). She then asks a child to find the letter 'd' and to pull it up onto the whiteboard or computer screen. She then clicks on the audio tool and clicks on 'd' to hear its sound. All of the children repeat the sound. Each child is then invited to select 'd', click on it to hear its sound and to say it at the same time. The teacher clicks on 'd' again and all of the children say the sound. How well did the children do?

Revisiting visual recognition of d

While still in the Sounds tab, the teacher clicks on the Asset bank, and each child gets a chance to circle the letter d in a word ('stand', 'damp', 'add' and 'Adam'), saying whether it is in the middle, the beginning or the end of the word. They do not read the words. Now the teacher can select the Follow-up tab and asset bank words. Another set of words will appear for the children to circle the letter 'd' in each word again, saying whether it is in the middle, the beginning or the end of the word. Finally, children are asked to complete this task on their PCM sheet, circling the letter d in each word. How well did the children do?

Revisiting writing d

The teacher then clicks on the Writing tab, and clicks on Show to get a demonstration of how to write the letter 'd'. The children form the letter in the damp sand using their index finger and saying the sound for d. Then the teacher clicks on Show again, and, using their own whiteboards and black marker pens, the children follow the instructions for forming the letter, saying the letter sound as they finish it. They can look at the whiteboard or computer screen to see how well they have done. The children can then use the Unit 2 PCM sheet for d again, where they will practise forming the letter d. Some children may benefit from work forming the letter using modelling clay.

Games to reinforce d, and all the letters sounds in Unit 2

The Unit 2 games (including all of the letter sounds taught by the end of Unit 2) were first introduced to the class through the daily Lesson Plans for Unit 3. These games will be motivating for the four children, but will also enable the teacher to observe and evaluate the success or otherwise of each pupil's contribution to each game played. Selecting the Sounds category for Games, each child in turn can have a go at identifying the letters from the sounds. Then they can use the Reading category to see these letter sounds in the context of words, and use the Spelling category to reinforce selecting letters to match the sounds they hear.

Reassess learning of Unit 2 Sounds

The next day, the teacher lays out for each child the letters 's, a, t, p, i, n, m, d' on a magnetic board. She asks each child to give the sound for each letter as she points to it. Then she re-arranges the letters and says each letter sound, asking them to point to the letter. Children still having difficulty can repeat the procedure above and spend more time playing the Unit 2 Games.

Assessment and catch-up work in preparation for Key Stage 1

Catch-up work for children having problems with blending and segmenting

Support work for blending for reading

Children who are slow to learn letter sounds may also have problems with blending (but not necessarily so). Other children may learn letter sounds with ease but nevertheless have difficulty in blending. What is important in the synthetic phonics approach is that children learn to track sequentially through words from left to right using letter-sound information, in order to read unfamiliar words. We recommend a smooth co-articulation of the sounds in words, spending as little time as possible pronouncing the letter sounds individually.

When children are faced with real words for blending practice, they may have seen them before and so try to recognise them on the basis of partial visual cues. This visual approach may slow down the acquisition of an extensive sight vocabulary, as many words look similar. The synthetic phonics method is designed to develop a form of sight word reading that is underpinned by all-through-the-word letter-sound information. Although slower learners often have short-term memory problems, we have found that sounding and blending practice actually increases their memory spans.

For children having difficulty with blending, we recommend carrying out some support work with *nonwords*; this means that they cannot guess what the item is, so the child has to blend the letter sounds together in order to pronounce it. You can tell the children that these are the names of children in a fictional book!

Assessment

For the assessment, you can use the nonwords on the *Phonics Bug Flashcards*. There are flashcards for the simple CVC nonwords used on Assessment Sheet 4 and Assessment Sheet 6, which contain adjacent consonants. For Key Stage 1, there are nonwords for Phase 5 and Phase 6 assessments after Units 27 and 30. The flashcards can also be printed off from the software (see 'Print Material' on page 19).

In this scenario, the class has been tested on Assessment Sheet 1, and the children know the letter sounds. They are then tested on Assessment Sheet 4. A small group of children have difficulty in reading these nonwords; it is useful to write on the assessment sheet the mistakes that they make, e.g. do they miss out letters or try to read the items as familiar words?

Catch-up

For support work, new nonwords can be found on the Catch-up: Nonwords flashcards. These occur after Unit 11 and Unit 12, and contain CVC nonwords, and nonwords with adjacent consonants.

Using these nonword cards, the child works through each nonword, blending the letters sounds from left to right. Our research shows that practising this approach is very effective in developing reading skills even in 12 year old secondary pupils.

It may be helpful to use plastic letters on a magnetic board while doing this, so that the letters can be pushed together from left to right as they blend. A game can be made by putting the magnetic letters into two piles, vowels and consonants, and getting the child to select two consonants and one vowel, and blending the letters together (which might produce some real words).

It would also be useful to make sure that the child applies their blending skills when reading text. Your session might include work with an appropriate *Phonics Bug* decodable reader; when the child hesitates over a word, they should be encouraged to sound and blend it.

Support work for segmenting for spelling

Segmenting for spelling involves children having awareness of phonemes in spoken words. However, research has shown that phonemic awareness skills are best developed through learning to read and spell.

First of all, make sure that the child can write or select magnetic letters for all of the letter sounds on Assessment Sheet 3. The children then carry out the segmentation test on Assessment Sheet 4. Read out each nonword clearly, repeating it until the child has heard it properly and can repeat it correctly. Ask the child to write down or select a magnetic letter for the first sound they hear. Then they should say the item again and pick out the next sound and write or select the appropriate letter. Continue like this until the whole item has been attempted, noting down the problems they experience. They may have problems like not repeating the item accurately, not keeping their place, or finding the vowel hard to identify.

The nonwords for segmentation practice are also available on flashcards. Work through these, helping the child segment the phonemes in sequential order; using nonwords will help them concentrate on the constituent phonemes. As each phoneme is segmented they should attempt to write it or select the appropriate magnetic letter. They can then sound and blend the letters to check their spelling.

Support work for reading and spelling vowel digraphs

All children find vowel digraphs difficult to read and spell accurately. It is important to get your pupils to recognise them as discrete units, but ultimately competence at reading and spelling vowel digraphs is going to depend to a great extent on word-specific learning.

Assessment and catch-up work in preparation for Key Stage 1

As the children work through the KS1 Units, those having particular difficulty will soon be spotted, especially as they work through the PCMs. You can assess them for their specific areas of difficulty by testing their spelling using Assessment sheets 8 and 9, and their reading using Assessment sheets 10 and 11 (also available as flashcards under Print Material, Phase 5 Assessment). The use of nonwords in the reading test helps to pick up children who cannot recognise vowel digraphs as units, in a situation where they cannot use word-specific knowledge. There is not always a 'correct' pronunciation of a vowel digraph, but context often gives a guide to how to pronounce them. For example, 'ea' has several alternative pronunciations but it always takes a long /e/ sound in front of the letter 'm', as in 'stream'.

Slower learners can reinforce their knowledge by working through the Games after a Unit has been completed. For example, in the Unit 17 Game for spelling, children can select the correct vowel digraph spelling for 'shadow', and for reading they can hear and then pick out the word 'crow' from a larger set of letters. However, as all the digraphs in the Unit are contained in these games sessions, for those having extreme difficulty you might like to make games for them using a set of cards with consonants on them, and a card for a specific vowel digraph or a rime. Using this procedure, they can learn useful rules about the pronunciation of vowel digraphs. For example, you might have cards displaying 'fl', 'cr', 'sn', and 'thr', and also the digraph 'ow'. They can add the digraph on to each consonant card and then pronounce for you the resulting word. Later on, you might give them cards where they learn that this sound is spelt 'oa' in the middle of words (as in 'toast'). Another example you can use is the fact that the spellings 'oi' and 'ai' occur in the middle of words, but are spelt 'oy' and 'ay' at the end of words. These games give the children a lot of exposure to word-specific spellings in a fun way, reinforce the idea that the two letters of the digraph make one sound, and introduce them to some phonics rules.

Assessment

Phonics Bug contains a variety of useful assessment resources to help you ensure that all children are progressing in line with national expectations throughout Reception, Year 1 and Year 2.

The resources help you gauge children's knowledge of the grapheme-phoneme correspondences and their ability to blend (using both real and non-words). These are the skills needed to reach the expected standard for the Phonics Screening Check in Year 1. You can also assess their knowledge of high-frequency/irregular (tricky) words. The resources can be used at regular intervals to provide an ongoing record of children's attainment. More information about the Phonics Screening Check is available in the *Phonics Bug Prepare and Assess Handbook*, along with a set of reading tests that will help familiarise pupils with the format of the Screening Check.

Ongoing formative assessment

Daily assessment is carried out in two ways. Firstly, through using the Whole Class Revision section of the Phoneme Sessions you can identify strengths and weaknesses at an early stage and intervene to support those children who need it during the guided independent work.

Additionally, you can monitor how well children complete the independent tasks in order to give an ongoing indicator of how each child is progressing. Feedback about progress should also be given to the children so that they know what they need to do to improve.

Children should also be assessed on their ability to use taught strategies to read unknown words. This should be done individually when they are reading their reading books to you. However, it is important that children should not be asked to guess an unknown word from context or use picture cues.

Self-assessment

Children should be encouraged to practise self-assessment, measured against the learning outcomes for the day. They can also reflect on their own performance through the inclusion of happy and sad faces on the PCMs, which they should tick in accordance with how confident they feel about the task. For further information, see page 21.

Summative assessment

Summative assessment (to be used formatively) is also recommended and resources are provided for this.

In *Phonics Bug Reception (Primary 1)*, we suggest that you undertake assessment activities regularly throughout the programme including after Unit 12 (Phase 4). This will inform any further teaching and/or consolidation that is deemed necessary before moving on to Units 13–30 in *Phonics Bug Key Stage 1 (Primary 2 & 3)*.

Here, in *Phonics Bug Key Stage 1 (Primary 2 & 3)*, we provide assessment activities which allow regular summative assessment after the Units within Phase 5 (to assess children's ability to read and spell words with new graphemes and alternative spellings) and activities for assessment after Unit 30 (to assess children's understanding of prefixes and suffixes).

Assessment and catch-up activities
Letter names and sounds

There may still be some children at this stage who are having difficulty remembering the letter sounds. These children will benefit from further reinforcement using the letter sound games for the Phoneme Sessions from *Phonics Bug Reception (Primary 1)*, and Assessments 1 to 3 can be used again to assess their progress.

Blending

There will be some children who still may not have mastered sounding and blending by the start of the second year of school. However, we have found even with Special Educational Needs children that by revisiting the earlier Units from the programme they can master this skill. If blending seems to be a problem for a child, you might like to re-administer Assessments 5 and 6 from *Phonics Bug Reception (Primary 1)*, as well as the catch-up activities recommended for blending.

Vowel digraphs/trigraphs and phonic rules

Vowel digraphs and trigraphs (covered in Units 9–22) are difficult for all children. This is where there is the greatest variability in English spelling (e.g. 'ea' has multiple pronunciations, and the long 'e' sound can be spelt in a number of different ways). Inevitably some learning has to be word-specific (e.g. 'head' versus 'bead'). It is also useful to teach certain phonic rules, such as split digraphs (i.e. silent or magic 'e'), although again there are word-specific exceptions that need to be learnt. There are also other useful rules covered in this programme, such as silent letters, and rules for when to double up the final consonant before adding a suffix. You can carry out Assessments 3 and 4 from *Phonics Bug Reception (Primary 1)* again with children who appear not to have made a good start on vowel digraphs and trigraphs before they start the new vowel digraphs and trigraphs (Units 14–22).

Delivery of assessment

The assessments for *Phonics Bug Key Stage 1 (Primary 2 & 3)* have been designed so that in each case there is a spelling assessment that can be delivered by the class teacher to quickly screen the whole class. The children who are found to have the greatest difficulty can then be selected to do the associated reading test, and the catch-up activities.

The chart on page 36 outlines the areas for assessment, together with suggestions for assessment methods. The necessary resource sheets are provided on pages 37–42.

Assessment

Phase 5 Assessment (after Unit 27)

You may wish to assess children on Phase 5 skills at regular periods throughout the teaching of Units 13-27. The assessment sheets described below are structured according to Unit-coverage, so you can work through the relevant parts of the sheets at your own pace.

Assessment area	Method
New graphemes and vowel digraphs/ trigraphs – Spelling	Carry out this spelling assessment with the whole class, as an initial screening test. It is unlikely that many children will master all vowel digraphs and trigraphs at this stage in their learning. However, it is important to assess at this stage how much consolidation work needs to be done. Explain the instructions to the whole class: 'Read each sentence and circle the missing word.' You could show some examples on the board first, e.g. The ____ is on fire. (house/howse) RESOURCE: ASSESSMENT SHEETS 8 & 9 *Note: Children will get some of these spelling questions right by chance if they use a guessing strategy, so this assessment may over-estimate their knowledge. This is more likely to happen with children having the greatest difficulty, so to overcome this you might like to work with them individually, helping them read the sentences.*
New graphemes and vowel digraphs/ trigraphs – Reading	While this reading assessment can be used for the whole class, you may find it is most useful when carried out with the children having the greatest difficulty with Assessments 8 and 9. Note the accuracy of the decoding of nonwords on Assessment Sheet 10. ('Nonwords' are used so that children cannot use a partial visual strategy to read them based on words they have seen before.) Note not only whether the child comes up with an acceptable pronunciation of a nonword, but whether the vowel pronunciation is an acceptable one in that letter context, e.g. 'ea' is variable, but always takes a long 'e' vowel sound in front of the letter 'm'. You might find it useful to tape-record their responses. RESOURCE: ASSESSMENT SHEETS 10 & 11 *The nonwords are also provided on flashcards which can be downloaded from the software (see page 19).*
Reading and spelling non-decodable common words	Use the words provided as flashcards to assess that children can read Phase 5 non-decodable common words (identified as 'tricky words' in *Letters and Sounds*). To assess spelling of these words, pronounce each one for the children to write or spell using their magnetic letters.

Catch-up activities for Assessment Sheets 8–11

Assessment area	Method
New graphemes, vowel digraphs and vowel trigraphs	For this catch-up work, children can be grouped, where possible, according to the type of difficulty they are having, and then revisit together the relevant Units and games, e.g. Unit 20 for the vowel digraph 'ir'.

Phase 6 Assessment (after Unit 30)

Assessment area	Method
Rules for adding suffixes and prefixes – Spelling	Carry out with groups or the whole class. Explain the instructions: 'Read each sentence and circle the missing word.' You could show some examples on the board first. For example: Have you hurt your _____? (knee/nee) RESOURCE: ASSESSMENT SHEET 12 *Note: See Assessment Sheet 8 note.*
Rules for adding suffixes and prefixes – Reading	While this reading assessment can be used for the whole class, you may find it is most useful when carried out with the children having the greatest difficulty with Assessment 12. Note the accuracy of the decoding of these further nonwords on Assessment Sheet 13. RESOURCE: ASSESSMENT SHEET 13 *The nonwords are also provided on flashcards which can be downloaded from the software (see page 19).*

Catch-up activities for Assessment Sheets 12 & 13

Assessment area	Method
Rules for adding suffixes and prefixes	For this catch-up work, children can be grouped, where possible, according to the type of difficulty they are having, and then revisit together the relevant units and games, e.g. Unit 28 for the suffix morpheme 'ing'.

Phonics Bug
Assessment sheet 8

New graphemes and vowel digraphs/trigraphs – Spelling

Name: _____ Date: _____

Unit	Cloze procedure sentence	Word selection	
13	Can you tell me _____ one? Please answer the _____ .	which fone	wich phone
14	Jack fell and is in _____ . Please can I have some _____ ?	payn cake	pain caik
15	Please _____ the car. Try not to get up to _____ .	cleen mischief	clean mischeef
16	The baby _____ all night. You can have _____ .	cried mien	cride mine
17	Jane has a pretty _____ in her hair. Please do not _____ the animals.	bow poak	boe poke
18	Poppy has a _____ dress. Can I play a _____ ?	blue toon	blew tune
19	Can you _____ me a picture? Where is my _____ , please?	draw bawl	drau ball
20	Give this to the _____ , please. Have you _____ this song?	gurl heard	girl herd
21	Please put the _____ away. Can you lend me a _____ coin?	toy pownd	toi pound

Assessment sheet 9

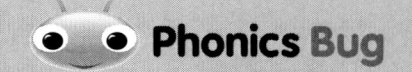

New graphemes and vowel digraphs/trigraphs – Spelling

Name: _____   Date: _____

Unit	Cloze procedure sentence	Word selection	
22	I do not have a hat to _____ .	wear	ware
23	After summer, I go to a new _____ .	school	skule
24	I am going to _____ home. I like the smell of Gran's _____ .	sycle scent	cycle sent
25	We have _____ today. Follow the _____ round the garden.	gym hedge	gim hej
26	Please _____ your hair. Please put down your _____ . We had an _____ crumble today.	coam knife apul	comb nife apple
27	I have a terrible _____ . The class has a drama _____ today. Stop at the next _____ . The football team gets a _____ train. A _____ came to the party.	ich seshun junction speshil magician	itch session junkshon special majishun
28	Tap your _____ with your fingers. At tea-time we like to have _____ . Do not _____ away from home. _____ and sit down, please.	head waffles wonder Come	hed woffles wander Cum

Phonics Bug

Assessment sheet 10

New graphemes and vowel digraphs/trigraphs – Reading

Name: _____ Date: _____

Unit	Nonword	Pronunciation guide	Blending notes
13	**phant**	As in 'fant'	
13	**bisual**	As in 'visual'	
14	**daim**	As in 'fame'	
14	**cay**	As in 'day'	
14	**pake**	As in 'bake'	
15	**feam**	As in 'beam'	
15	**heeb**	As in 'sheep'	
15	**beve**	As in 'Eve'	
16	**kigh**	As in 'nigh'	
16	**nied**	As in 'tied'	
16	**cly**	As in 'fly'	
16	**dife**	As in 'strife'	
17	**fow**	As in 'blow' or 'cow'	
17	**boam**	As in 'foam'	
17	**cose**	As in 'hose'	
18	**bued**	As in 'sued'	
18	**bew**	As in 'new'	
18	**fube**	As in 'tube'	

Assessment sheet 11

New graphemes and vowel digraphs/trigraphs – Reading

Name: _____ Date: _____

Unit	Nonword	Pronunciation guide	Blending notes
19	nawn	As in 'drawn'	
19	paum	As in 'drawn'	
20	thirk	As in 'shirt'	
20	gert	As in 'bert'	
20	kearn	As in 'herd'	
21	voim	As in 'coin'	
21	doy	As in 'toy'	
22	bleer	As in 'beer'	
22	sare	As in 'pear'	
23	carn	Hard 'k' sound	
23	kint	Hard 'k' sound	
24	cem	Soft c sound (sem)	
24	dence	Soft c sound (dense)	
25	dinge	Soft g sound (dinj)	
25	gyl	Soft g sound (jil)	
26	somb	Silent b (som)	
26	kneb	Silent k (neb)	
27	wab	Short vowel o (wob)	

Phonics Bug

Assessment sheet 12

Rules for adding suffixes and prefixes – Spelling

Name: _____   Date: _____

Unit	Cloze procedure sentence	Word selection	
28	My sister's _____ is in June.	weeding	wedding
28	I fell and _____ my t-shirt. That is a nice _____ jacket.	ripped padded	rippt paded
28	The cat is _____ the dog. We saw the ice _____ on TV.	chasing skateing	chaseing skating
28	I _____ you would be here. We had _____ cheese on toast.	hoped gratted	hopped grated
29	We saw the _____ at the circus.	clownz	clowns
29	Count the _____ on the shelf. How many _____ will we need? The silver _____ need cleaning. Pet rabbits live in _____ .	glasses boxses dishs hutches	glases boxes dishes hutchs
30	Reset the DVD to _____ the film.	reeplai	replay
30	On our return, we had to _____ the cases.	unnpak	unpack
30	The water bottle needs _____ . Remember the TV has to be _____ . Tracey _____ her new doll. The driver _____ his lorry.	refilling unplugged unndresses reloaded	reefilling unplugd undresses reeloaded

Assessment sheet 13

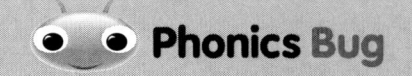

Rules for adding suffixes and prefixes – Reading

Name: _____   Date: _____

Unit	Nonword	Pronunciation guide	Blending notes
28	**dobing**	Long vowel 'o' as in 'robing'	
28	**kobbing**	Short vowel 'o' as in 'shopping'	
28	**tropped**	Short vowel 'o' as in 'dropped'	
28	**hobed**	Long vowel 'o' as in 'robed'	
29	**unfoll**	See if prefix pronounced as one unit i.e. /un/	
29	**rebick**	See if prefix pronounced as one unit i.e. /re/	
30	**unbroded**	See if prefix 'un' and suffix 'ed' each pronounced as one unit i.e. /un/ and /ed/	
30	**relinding**	See if prefix 're' and suffix 'ing' each pronounced as one unit i.e. /re/ and /ing/	

Guide to teaching Sessions

Every Phoneme Session in the programme follows exactly the same pattern of teaching (with the exception of Unit 1), as does every Language Session. There is a Language Session for each unit (group of letters). The pattern and delivery method of teaching each Session is described here. You are advised to use these pages to familiarise yourself with the method of teaching before you begin the programme. Pages 43-106 give you a detailed plan describing the content of each Session. There is also a 'Guide' button on the software, which will act as an *aide-memoire*.

Limited interactive whiteboard access

If you have only limited access to an interactive whiteboard, you can:

- Use the resource cards and writing on the board to substitute for the Reading Teaching Elements, the asset bank contents and free-writing on screen.
- Use magnetic letters for all uses of the electronic Magnetic letters.
- Carry out your own demonstrations of letter formation, letter-sound articulation and blending.

Generic lesson guidance

Remember that each Phoneme and Language Session should feature the following:

- The Alphabet song to begin and end every Session (if letter names are taught)
- Learning intentions and desired outcomes discussed at the beginning of each lesson
- Learning outcomes discussed at the end of each lesson
- The necessary next steps (online pupil games, relevant Unit PCMs for guided independent work, and relevant reading books)

The target phonemes are stated at the start of each session

Unit 26

Target phoneme /r/ written as 'wr'

INTRODUCTION
- Play the alphabet song twice, once with voice accompaniment, children listening and singing along with accompaniment, and once with children singing along to the music without voice accompaniment.
- Discuss with the children the learning intentions for the day.

REVISION
(previously taught grapheme–phoneme correspondences; blending phonemes for reading; segmenting spoken words for spelling)
- Go through the Revision screens at a brisk pace.
- Watch out for any children who have not remembered the phonemes or the graphemes.

LESSON

Sounds
- Choose the relevant lesson session.
- Say the phoneme /r/, and ask the children to repeat it after you. Make sure you keep the sound pure and encourage the children to do the same.
- Explain that 'wr' at the beginning of words sounds /r/ as in "write" ("silent 'w'").

Visual Search
- Bring up the words from the asset bank onto the Work area. Ask the children to highlight the 'wr' in each of the words. Do not pronounce the words.

Reading
- Click the Reading tab to see the word.
- Click Blend to watch and hear the Bug's demonstration of how to blend the word. Click Undo and ask a child to come to the Work area and move the arrow. Encourage the whole class to blend the phonemes out loud as the arrow is moving along.
- Work through each of the words in sequence.

Spelling
- The children return to their seats.
- Start by selecting the Words tab. Click Say to hear the word and ask the children to repeat it, then ask the children to use pencil and paper or their magnetic letters to make the word, saying the word every time they write down or look for a letter. Ask a child to come up to the Work area to make the word. Did everyone get it right?
- Ask a child to use the arrow to push the letters together. Encourage the class to blend the word together out loud.
- Repeat for the remaining word under the Words tab.
- Under the Pictures tab, click Show to display each image and repeat the process for each one. (See pages 8–9 and 12–13.)

Writing
- Ask the children to find the letters 'w' and 'r' among their magnetic letters and to feel the shape of them. Click Show and ask the children to look and listen as the lowercase letters are formed.
- Ask a child to direct you how to write the letters as you write them on the empty Work area.
- Ask the child to write them on the dashed lines, then ask the children to practise writing 'wr' themselves.
- Select uppercase and repeat.

Follow-up
- Click Say to hear the sentence. Repeat the sentence, then dictate it slowly and deliberately for the children to write it. Then click Show to reveal the correct answer. (See page 13.)

WRAP-UP
- Recap the learning intentions with the children.
- Play the alphabet song and encourage the children to sing along, signifying the end of the session.

Learning intentions are to:
- recap what we know
- say the /r/ phoneme
- learn different ways to spell the /r/ phoneme
- read and spell words of more than one syllable
- write a dictated sentence

Focus content: revision

Letters and Sounds
r — Unit 4

Reading
print, rock, rag, rim

Writing and Spelling
red, ran, rug, rid

Focus content: lesson

Sounds
/r/

Visual search
wrinkled, wring, wriggle, wrong

Reading
Audio: wrist, write, wrestle, wreck
No audio: wrong, wrote, wriggle, wrinkle

Spelling
Words tab: wrap, write
Pictures tab: wren, wrapper

Writing
wr

Follow-up
Dictation
Wrap the present and write your name on the card.

Next steps
- Play the online pupil games for Unit 25
- Complete the phoneme PCM for Unit 26 (wr)
- Read the Phonics Bug books that practise /j/ alternatives: *Different Homes*, *Giant George and the Robin*

This panel gives you at-a-glance information about the content of the session

Suggested next steps in the form of guided independent work and Phonics Bug reading books are given throughout

Guide to teaching Sessions

The daily lesson plans
Each Phoneme Session is divided into Revision and Lesson (with the exception of Unit 1, Sessions 1-4). The Revision Session ensures that the children have retained all the teaching from their previous Sessions. Each Language session is divided into Irregular (key words) and Lesson. Remember that the programme is effective if the children are active participants in the lessons.

Alphabet song
The Alphabet Song, automatically highlighting the letters, can begin and end every Session. It helps children to learn the alphabet and to practise letter-name correspondence. One version of the song includes accompaniment and singing, but before long the children can sing the song on their own, so the second version of the song needs only the accompaniment with one child coming out to point to the letters as they are sung. The software provides for singing in both lower case and upper case letters.

Glossary of terms
Adjacent consonants two or more letters that represent two or more phonemes, e.g. 'fr' beginning the word "fridge"

Blend drawing together the constituent phonemes of a written word in order to read it

Digraph two successive letters that represent one phoneme, e.g. 'oa', 'ck', etc.

Grapheme letter or combination of letters that represent a phoneme, e.g. 'r', 'ch'

Phoneme the smallest unit of sound that changes a word's meaning; it can be represented by one or several letters, e.g. /a/ or /sh/

Segment breaking down the sounds of a spoken word into phonemes in order to spell it

Trigraph three successive letters representing one phoneme, e.g. 'igh'

Language sessions enable children to apply the skills taught in prior sessions to read and spell irregular/high-frequency words, captions and sentences

Unit 26

Language session
After: alternatives for /l/, /m/, /n/, /r/

INTRODUCTION
- Play the alphabet song twice, once with voice accompaniment, children listening and singing along with accompaniment, and once with children singing along to the music without voice accompaniment.
- Discuss with the children the learning intentions for the day.

HIGH-FREQUENCY WORDS
Reading
- Select the H-F words part of the session.
- Click Show to display the words, and ask the children to read them.
- Click Answer to listen to the word being read.
- Ask the children about the punctuation mark. Did the children remember it is called an "apostrophe"?

Spelling
- Click Say to hear the words, and ask the children to repeat each word. Put the word into a sentence so that the children understand its meaning, for example, "I don't like pickle", "We can't play outdoors because it's raining", "Mary didn't eat all of her lunch".
- (i) You may want to explain to the children when appropriate that:
  – "don't" stands for "do not" – the apostrophe replaces the 'o' of "not"
  – "can't" stands for "cannot" – the apostrophe replaces the 'no' of "not"
  – "didn't" stands for "did not" – the apostrophe replaces the 'o' of "not"
- Say the target word, and ask the children to repeat it again. Ask the class to give each letter, and ask a child to come up to the Work area and drag up the correct letters into the spaces provided. Point out that the apostrophe is already on the screen.
- Ask the class to read the word, and click Say for them to hear it again.
- Repeat for the remaining words.

LESSON
Reading
- Click Show to display the sentences, and ask the children to read them.
- Click Answer to reveal whether they are right.
- Point out the use of direct speech again and the use of speech marks (see Unit 23).

Spelling and Writing
- The children return to their seats.
- Remind the children about the dictation procedure.
- Click Say to hear the first sentence, and ask the children to repeat it.
- Slowly and distinctly dictate the sentence, asking the children to tell you how to write the words.
- Click Answer to reveal the sentence. Did the children tell you how to write it correctly?
- Repeat for the second sentence asking the children to write it using pencil and paper or their magnetic letters. (See page 13.)

Follow-up
- Write "do not", "cannot" and "did not" on the Work area.
- Ask the children to write the short version (contraction) with an apostrophe.
- Then reverse the procedure: write the shortened version on the Work area and ask the children to write the full version.
- Ask the children to write their own sentence containing any of don't, can't or didn't.

WRAP-UP
- Recap the learning intentions with the children.
- Play the alphabet song again and encourage the children to sing along, signifying the end of the session.

Notes to the teacher explain any particular points or exceptions

---

Learning intentions are provided for each session

Learning intentions are to:
- learn to read and spell irregular words with an apostrophe – "don't", "can't" and "didn't"
- write sentences from dictation which include "don't", "can't" and "didn't"

Focus content: h-f words

Reading
don't, can't, didn't

Spelling
don't, can't, didn't

Focus content: lesson

Reading
The sign said: 'Don't climb this apple tree', but I did.
I fell and hurt my wrist.
Now I can't write.

Spelling and Writing
I knew I was wrong, but I didn't think.
It was a hard but simple lesson.

Follow-up
Children write their own sentence containing any of don't, can't or didn't.

Next steps
- Play the online language pupil games for Unit 26
- Complete the language PCM for Unit 26
- Read the Phonics Bug books that practise /l/, /m/, /n/, /r/ alternatives: Dinosaurs, The Purple Muncher

Unit 13

Target phoneme /zh/ written as 's'

INTRODUCTION
- Play the alphabet song twice, once with voice accompaniment, children listening and singing along with accompaniment, and once with children singing along to the music without voice accompaniment.
- Discuss with the children the learning intentions for the day.

REVISION
[previously taught grapheme–phoneme correspondences; blending phonemes for reading; segmenting spoken words for spelling]
- Go through the Revision screens at a brisk pace.
- Watch out for any children who have not remembered the phonemes or the graphemes.

LESSON
Sounds
- Choose the relevant Lesson session.
- Say the phoneme /zh/, and ask the children to repeat it after you. Make sure you keep the sound pure and encourage the children to do the same.
- Explain that the /zh/ sound is spelled with an 's' before 'ure', 'ion', or 'ual'.

Visual Search
- Bring up the words from the asset bank onto the Work area. Ask children to highlight the letter for /zh/ in each of the words, saying whether it is at the beginning, the middle or the end of the word. Do not pronounce the words.

Reading
- Click the Reading tab to see the word and syllables.
- Click Blend to watch and hear the Bug's demonstration of how to blend the syllables and the word. Click Undo and ask a child to come to the Work area and move the arrow. Encourage the whole class to blend the phonemes of the syllables and then the sounds of the word out loud as the arrow is moving along.
- Work through each of the words in sequence.
- ⓘ For the words "measure", "treasure" and "pleasure", you may want to teach that 'ea' sounds short /e/ in this first session; it is taught more fully later in Unit 27. Similarly, for the word "leisure", you may want to point out the unusual 'ei' grapheme for the short /e/ sound; 'g' can also sound /zh/ as in "beige".

Spelling
- The children return to their seats.
- Start by selecting the Words tab. Click Say to hear the word and ask the children to repeat it, then ask the children to use their magnetic letters to make the word, saying the word every time they look for a letter. Ask a child to come up to the Work area to make the word. Did everyone get it right?
- Ask a child to use the arrow to push the letters together. Encourage the class to blend the word together out loud.
- Repeat for the remaining words under the Words tab.
- Under the Pictures tab, click Show to display each image and repeat the process for each one. (See pages 8–9, 12.)

Writing
- Ask the children to find the letter 's' among their magnetic letters and to feel the shape of it. Click Show and ask the children to look and listen as the lowercase letter is formed.
- Ask a child to direct you how to write the letter as you write it on the empty Work area.
- Ask the child to write it on the dashed lines, then ask the children to practise writing the letter 's' themselves.
- Select uppercase and repeat.

Follow-up
- Click Say to hear the sentence. Repeat the sentence, then dictate it slowly and deliberately for the children to write it. Then click Show to reveal the correct answer. (See page 13.)

WRAP-UP
- Recap the learning intentions with the children.
- Play the alphabet song and encourage the children to sing along, signifying the end of the session.

Learning intentions are to:
- recap what we know
- say the /zh/ phoneme
- find the letter 's'
- read and spell words of one syllable or more with /zh/ in
- write a dictated sentence

Focus content: revision

Letters and Sounds
sh Unit 8
Reading
ship, flash, fish, shell
Writing and Spelling
shop, cash, rush, shed

Focus content: lesson

Sounds
/zh/

Visual search

treasure, erosion, television, usual

Reading

Audio: vision, treasure, usual, leisure

No audio: pleasure, casual, erosion

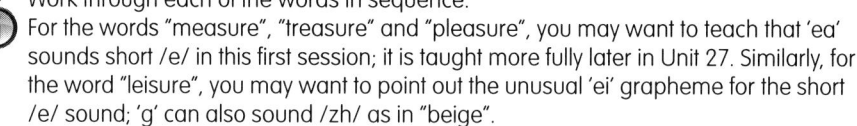

Spelling

Words tab: usual, division

Pictures tab: treasure, measure

Writing

s

Follow-up

Dictation

We need to measure the television.

Next steps
- Play the online pupil games for Unit 12
- Complete the phoneme PCM for Unit 13 (zh)
- Read the Phonics Bug books for Unit 12: A Job for Jim, A Little Green Monster, At the Dentist, Be a Cress Barber, Cool Cars, Fantastic Fish, Look What We Can Do!, Monsters!, Pompom Pets, Sea Fishing, Sid and the Boxer Pup, Sid and the Haircut, Sid Snaps, Snails, Springs and Things, Stop Helping!, Stuck in a Trap, The Bright Stars, There's Something in the Garden, Trains

Unit 13

Target phoneme /w/ written as 'wh'

INTRODUCTION
- Play the alphabet song twice, once with voice accompaniment, children listening and singing along with accompaniment, and once with children singing along to the music without voice accompaniment.
- Discuss with the children the learning intentions for the day.

REVISION
[previously taught grapheme–phoneme correspondences; blending phonemes for reading; segmenting spoken words for spelling]
- Go through the Revision screens at a brisk pace.
- Watch out for any children who have not remembered the phonemes or the graphemes.

LESSON

Sounds
- Choose the relevant lesson session.
- Select and drag the digraph 'wh' on to the Work area. Click on the digraph to hear how to say the phoneme /w/.
- Say the phoneme /w/, and ask the children to repeat it after you. Make sure you keep the sound pure and encourage the children to do the same.

Visual Search
- Bring up the words from the asset bank onto the Work area. Ask the children to highlight the 'wh' in each of the words, saying whether it is at the beginning, the middle or the end of the word. Do not pronounce the words.

Reading
- Click the Reading tab to see the word.
- Click Blend to watch and hear the Bug's demonstration of how to blend the word. Click Undo and ask a child to come to the Work area and move the arrow. Encourage the whole class to blend the phonemes out loud as the arrow is moving along.
- Work through each of the words in sequence.
- Point out that "which" and "when" are question words like "what", "why" and "who".

Spelling
- The children return to their seats.
- Start by selecting the Words tab. Click Say to hear the word and ask the children to repeat it, then ask the children to use their magnetic letters to make the word, saying the word every time they look for a letter. Ask a child to come up to the Work area to make the word. Did everyone get it right?
- Ask a child to use the arrow to push the letters together. Encourage the class to blend the word together out loud.
- Repeat for the remaining words under the Words tab.
- Under the Pictures tab, click Show to display each image and repeat the process for each one. (See page 8.)
- Select the Spelling video and play it once through.

Writing
- Ask the children to find the letters 'w' and 'h' among their magnetic letters and to feel the shape of them. Click Show and ask the children to look and listen as the lowercase letters are formed.
- Ask a child to direct you how to write the letters as you write them on the empty Work area.
- Ask the child to write it on the dashed lines, then ask the children to practise writing the letters 'wh' themselves.
- Select uppercase and repeat.

Follow-up
- Click Say to hear the sentence. Repeat the sentence, then dictate it slowly and deliberately for the children to write it. Then click Show to reveal the correct answer. (See page 13.)

WRAP-UP
- Recap the learning intentions with the children.
- Play the alphabet song and encourage children to sing along, signifying the end of the session.

Learning intentions are to:
- recap what we know
- say the /w/ phoneme
- find the letters 'wh'
- read and spell words of one syllable or more with 'wh' in
- write a dictated sentence

Focus content: revision

Letters and Sounds
w ➔ Unit 6

Reading
win, wick, swim, wigwam

Writing and Spelling
web, will, twig, wagon

Focus content: lesson

Sounds
/w/

Visual search
whip, wham, whiz, when

Reading
Audio: whip, wham, whizz, when
No audio: which, whist, whack, whiplash

Spelling
Words tab: when, whizz
Pictures tab: whisk, whiff
Video: wet, when

Writing
wh

Follow-up
Dictation
The whip went whack!

Next steps
- Play the online pupil games for Unit 12
- Complete the phoneme PCM for Unit 13 (wh)
- Read the Phonics Bug books for Unit 12: A Job for Jim, A Little Green Monster, At the Dentist, Be a Cress Barber, Cool Cars, Fantastic Fish, Look What We Can Do!, Monsters!, Pompom Pets, Sea Fishing, Sid and the Boxer Pup, Sid and the Haircut, Sid Snaps, Snails, Springs and Things, Stop Helping!, Stuck in a Trap, The Bright Stars, There's Something in the Garden, Trains

Unit 13

Target phoneme /f/ written as 'ph'

INTRODUCTION
- Play the alphabet song twice, once with voice accompaniment, children listening and singing along with accompaniment, and once with children singing along to the music without voice accompaniment.
- Discuss with the children the learning intentions for the day.

REVISION
(previously taught grapheme–phoneme correspondences; blending phonemes for reading; segmenting spoken words for spelling)
- Go through the Revision screens at a brisk pace.
- Watch out for any children who have not remembered the phonemes or the graphemes.

LESSON

Sounds
- Choose the relevant lesson session.
- Select and drag the digraph 'ph' on to the Work area. Click on the digraph to hear how to say the phoneme /f/.
- Say the phoneme /f/, and ask the children to repeat it after you. Make sure you keep the sound pure and encourage the children to do the same.

Visual Search
- Bring up the words from the asset bank onto the Work area. Ask the children to highlight the 'ph' in each of the words, saying whether it is at the beginning, the middle or the end of the word. Do not pronounce the words.

Reading
- Click the Reading tab to see the word and syllables.
- Click Blend to watch and hear the Bug's demonstration of how to blend the syllables and the word. Click Undo and ask a child to come to the Work area and move the arrow. Encourage the whole class to blend the phonemes of the syllables and then the sounds of the word out loud as the arrow is moving along.
- Work through each of the words in sequence.
- (i) You may wish to point out that the two 'o' letters in "photo" sound the long vowel /ō/.

Spelling
- The children return to their seats.
- Start by selecting the Words tab. Click Say to hear the word and ask the children to repeat it, then ask the children to use their magnetic letters to make the word, saying the word every time they look for a letter. Ask a child to come up to the Work area to make the word. Did everyone get it right?
- Ask a child to use the arrow to push the letters together. Encourage the class to blend the word together out loud.
- Repeat for the remaining words under the Words tab.
- Under the Pictures tab, click Show to display the images and repeat the process for each one. (See page 12.)

Writing
- Ask children to find the letters 'p' and 'h' among their magnetic letters and to feel the shape of them. Click Show and ask children to look and listen as the lowercase letters are formed.
- Ask a child to direct you how to write the letters as you write them on the empty Work area.
- Ask the child to write them on the dashed lines, then ask the children to practise writing 'ph' themselves.
- Select uppercase and repeat.

Follow-up
- Click Say to hear the sentence. Repeat the sentence, then dictate it slowly and deliberately for the children to write it. Then click Show to reveal the correct answer. (See page 13.)

WRAP-UP
- Recap the learning intentions with the children.
- Play the alphabet song and encourage the children to sing along, signifying the end of the session.

Learning intentions are to:
- recap what we know
- say the /f/ phoneme
- find the letters 'ph'
- read and spell words of one syllable or more with 'ph' in
- write a dictated sentence

Focus content: revision

Letters and Sounds
f ⊙ Unit 5
Reading
fun, puff, fan, fin
Writing and Spelling
if, fit, fib, cuff

Focus content: lesson

Sounds
/f/
Visual search
dolphin, graph, elephant, Philip
Reading
Audio: dolphin, graph, elephant, Philip
No audio: photo, phonics, alphabet, phantom
Spelling
Words tab: photo, orphan
Pictures tab: elephant, dolphin
Writing
ph
Follow-up
Dictation
Look at the photo of the dolphin.

Next steps
- Play the online pupil games for Unit 12
- Complete the phoneme PCM for Unit 13 (ph)
- Read the Phonics Bug books for Unit 12: A Job for Jim, A Little Green Monster, At the Dentist, Be a Cress Barber, Cool Cars, Fantastic Fish, Look What We Can Do!, Monsters!, Pompom Pets, Sea Fishing, Sid and the Boxer Pup, Sid and the Haircut, Sid Snaps, Snails, Springs and Things, Stop Helping!, Stuck in a Trap, The Bright Stars, There's Something in the Garden, Trains

Unit 13

Language session

After: zh, wh, ph

INTRODUCTION
- Play the alphabet song twice, once with voice accompaniment, children listening and singing along with accompaniment, and once with children singing along to the music without voice accompaniment.
- Discuss with the children the learning intentions for the day.

IRREGULAR

Reading
- Select the Irregular part of the session.
- Click Show to display the words, and ask the children to read them.
- Click Answer to listen to the word being read.
- Explain that in "their", 'eir' sounds /air/.

Spelling
- Click Say to hear the words, and ask the children to repeat each word. Put the word into a sentence so that the children understand its meaning, for example, "Oh! What a terrible noise!", "They went to collect their coats".
- Say the target word, and ask the children to repeat it again. Ask the class to give each letter, and ask a child to come up to the Work area and drap up the correct letters into the spaces provided.
- Ask the class to read the word and click Say for them to hear it again.
- Repeat for the remaining word.

LESSON

Reading
- Click Show to display the sentences, and ask the children to read them.
- Click Answer to reveal whether they are right.

Spelling and Writing
- The children return to their seats.
- Remind the children about the dictation procedure.
- Click Say to hear the first sentence, and ask the children to repeat it.
- Slowly and distinctly dictate the sentence, while the children tell you how to write it.
- Click Answer to reveal the sentence. Did the children tell you what to write correctly?
- Repeat for the second sentence. This time ask the children to write it using pencil and paper or their magnetic letters. (See page 13.)

Follow-up
- Display the picture and ask the children questions relating to it, to promote discussion and stimulate their thinking skills. You might ask: "What are the children doing? Where do you think the children are? Is this something you would like to do? Why, or why not?"
- Encourage the children to come up with sentences using words they have learnt in the programme – perhaps asking their own question about the picture.
- Write up on the Work area one or more good sentences or questions suggested by the children to further the discussion.

WRAP-UP
- Recap the learning intentions with the children.
- Play the alphabet song again and encourage the children to sing along, signifying the end of the session.

Learning intentions are to:
- learn to read and spell irregular words "oh" and "their"
- write sentences from dictation with one- and two-syllable words
- contribute to discussion, learning to ask their own questions

Focus content: irregular

Reading
oh, their

Spelling
oh, their

Focus content: lesson

Reading
Philip and Sophie swam with the dolphins. Oh, it was such a pleasure! Which of their photos do you like best?

Spelling and Writing
When did they swim with the dolphins? Their trip was last summer.

Follow-up
Picture shows: children swimming with dolphins

Next steps
- Play the online language pupil games for Unit 13
- Complete the language PCM for Unit 13
- Read the Phonics Bug books that practise wh, ph: Keeping a Pet, Up in a Tree, Whizz!

Unit 14

Target phoneme /ai/ written as 'ay'

INTRODUCTION
- Play the alphabet song twice, once with voice accompaniment, children listening and singing along with accompaniment, and once with children singing along to the music without voice accompaniment.
- Discuss with the children the learning intentions for the day.

REVISION
[previously taught grapheme–phoneme correspondences; blending phonemes for reading; segmenting spoken words for spelling]
- Go through the Revision screens at a brisk pace.
- Watch out for any children who have not remembered the phonemes or the graphemes.

LESSON

Sounds
- Choose the relevant lesson session.
- Select and drag the digraph 'ay' on to the Work area. Click on the digraph to hear how to say the phoneme /ai/.
- Say the phoneme /ai/, and ask the children to repeat it after you. Make sure you keep the sound pure and encourage the children to do the same.
- Explain to the children that 'ay' is generally used at the end of a word or syllable. It is a vowel digaraph.

Visual Search
- Bring up the words from the asset bank onto the Work area. Ask the children to highlight the 'ay' in each of the words, saying whether it is at the beginning, the middle or the end of the word. Do not pronounce the words.

Reading
- Click the Reading tab to see the word.
- Click Blend to watch and hear the Bug's demonstration of how to blend the word. Click Undo and ask a child to come to the Work area and move the arrow. Encourage the whole class to blend the phonemes out loud as the arrow is moving along.
- Work through each of the words in sequence.

Spelling
- The children return to their seats.
- Start by selecting the Words tab. Click Say to hear the word and ask the children to repeat it, then ask the children to use their magnetic letters to make the word, saying the word every time they look for a letter. Ask a child to come up to the Work area to make the word. Did everyone get it right?
- Ask a child to use the arrow to push the letters together. Encourage the class to blend the word together out loud.
- Repeat for the remaining word under the Words tab.
- Under the Pictures tab, click Show to display each image and repeat the process for each one. (See pages 8–9.)

Writing
- Ask the children to find the letters 'a' and 'y' among their magnetic letters and to feel the shape of them. Click Show and ask the children to look and listen as the lowercase letters are formed.
- Ask a child to direct you how to write the letters as you write them on the empty Work area.
- Ask the child to write them on the dashed lines, then ask the children to practise writing the letters 'ay' themselves.
- Select uppercase and repeat.

Follow-up
- Click Say to hear the sentence. Repeat the sentence, then dictate it slowly and deliberately for the children to write it. Then click Show to reveal the correct answer. (See page 13.)

WRAP-UP
- Recap the learning intentions with the children.
- Play the alphabet song and encourage the children to sing along, signifying the end of the session.

Learning intentions are to:
- recap what we know
- learn different ways to spell the /ai/ phoneme
- read and spell words of one syllable or more
- write a dictated sentence

Focus content: revision

Letters and Sounds
ai ↵ Unit 9
Reading
rain, tail, nail, snail
Writing and Spelling
sail, wait, main, train

Focus content: lesson

Sounds
/ai/
Visual search
may, play, tray, stay
Reading
Audio: say, pray, Kay, away
No audio: day, clay, spray, stay
Spelling
Words tab: stray, Sunday
Pictures tab: hay, tray
Writing
ay
Follow-up
Reinforce: 4 steps for reading syllables, using "Sunday" (see page 12) graphemes 'ai' and 'ay' as same vowel sound /ai/
Dictation
Can you play with me today?

Next steps
- Play the online pupil games for Unit 13
- Complete the phoneme PCM for Unit 14 (ay)
- Read the Phonics Bug books that practise wh, ph: Keeping a Pet, Up in a Tree, Whizz!

Unit 14

Target phoneme /ai/ written as 'a–e'

INTRODUCTION
- Play the alphabet song twice, once with voice accompaniment, children listening and singing along with accompaniment, and once with children singing along to the music without voice accompaniment.
- Discuss with the children the learning intentions for the day.

REVISION
[previously taught grapheme–phoneme correspondences; blending phonemes for reading; segmenting spoken words for spelling]
- Go through the Revision screens at a brisk pace.
- Watch out for any children who have not remembered the phonemes or the graphemes.

LESSON
Sounds
- Choose the relevant lesson session.
- Say the phoneme /ai/, and ask the children to repeat it after you. Make sure you keep the sound pure and encourage the children to do the same.
- Explain to the children that 'a–e' is called a 'split digraph'. The silent 'e' changes /a/ to /ai/.

Visual Search
- Bring up the words from the asset bank onto the Work area. Ask the children to highlight the 'a–e' in each of the words. Do not pronounce the words.

Reading
- Click the Reading tab to see the word.
- Click Blend to watch and hear the Bug's demonstration of how to blend the word. Click Undo and ask a child to come to the Work area and move the arrow. Encourage the whole class to blend the phonemes out loud as the arrow is moving along.
- Work through each of the words in sequence.

Spelling
- The children return to their seats.
- Start by selecting the Words tab. Click Say to hear the word and ask the children to repeat it, then ask the children to use their magnetic letters to make the word, saying the word every time they look for a letter. Ask a child to come up to the Work area to make the word. Did everyone get it right?
- Ask a child to use the arrow to push the letters together. Encourage the class to blend the word together out loud.
- Repeat for the remaining words under the Words tab.
- Under the Pictures tab, click Show to display each image and repeat the process for each one. (See pages 8–9.)

Writing
- Ask the children to find the letters 'a', 't' and 'e' among their magnetic letters and to feel the shape of them. Click Show and ask children to look and listen as the lowercase letters are formed.
- Ask a child to direct you how to write the letters as you write them on the empty Work area.
- Ask the child to write them on the dashed lines, then ask the children to practise writing 'ate' themselves.
- Select uppercase and repeat.

Follow-up
- Click Say to hear the sentence. Repeat the sentence, then dictate it slowly and deliberately for the children to write it. Then click Show to reveal the correct answer. (See page 13.)

WRAP-UP
- Recap the learning intentions with the children.
- Play the alphabet song and encourage the children to sing along, signifying the end of the session.

Learning intentions are to:
- recap what we know
- learn different ways to spell the /ai/ phoneme
- read and spell words of one syllable or more
- write a dictated sentence

Focus content: revision

Letters and Sounds
ay

Reading
stray, Sunday, hay, tray

Writing and Spelling
may, clay, spray, away

Focus content: lesson

Sounds
/ai/

Visual search
ate, safe, spade, pancake

Reading
Audio: ape, name, snake, plate
No audio: came, shake, scrape, make

Spelling
Words tab: made, take
Pictures tab: spade, grapes

Writing
ate

Follow-up
Reinforce: 4 steps for reading syllables, using "pancake" (see page 12) silent 'e' not counting as a vowel sound in a syllable
Dictation
Scrape the mud off your trainers.

Next steps
- Play the online pupil games for Unit 13
- Complete the phoneme PCM for Unit 14 (a–e)
- Read the Phonics Bug books that practise wh, ph: Keeping a Pet, Up in a Tree, Whizz!

Unit 14

Target phoneme /ai/ written as 'eigh', 'ey', 'ei'

INTRODUCTION
- Play the alphabet song twice, once with voice accompaniment, children listening and singing along with accompaniment, and once with children singing along to the music without voice accompaniment.
- Discuss with the children the learning intentions for the day.

REVISION
[previously taught grapheme–phoneme correspondences; blending phonemes for reading; segmenting spoken words for spelling]
- Go through the Revision screens at a brisk pace.
- Watch out for any children who have not remembered the phonemes or the graphemes.

LESSON
Sounds
- Choose the relevant lesson session.
- Say the phoneme /ai/, and ask the children to repeat it after you. Make sure you keep the sound pure and encourage the children to do the same.
- Explain that you are going to look at some more ways to spell the /ai/ phoneme. Introduce the children to the spellings 'eigh', 'ey' and 'ei'. Mention too that 'aigh' sounds /ai/ as in "straight", and 'ea' sounds /ai/ as in "break" and "great".

Visual Search
- Bring up the words from the asset bank onto the Work area. Ask the children to highlight the 'eigh', 'ey' or 'ei' in each of the words, saying whether it is at the beginning, the middle or the end of the word. Do not pronounce the words.

Reading
- Click the Reading tab to see the word.
- Click Blend to watch and hear the Bug's demonstration of how to blend the word. Click Undo and ask a child to come to the Work area and move the arrow. Encourage the whole class to blend the phonemes out loud as the arrow is moving along.
- Work through each of the words in sequence.

Spelling
- The children return to their seats.
- Start by selecting the Words tab. Click Say to hear the word and ask the children to repeat it, then ask the children to use their magnetic letters to make the word, saying the word every time they look for a letter. Ask a child to come up to the Work area to make the word. Did everyone get it right?
- Ask a child to use the arrow to push the letters together. Encourage the class to blend the word together out loud.
- Repeat for the remaining word under the Words tab.
- Under the Pictures tab, click Show to display each image and repeat the process for each one. (See pages 8–9.)
- Select the Spelling video and play it once through.

Writing
- Ask the children to find the letters 'e', 'i', 'g', and 'h' among their magnetic letters and to feel the shape of them. Click Show and ask the children to look and listen as the lowercase letters are formed.
- Ask a child to direct you how to write the letters as you write them on the empty Work area.
- Ask the child to write them on the dashed lines, then ask the children to practise writing 'eigh' themselves.
- Repeat for 'ey' and 'ei'.

Follow-up
- Click Say to hear the sentence. Repeat the sentence, then dictate it slowly and deliberately for the children to write it. Then click Show to reveal the correct answer. (See page 13.)

WRAP-UP
- Recap the learning intentions with the children.
- Play the alphabet song and encourage the children to sing along, signifying the end of the session.

Learning intentions are to:
- recap what we know
- learn different ways to spell the /ai/ phoneme
- read and spell words of one syllable or more
- write a dictated sentence

Focus content: revision

Letters and Sounds
a–e
Reading
made, take, spade, grapes
Writing and Spelling
came, shake, scrape, make

Focus content: lesson

Sounds
/ai/
Visual search
weigh, obey, reign, hey
Reading
Audio: weight, they, reins, convey
No audio: neigh, prey, vein, freight
Spelling
Words tab: prey, survey
Pictures tab: grey
Video: rain, day, name, grey
Writing
eigh, ey, ei
Follow-up
Dictation
They held the reins of the sleigh.

Next steps
- Play the online pupil games for Unit 13
- Complete the phoneme PCM for Unit 14 (eigh, ey, ei)
- Read the Phonics Bug books that practise wh, ph: Keeping a Pet, Up in a Tree, Whizz!

Unit 14

Language session

After: ay, a-e, eigh/ey/ei

INTRODUCTION
- Play the alphabet song twice, once with voice accompaniment, children listening and singing along with accompaniment, and once with children singing along to the music without voice accompaniment.
- Discuss with the children the learning intentions for the day.

HIGH-FREQUENCY WORDS

Reading
- Select the H-F words part of the session.
- Click Show to display the words, and ask the children to read them.
- Click Answer to listen to the word being read.

Spelling
- Click Say to hear the words, and ask the children to repeat each word. Put the word into a sentence so that the children understand its meaning, for example, "Mr and Mrs Smith went on holiday."
- Say the target word, and ask the children to repeat it again. Ask the class to give each letter, and ask a child to come up to the Work area and drag up the correct letters into the spaces provided.
- Ask the class to read the word and click Say for them to hear it again.
- Repeat for the remaining words.

LESSON

Reading
- Click Show to display the sentences, and ask the children to read them.
- Click Answer to reveal whether they are right.

Spelling and Writing
- The children return to their seats.
- Remind the children about the dictation procedure.
- Click Say to hear the first sentence, and ask the children to repeat it.
- Slowly and distinctly dictate the sentence, while the children tell you how to write it.
- Click Answer to reveal the sentence. Did the children tell you what to write correctly?
- Point out that in "have", 'a' takes the short vowel sound /a/; 'e' is silent for reading, but is needed for spelling.
- Repeat for the second and third sentences, asking the children to write them using pencil and paper or their magnetic letters. (See page 12.)

Follow-up
- Display the picture and ask the children questions relating to it, to promote discussion and stimulate their thinking skills. You might ask, "Why is the box up in the loft? Who put the box up in the loft? What do you think might be in the box? What if the children can't open the lock? How will they be able to find out what is in the box?"
- Encourage the children to come up with sentences using words they have learnt in the programme – perhaps asking their own question about the picture.
- Write up on the Work area one or more good sentences or questions suggested by the children to further the discussion.

WRAP-UP
- Recap the learning intentions with the children.
- Play the alphabet song again and encourage the children to sing along, signifying the end of the session.

Learning intentions are to:
- learn to read and spell irregular words "Mr" and "Mrs"
- write sentences from dictation with one- and two-syllable words
- contribute to discussion, learning to ask their own questions

Focus content: h-f words

Reading
Mr, Mrs

Spelling
Mr, Mrs

Focus content: lesson

Reading
Gail and Ray are twins. They are eight today. Mr and Mrs Blane made a cake for their party.

Spelling and Writing
They have to hunt for the grey party box. It is in the loft. They have to try to open the lock.

Follow-up
Picture shows: children opening the lock on the party box.

Next steps
- Play the online language pupil games for Unit 14
- Complete the language PCM for Unit 14
- Read the Phonics Bug books that practise /ai/ alternatives: Dave's Big Day, I Will Amaze You, The Runaway Train

Unit 15

Target phoneme /ee/ written as 'ea'

INTRODUCTION
- Play the alphabet song twice, once with voice accompaniment, children listening and singing along with accompaniment, and once with children singing along to the music without voice accompaniment.
- Discuss with the children the learning intentions for the day.

REVISION
[previously taught grapheme–phoneme correspondences; blending phonemes for reading; segmenting spoken words for spelling]
- Go through the Revision screens at a brisk pace.
- Watch out for any children who have not remembered the phonemes or the graphemes.

LESSON

Sounds
- Choose the relevant lesson session.
- Select and drag the digraph 'ea' on to the Work area. Click on the digraph to hear how to say the phoneme /ee/.
- Say the phoneme /ee/, and ask the children to repeat it after you. Make sure you keep the sound pure and encourage the children to do the same.

Visual Search
- Bring up the words from the asset bank onto the Work area. Ask the children to highlight the 'ea' in each of the words, saying whether it is at the beginning, the middle or the end of the word. Do not pronounce the words.

Reading
- Click the Reading tab to see the word.
- Click Blend to watch and hear the Bug's demonstration of how to blend the word. Click Undo and ask a child to come to the Work area and move the arrow. Encourage the whole class to blend the phonemes out loud as the arrow is moving along.
- Work through each of the words in sequence.

Spelling
- The children return to their seats.
- Start by selecting the Words tab. Click Say to hear the word and ask the children to repeat it, then ask the children to use their magnetic letters to make the word, saying the word every time they look for a letter. Ask a child to come up to the Work area to make the word. Did everyone get it right?
- Ask a child to use the arrow to push the letters together. Encourage the class to blend the word together out loud.
- Repeat for the remaining word under the Words tab.
- Under the Pictures tab, click Show to display the images and repeat the process for each word. (See pages 8–9.)

Writing
- Ask the children to find the letters 'e' and 'a' among their magnetic letters and to feel the shape of them. Click Show and ask the children to look and listen as the lowercase letters are formed.
- Ask a child to direct you how to write the letters as you write them on the empty Work area.
- Ask the child to write them on the dashed lines, then ask the children to practise writing the letters 'ea' by themselves.
- Select uppercase and repeat.

Follow-up
- Click Say to hear the sentence. Repeat the sentence, then dictate it slowly and deliberately for the children to write it. Then click Show to reveal the correct answer. (See page 13.)

WRAP-UP
- Recap the learning intentions with the children.
- Play the alphabet song and encourage the children to sing along, signifying the end of the session.

Learning intentions are to:
- recap what we know
- say the /ee/ phoneme
- learn different ways to spell the /ee/ phoneme
- read and spell words of one syllable or more
- write a dictated sentence

Focus content: revision

Letters and Sounds
ee ⟲ Unit 9

Reading
green, feet, sheep, bee

Writing and Spelling
peel, sleep, tree, see

Focus content: lesson

Sounds
/ee/

Visual search
eat, tea, clean, reach

Reading
Audio: eat, leaf, meal, teapot
No audio: beak, seat, each, seaweed

Spelling
Words tab: beach, heat
Pictures tab: seal, teapot

Writing
ea

Follow-up
Reinforce:
4 steps for reading syllables, using "seaweed" and "teapot" (see p.12)
graphemes 'ea' and 'ee' as same vowel sound /ee/
Dictation
We had a picnic meal on the beach.

Next steps
- Play the online pupil games for Unit 14
- Complete the phoneme PCM for Unit 15 (ea)
- Read the Phonics Bug books that practise /ai/ alternatives: Dave's Big Day, I Will Amaze You, The Runaway Train

Unit 15

Target phoneme /ee/ written as 'e–e'

INTRODUCTION
- Play the alphabet song twice, once with voice accompaniment, children listening and singing along with accompaniment, and once with children singing along to the music without voice accompaniment.
- Discuss with the children the learning intentions for the day.

REVISION
[previously taught grapheme–phoneme correspondences; blending phonemes for reading; segmenting spoken words for spelling]
- Go through the Revision screens at a brisk pace.
- Watch out for any children who have not remembered the phonemes or the graphemes.

LESSON

Sounds
- Choose the relevant lesson session.
- Say the phoneme /ee/, and ask the children to repeat it after you. Make sure you keep the sound pure and encourage the children to do the same.
- Explain to children that 'e–e' is called a 'split digraph'. The silent 'e' at the end changes /e/ in the middle to /ee/.

Visual Search
- Bring up the words from the asset bank onto the Work area. Ask children to highlight the 'e–e' in each of the words. Do not pronounce the words.

Reading
- Click the Reading tab to see the word.
- Click Blend to watch and hear the Bug's demonstration of how to blend the word. Click Undo and ask a child to come to the Work area and move the arrow. Encourage the whole class to blend the phonemes out loud as the arrow is moving along.
- Work through each of the words in sequence.

Spelling
- The children return to their seats.
- Start by selecting the Words tab. Click Say to hear the word and ask the children to repeat it, then ask the children to use their magnetic letters to make the word, saying the word every time they look for a letter. Ask a child to come up to the Work area to make the word. Did everyone get it right?
- Ask a child to use the arrow to push the letters together. Encourage the class to blend the word together out loud.
- Repeat for the remaining word under the Words tab.
- Under the Pictures tab, click Show to display the images and repeat the process for each word. (See pages 8–9 and 12.)

Writing
- Ask the children to find the letters 'e', 'v' and 'e' among their magnetic letters and to feel the shape of them. Click Show and ask the children to look and listen as the lowercase letters are formed.
- Ask a child to direct you how to write the letters as you write them on the empty Work area.
- Ask the child to write them on the dashed lines, then ask the children to practise writing the letters 'eve' by themselves.
- Select uppercase and repeat.

Follow-up
- Click Say to hear the sentence. Repeat the sentence, then dictate it slowly and deliberately for the children to write it. Then click Show to reveal the correct answer. (See page 13.)

WRAP-UP
- Recap the learning intentions with the children.
- Play the alphabet song and encourage children to sing along, signifying the end of the session.

Learning intentions are to:
- recap what we know
- say the /ee/ phoneme
- learn different ways to spell the /ee/ phoneme
- read and spell words of one syllable or more
- write a dictated sentence

Focus content: revision

Letters and Sounds
ea sounding /ee/
Reading
beach, heat, seal, teapot
Writing and Spelling
beak, seat, each, seaweed

Focus content: lesson

Sounds
/ee/
Visual search
extreme, phoneme, scheme, morpheme
Reading
Audio: these, Pete, Eve, theme
No audio: swede, compete, Steve, gene
Spelling
Words tab: Steve, delete, compete
Pictures tab: athlete, concrete
Writing
eve
Follow-up
Reinforce: 4 steps for reading syllables, using "complete" and "athlete" (see page 12)
Dictation
Steve was held up in a stream of cars.

Next steps
- Play the online pupil games for Unit 14
- Complete the phoneme PCM for Unit 15 (e–e)
- Read the Phonics Bug books that practise /ai/ alternatives: Dave's Big Day, I Will Amaze You, The Runaway Train

Unit 15

Target phoneme /ee/ written as 'ie', 'ey', 'y'

INTRODUCTION
- Play the alphabet song twice, once with voice accompaniment, children listening and singing along with accompaniment, and once with children singing along to the music without voice accompaniment.
- Discuss with the children the learning intentions for the day.

REVISION
[previously taught grapheme–phoneme correspondences; blending phonemes for reading; segmenting spoken words for spelling]
- Go through the Revision screens at a brisk pace.
- Watch out for any children who have not remembered the phonemes or the graphemes.

LESSON

Sounds
- Choose the relevant lesson session.
- Select and drag the digraph 'ie' on to the Work area. Click on the digraph to hear how to say the phoneme /ee/. Repeat for 'ey' and 'y'.
- Say the phoneme /ee/, and ask the children to repeat it after you. Make sure you keep the sound pure and encourage the children to do the same.
- Explain that you are going to look at some more ways to spell the /ee/ sound.
- ⓘ When relevant, mention that 'eo' sounds /ee/ as in "people"; 'ei' following 'c' sounds /ee/ as in "receive"; and that 'ie' sounds /e/ as in "friends".

Visual Search
- Bring up the words from the asset bank onto the Work area. Ask the children to highlight the 'ie', 'ey' or 'y' in each of the words, saying whether it is at the beginning, the middle or the end of the word. Do not pronounce the words.

Reading
- Click the Reading tab to see the word.
- Click Blend to watch and hear the Bug's demonstration of how to blend the word. Click Undo and ask a child to come to the Work area and move the arrow. Encourage the whole class to blend the phonemes out loud as the arrow is moving along.
- Work through each of the words in sequence.

Spelling
- The children return to their seats.
- Start by selecting the Words tab. Click Say to hear the word and ask the children to repeat it, then ask the children to use their magnetic letters to make the word, saying the word every time they look for a letter. Ask a child to come up to the Work area to make the word. Did everyone get it right?
- Ask a child to use the arrow to push the letters together. Encourage the class to blend the word together out loud.
- Repeat for the remaining word under the Words tab.
- Under the Pictures tab, click Show to display the images and repeat the process for each word. (See pages 8–9.)
- Select the Spelling video and play it once through.

Writing
- Ask the children to find the letters 'i' and 'e' among their magnetic letters and to feel the shape of them. Click Show and ask the children to look and listen as the lowercase letters are formed.
- Ask a child to direct you how to write the letters as you write them on the empty Work area.
- Ask the child to write them on the dashed lines, then ask the children to practise writing the letters themselves.
- Repeat for 'ey' and 'y'.

Follow-up
- Use the arrow to select the sentence. Click Say to hear the sentence. Repeat the sentence and dictate it slowly and deliberately for the children to write it. Then click Show to reveal the correct answer. (See page 13.)

WRAP-UP
- Recap the learning intentions with the children.
- Play the alphabet song and encourage the children to sing along, signifying the end of the session.

Learning intentions are to:
- recap what we know
- say the /ee/ phoneme
- learn different ways to spell the /ee/ phoneme
- read and spell words of one syllable or more
- write a dictated sentence

Focus content: revision

Letters and Sounds
e-e
Reading
swede, delete, compete, athlete
Writing and Spelling
Steve, complete, stampede, gene

Focus content: lesson

Sounds
/ee/
Visual search
shriek, monkey, pony, trolley
Reading
Audio: brief, shield, hockey, very
No audio: belief, chief, floppy, donkey
Spelling
Words tab: field, happy
Pictures tab: key, thief
Video: feet, sea, these, thief, key, sadly
Writing
ie, ey, y
Follow-up
Reinforce: 5 steps for spelling syllables (see page 12)
Dictation
The thief took the key.

Next steps
- Play the online pupil games for Unit 14
- Complete the phoneme PCM for Unit 15 (ie, ey, y)
- Read the Phonics Bug books that practise /ai/ alternatives: Dave's Big Day, I Will Amaze You, The Runaway Train

Unit 15

Language session

After: ea, ee, ie/ey/y

INTRODUCTION
- Play the alphabet song twice, once with voice accompaniment, children listening and singing along with accompaniment, and once with children singing along to the music without voice accompaniment.
- Discuss with the children the learning intentions for the day.

IRREGULAR

Reading
- Select the Irregular part of the session.
- Explain to the children that the letters 'ed' can sound /t/. Examples are 'looked', 'called' and 'asked'.
- Click Show to display the words, and ask the children to read them.
- Click Answer to listen to the word being read.

Spelling
- Click Say to hear the words, and ask the children to repeat each word. Put the word into a sentence so that the children understand its meaning, for example, "He looked for a chocolate bar in the cupboard".
- Say the target word, and ask the children to repeat it again. Ask the class to give each letter, and ask a child to come up to the Work area and drag up the correct letters into the spaces provided.
- Ask the class to read the word and click Say for them to hear it again.
- Repeat for the remaining words.

LESSON

Reading
- Click Show to display the sentences, and ask the children to read them.
- Click Answer to reveal whether they are right.

Spelling and Writing
- The children return to their seats.
- Remind the children about words consisting of syllables; about vowel digraphs 'ea' and 'ee' which have the long /e/ sound; and about 'ed' sounding /t/. Remind the children about the dictation procedure.
- Click Say to hear the first sentence, and ask the children to repeat it.
- Slowly and distinctly dictate the sentence, while the children tell you how to write it.
- Click Answer to reveal the sentence. Did the children tell you what to write correctly?
- Repeat for the second sentence. This time ask the children to write it using pencil and paper or their magnetic letters. (See page 13.)

Follow-up
- Display the picture and ask the children questions relating to it, to promote discussion and stimulate their thinking skills. You might ask "How do you know the child has fallen from a tree? Why do you think this happened? What do you think will happen next? What if the child had been playing alone when this happened?"
- Encourage the children to come up with sentences using words they have learnt in the programme – perhaps asking their own question about the picture.
- Write up on the Work area one or more good sentences or questions suggested by the children to further the discussion.

WRAP-UP
- Recap the learning intentions with the children.
- Play the alphabet song again and encourage the children to sing along, signifying the end of the session.

Learning intentions are to:
- learn to read and spell words that end in 'ed' (sounding /t/)
- read sentences which have words ending in 'ed' and alternative spellings for /ee/
- write sentences from dictation
- contribute to discussion, learning to ask their own questions

Focus content: irregular

Reading
looked, called, asked

Spelling
looked, called, asked

Focus content: lesson

Reading
Eve looked at the peach tree. She can reach up for a fuzzy peach.

Spelling and Writing
Eve and I went to the shop. We asked for a pot of cream.

Follow-up
Picture shows: children in the garden at a peach tree; one of the children falling from the tree.

Next steps
- Play the online language pupil games for Unit 15
- Complete the language PCM for Unit 15
- Read the Phonics Bug books that practise /ee/ alternatives: Babysitting Barney, Easy-Peasy!, Sunny Days, Rainy Days

Unit 16

Target phoneme /igh/ written as 'ie'

INTRODUCTION
- Play the alphabet song twice, once with voice accompaniment, children listening and singing along with accompaniment, and once with children singing along to the music without voice accompaniment.
- Discuss with the children the learning intentions for the day.

REVISION
[previously taught grapheme–phoneme correspondences; blending phonemes for reading; segmenting spoken words for spelling]
- Go through the Revision screens at a brisk pace.
- Watch out for any children who have not remembered the phonemes or the graphemes.

LESSON

Sounds
- Choose the relevant lesson session.
- Select and drag the digraph 'ie' on to the Work area. Click on the digraph to hear how to say the phoneme /igh/.
- Say the phoneme /igh/, and ask the children to repeat it after you. Make sure you keep the sound pure and encourage the children to do the same.

Visual Search
- Bring up the words from the asset bank onto the Work area. Ask children to highlight the 'ie' in each of the words. Do not pronounce the words.

Reading
- Click the Reading tab to see the word.
- Click Blend to watch and hear the Bug's demonstration of how to blend the word. Click Undo and ask a child to come to the Work area and move the arrow. Encourage the whole class to blend the phonemes out loud as the arrow is moving along.
- Work through each of the words in sequence.

Spelling
- The children return to their seats.
- Start by selecting the Words tab. Click Say to hear the word and ask the children to repeat it, then ask the children to use their magnetic letters to make the word, saying the word every time they look for a letter. Ask a child to come up to the Work area to make the word. Did everyone get it right?
- Ask a child to use the arrow to push the letters together. Encourage the class to blend the word together out loud.
- Repeat for the remaining word under the Words tab.
- Under the Pictures tab, click Show to display the images and repeat the process for each one. (See pages 8–9.)

Writing
- Ask children to find the letters 'i' and 'e' among their magnetic letters and to feel the shape of them. Click Show and ask children to look and listen as the lowercase letters are formed.
- Ask a child to direct you how to write the letters as you write them on the empty Work area.
- Ask the child to write them on the dashed lines, then ask the children to practise writing the letters 'ie' themselves.
- Select uppercase and repeat.

Follow-up
- Click Say to hear the sentence. Repeat the sentence, then dictate it slowly and deliberately for the children to write it. Then click Show to reveal the correct answer. (See page 13.)

WRAP-UP
- Recap the learning intentions with the children.
- Play the alphabet song and encourage the children to sing along, signifying the end of the session.

Learning intentions are to:
- recap what we know
- say the /igh/ phoneme
- learn different ways to spell the /igh/ phoneme
- read and spell words of one syllable or more
- write a dictated sentence

Focus content: revision

Letters and Sounds
igh Unit 9
Reading
fight, flight, light, night
Writing and Spelling
sigh, right, bright, tonight

Focus content: lesson

Sounds
/igh/
Visual search
tie, pie, ties, lies
Reading
Audio: tie, pie, ties, lies
No audio: flies, cried, magpie, fried
Spelling
Words tab: tried, lie
Pictures tab: tie, pie
Writing
ie
Follow-up
Reinforce: 4 steps for reading syllables, using "magpie" (see page 12) grapheme 'ie' as one vowel sound /igh/
Dictation
It is not right to lie.

Next steps
- Play the online games for Unit 15
- Complete the phoneme PCM for Unit 16 (ie)
- Read the Phonics Bug books that practise /ee/ alternatives: Babysitting Barney, Easy-Peasy!, Sunny Days, Rainy Days

Unit 16

Target phoneme /igh/ written as 'i–e'

INTRODUCTION
- Play the alphabet song twice, once with voice accompaniment, children listening and singing along with accompaniment, and once with children singing along to the music without voice accompaniment.
- Discuss with the children the learning intentions for the day.

REVISION
[previously taught grapheme–phoneme correspondences; blending phonemes for reading; segmenting spoken words for spelling]
- Go through the Revision screens at a brisk pace.
- Watch out for any children who have not remembered the phonemes or the graphemes.

LESSON

Sounds
- Choose the relevant lesson session.
- Say the phoneme /igh/, and ask the children to repeat it after you. Make sure you keep the sound pure and encourage the children to do the same.
- Explain to the children that 'i–e' is called a 'split digraph'. The silent 'e' changes /i/ to /igh/. So, 'i–e' sounds /igh/ as in "hive" and "alive", but sounds /i/ in "give", "live".

Visual Search
- Bring up the words from the asset bank onto the Work area. Ask children to highlight the 'i–e' in each of the words. Do not pronounce the words.

Reading
- Click the Reading tab to see the word.
- Click Blend to watch and hear the Bug's demonstration of how to blend the word. Click Undo and ask a child to come to the Work area and move the arrow. Encourage the whole class to blend the phonemes out loud as the arrow is moving along.
- Work through each of the words in sequence.

Spelling
- The children return to their seats.
- Start by selecting the Words tab. Click Say to hear the word and ask the children to repeat it, then ask the children to use their magnetic letters to make the word, saying the word every time they look for a letter. Ask a child to come up to the Work area to make the word. Did everyone get it right?
- Ask a child to use the arrow to push the letters together. Encourage the class to blend the word together out loud.
- Repeat for the remaining word under the Words tab.
- Under the Pictures tab, click Show to display the images and repeat the process for each word. (See pages 8–9.)

Writing
- Ask the children to find the letters 'r', 'i', 'p' and 'e' among their magnetic letters and to feel the shape of them. Click Show and ask the children to look and listen as the lowercase letters are formed.
- Ask a child to direct you how to write the letters as you write them on the empty Work area.
- Ask the child to write them on the dashed lines, then ask the children to practise writing the letters "ripe" by themselves.
- Select uppercase and repeat.

Follow-up
- Click Say to hear the sentence. Repeat the sentence, then dictate it slowly and deliberately for the children to write it. Then click Show to reveal the correct answer. (See page 13.)

WRAP-UP
- Recap the learning intentions with the children.
- Play the alphabet song and encourage the children to sing along, signifying the end of the session.

Learning intentions are to:
- recap what we know
- say the /igh/ phoneme
- learn different ways to spell the /igh/ phoneme
- read and spell words of one syllable or more
- write a dictated sentence

Focus content: revision

Letters and Sounds
ie

Reading
tried, lie, pie, tie

Writing and Spelling
flies, cried, magpie, fried

Focus content: lesson

Sounds
/igh/

Visual search
slide, prize, smile, five

Reading
Audio: hide, time, pine, strike
No audio: kite, pipe, drive, sunshine

Spelling
Words tab: tide, strike
Pictures tab: bike, bride

Writing
ripe

Follow-up
Reinforce: 4 steps for reading syllables, using "sunshine" (see p. 12) silent 'e' not as a vowel sound
Dictation I went for a ride on my bike.

Next steps
- Play the online pupil games for Unit 15
- Complete the phoneme PCM for Unit 16 (i-e)
- Read the Phonics Bug books that practise /ee/ alternatives: Babysitting Barney, Easy-Peasy!, Sunny Days, Rainy Days

Unit 16

Target phoneme /igh/ written as 'y'

INTRODUCTION
- Play the alphabet song twice, once with voice accompaniment, children listening and singing along with accompaniment, and once with children singing along to the music without voice accompaniment.
- Discuss with the children the learning intentions for the day.

REVISION
[previously taught grapheme–phoneme correspondences; blending phonemes for reading; segmenting spoken words for spelling]
- Go through the Revision screens at a brisk pace.
- Watch out for any children who have not remembered the phonemes or the graphemes.

LESSON
Sounds
- Choose the relevant lesson session.
- Select and drag the letter 'y' on to the Work area. Click on the letter to hear how to say the phoneme /igh/.
- Say the phoneme /igh/, and ask the children to repeat it after you. Make sure you keep the sound pure and encourage the children to do the same.
- Explain that 'y' counts as a vowel at the end of a word or syllable. Point out that 'y' used as a vowel can sound /igh/ as in "sky", and 'ey' can sound /igh/ as in "eye".

Visual Search
- Bring up the words from the asset bank onto the Work area. Ask the children to highlight the 'y' in each of the words, saying whether it is at the middle or the end of the word. Note that the 'y' comes at the end of a word or syllable. Do not pronounce the words.

Reading
- Click the Reading tab to see the word.
- Click Blend to watch and hear the Bug's demonstration of how to blend the word. Click Undo and ask a child to come to the Work area and move the arrow. Encourage the whole class to blend the phonemes out loud as the arrow is moving along.
- Work through each of the words in sequence.

Spelling
- The children return to their seats.
- Start by selecting the Words tab. Click Say to hear the word and ask the children to repeat it, then ask the children to use their magnetic letters to make the word, saying the word every time they look for a letter. Ask a child to come up to the Work area to make the word. Did everyone get it right?
- Ask a child to use the arrow to push the letters together. Encourage the class to blend the word together out loud.
- Repeat for the remaining word under the Words tab.
- Under the Pictures tab, click Show to display the images and repeat the process for each word. (See pages 8–9.)
- Select the Spelling video and play it once through.

Writing
- Ask children to find the letter 'y' among their magnetic letters and to feel the shape of it. Click Show and ask children to look and listen as the lowercase letter is formed.
- Ask a child to direct you how to write the letter as you write it on the empty Work area.
- Ask the child to write it on the dashed lines, then ask the children to practise writing the letter 'y' themselves.
- Select uppercase and repeat.

Follow-up
- Click Say to hear the sentence. Repeat the sentence, then dictate it slowly and deliberately for the children to write it. Then click Show to reveal the correct answer. (See page 13.)

WRAP-UP
- Recap the learning intentions with the children.
- Play the alphabet song and encourage the children to sing along, signifying the end of the session.

Learning intentions are to:
- recap what we know
- say the /igh/ phoneme
- learn different ways to spell the /igh/ phoneme
- read and spell words of one syllable or more
- write a dictated sentence

Focus content: revision

Letters and Sounds
i–e

Reading
tide, strike, bike, bride

Writing and Spelling
kite, pipe, drive, sunshine

Focus content: lesson

Sounds
/igh/

Visual search
why, fry, dry, skylight

Reading
Audio: by, shy, fly, myself
No audio: sly, try, cry, spy

Spelling
Words tab: why, fry
Pictures tab: sky, fly
Video: tie, light, fine, cry

Writing
y

Follow-up
Reinforce: 4 steps for reading syllables, using "skylight" and "myself" (see page 12); 'y' counting as a vowel
Dictation
I am shy and like to be by myself.

Next steps
- Play the online pupil games for Unit 15
- Complete the phoneme PCM for Unit 16 (y)
- Read the Phonics Bug books that practise /ee/ alternatives: Babysitting Barney, Easy-Peasy!, Sunny Days, Rainy Days

Unit 16

Target phoneme /igh/ written as 'i'

INTRODUCTION
- Play the alphabet song twice, once with voice accompaniment, children listening and singing along with accompaniment, and once with children singing along to the music without voice accompaniment.
- Discuss with the children the learning intentions for the day.

REVISION
- Go through the Revision screens at a brisk pace.
- Watch out for any children who have not remembered the phonemes or the graphemes.

LESSON

Sounds
- Choose the relevant lesson session.
- Select and drag the letter 'i' on to the Work area. Click on the letter to hear how to say the phoneme /igh/.
- Say the phoneme /igh/, and ask the children to repeat it after you. Make sure you keep the sound pure and encourage the children to do the same.

Visual Search
- Bring up the words from the asset bank onto the Work area. Ask the children to highlight the 'i' in each of the words, saying whether it is at the beginning, the middle or the end of the word. Do not pronounce the words.

Reading
- Click the Reading tab to see the word.
- Click Blend to watch and hear the Bug's demonstration of how to blend the word. Click Undo and ask a child to come to the Work area and move the arrow. Encourage the whole class to blend the phonemes out loud as the arrow is moving along.
- Work through each of the words in sequence.

Spelling
- The children return to their seats.
- Start by selecting the Words tab. Click Say to hear the word and ask the children to repeat it, then ask the children to use their magnetic letters to make the word, saying the word every time they look for a letter. Ask a child to come up to the Work area to make the word. Did everyone get it right?
- Ask a child to use the arrow to push the letters together. Encourage the class to blend the word together out loud.
- Repeat for the remaining word under the Words tab.
- Under the Pictures tab, click Show to display the images and repeat the process for each word. (See pages 8–9.)

Writing
- Ask the children to find the letter 'i' among their magnetic letters and to feel the shape of it. Click Show and ask the children to look and listen as the lowercase letter is formed.
- Ask a child to direct you how to write the letter as you write it on the empty Work area.
- Ask the child to write it on the dashed lines, then ask the children to practise writing the letter 'i' themselves.
- Select uppercase and repeat.

FOLLOW-UP
- Click Say to hear the sentence. Repeat the sentence, then dictate it slowly and deliberately for the children to write it. Then click Show to reveal the correct answer. (See page 13.)

WRAP-UP
- Recap the learning intentions with the children.
- Play the alphabet song and encourage the children to sing along, signifying the end of the session.

Learning intentions are to:
- recap what we know
- say the /igh/ phoneme
- learn different ways to spell the /igh/ phoneme
- read and spell words of one syllable or more
- write a dictated sentence

Focus content: revision

Letters and Sounds
y

Reading
why, fry, sky, fly

Writing and Spelling
sly, try, cry, spy

Focus content: lesson

Sounds
/igh/

Visual search
mind, child, blind, wild

Reading
Audio: find, mild, mind, behind
No audio: grind, rind, remind

Spelling
Words tab: kind, wild
Pictures tab: child, blind

Writing
i

Follow-up
Reinforce:
• 4 steps for reading syllables, using 2-syllable words "behind" and "remind" (see page 12)
• grapheme 'i' sounding /igh/ before consonant blends 'ld', 'nd', 'nt'

Dictation

Be kind to the child.

Next steps
- Play the online pupil games for Unit 15
- Complete the phoneme PCM for Unit 16 (i)
- Read the Phonics Bug books that practise /ee/ alternatives: Babysitting Barney, Easy-Peasy!, Sunny Days, Rainy Days

Language session

After: ie, i-e, y, i

INTRODUCTION
- Play the alphabet song twice, once with the children listening and singing along with accompaniment, and once listening to the music without voice accompaniment.
- Discuss with the children the learning intentions.

IRREGULAR

Reading
- Select the Irregular part of the session.
- Click Show to display the words, and ask the children to read them.
- Click Answer to listen to the word being read.

Spelling
- Click Say to hear the words, and ask the children to repeat the word into a sentence so that the children understand their meaning, like a glass of water", "Where shall we go on holiday?"
- Point out that in "water", 'a' sounds /o/, and in "where" sounds /air/.
- Say the target word, and ask the children to repeat it again. Ask the class to give each letter, and ask a child to come up to the Work area and drag up the correct letters into the spaces provided.
- Ask the class to read the word and click Say for them to hear it again.
- Repeat for the remaining words.

LESSON

Reading
- Click Show to display the sentences, and ask the children to read them.
- Click Answer to reveal whether they are right.

Spelling and Writing
- The children return to their seats.
- Remind the children about the dictation procedure.
- Click Say to hear the caption/sentence and ask the children to repeat it.
- Slowly and distinctly dictate the caption/sentence, while the children write it using pencil and paper or their magnetic boards.
- Click Answer to reveal the caption/sentence. Did the children write it correctly? Ask the children to add one or two more items they could take with them.
- Repeat for the second caption/sentence. This time as you slowly and distinctly dictate the sentence, ask the children to tell you how to write the words.
- Click Answer to reveal the sentence. Did the children tell you what to write correctly? (See page 13.)

Follow-up
- Display the picture and ask the children questions relating to it, to promote discussion and stimulate their thinking skills, such as: "How do you know what kind of day it is in the picture?"
- Encourage the children to come up with sentences using words they have learnt in the programme – perhaps asking their own questions.
- Write up on the Work area one or more good sentences to enable the children to further the discussion.

WRAP-UP
- Recap the learning intentions with the children.
- Play the alphabet song again and encourage the children to join in at the end of the session.

Unit 16

Learning intentions are to:
- learn to read and spell irregular words "water" and "where"
- write sentences from dictation, including a three-syllable word
- contribute to discussion, learning to ask their own questions

Focus content: irregular

Reading
water, where

Spelling
water, where

Focus content: lesson

Reading
Let us go outside in the sunshine. What will each child need to take?

Spelling and Writing
Sunglasses, fly spray Where is my cup of water?

Follow-up
Picture shows: children going outside to play: sunglasses, fly spray, etc.

Next steps
- Play the online language pupil games for Unit 16
- Complete the language PCM for Unit 16
- Read the Phonics Bug books that practise /igh/ alternatives: Butterfly Pie, Flying High, I Spy

---

Handwritten notes:

5/3 laptop didn't work! so practised 'water' + 'where' on whiteboards + did dictation - "where is my cup of water?"

worked up to take in spelling 18/11 looking in phonics books many need more reinforcement. Teach again using the program?

20/11 worked upto + including spelling, pictures tab, grapes.

Unit 17

Target phoneme /oa/ written as 'ow'

INTRODUCTION
- Play the alphabet song twice, once with voice accompaniment, children listening and singing along with accompaniment, and once with children singing along to the music without voice accompaniment.
- Discuss with the children the learning intentions for the day.

REVISION
[previously taught grapheme–phoneme correspondences; blending phonemes for reading; segmenting spoken words for spelling]
- Go through the Revision screens at a brisk pace.
- Watch out for any children who have not remembered the phonemes or the graphemes.

LESSON

Sounds
- Choose the relevant lesson session.
- Select and drag the digraph 'ow' on to the Work area. Click on the digraph to hear how to say the phoneme /oa/.
- Say the phoneme /oa/, and ask the children to repeat it after you. Make sure you keep the sound pure and encourage the children to do the same.
- Explain that 'ow' is used at the end of a word and, when relevant, before 'n' at the end of a word.

Visual Search
- Bring up the words from the asset bank onto the Work area. Ask the children to highlight the 'ow' in each of the words, saying whether it is at the beginning, the middle or the end of the word. Do not pronounce the words.

Reading
- Click the Reading tab to see the word.
- Click Blend to watch and hear the Bug's demonstration of how to blend the word. Click Undo and ask a child to come to the Work area and move the arrow. Encourage the whole class to blend the phonemes out loud as the arrow is moving along.
- Work through each of the words in sequence.

Spelling
- The children return to their seats.
- Start by selecting the Words tab. Click Say to hear the word and ask the children to repeat it, then ask the children to use their magnetic letters to make the word, saying the word every time they look for a letter. Ask a child to come up to the Work area to make the word. Did everyone get it right?
- Ask a child to use the arrow to push the letters together. Encourage the class to blend the word together out loud.
- Repeat for the remaining word under the Words tab.
- Under the Pictures tab, click Show to display the images and repeat the process for each word. (See pages 8–9 and 12.)

Writing
- Ask the children to find the letters 'o' and 'w' among their magnetic letters and to feel the shape of them. Click Show and ask the children to look and listen as the lowercase letters are formed.
- Ask a child to direct you how to write the letters as you write them on the empty Work area.
- Ask the child to write them on the dashed lines, then ask the children to practise writing the letters 'ow' by themselves.
- Select uppercase and repeat.

Follow-up
- Click Say to hear the sentence. Repeat the sentence, then dictate it slowly and deliberately for the children to write it. Then click Show to reveal the correct answer. (See page 13.)

WRAP-UP
- Recap the learning intentions with the children.
- Play the alphabet song and encourage the children to sing along, signifying the end of the session.

Learning intentions are to:
- recap what we know
- say the /oa/ phoneme
- learn different ways to spell the /oa/ phoneme
- read and spell words of one syllable or more
- write a dictated sentence

Focus content: revision

Letters and Sounds
oa Unit 9
Reading
foam, loaf, goat, toad
Writing and Spelling
soap, float, toast, Joan

Focus content: lesson

Sounds
/oa/
Visual search
blow, arrow, yellow, elbow
Reading
Audio: snow, throw, barrow
No audio: flow, grows, sparrow, window
Spelling
Words tab: crow, follow
Pictures tab: rainbow, pillow
Writing
ow
Follow-up
Reinforce: 4 steps for reading syllables, using "sparrow" and "window" (see page 12)
Dictation
Joan hurt her elbow.

Next steps
- Play the online pupil games for Unit 16
- Complete the phoneme PCM for Unit 17 (ow)
- Read the Phonics Bug books that practise /igh/ alternatives: Butterfly Pie, Flying High, I Spy

Unit 17

Target phoneme /oa/ written as 'o–e'

INTRODUCTION
- Play the alphabet song twice, once with voice accompaniment, children listening and singing along with accompaniment, and once with children singing along to the music without voice accompaniment.
- Discuss with the children the learning intentions for the day.

REVISION
[previously taught grapheme–phoneme correspondences; blending phonemes for reading; segmenting spoken words for spelling]
- Go through the Revision screens at a brisk pace.
- Watch out for any children who have not remembered the phonemes or the graphemes.

LESSON

Sounds
- Choose the relevant lesson session.
- Say the phoneme /oa/, and ask the children to repeat it after you. Make sure you keep the sound pure and encourage the children to do the same.
- Explain to children that 'o–e' is called a 'split digraph'. The silent 'e' changes /o/ to /oa/. You may also want to explain that 'o–e' sounds /u/ in "done", "come", "some".

Visual Search
- Bring up the words from the asset bank onto the Work area. Ask the children to highlight the 'o–e' in each of the words. Do not pronounce the words.

Reading
- Click the Reading tab to see the word.
- Click Blend to watch and hear the Bug's demonstration of how to blend the word. Click Undo and ask a child to come to the Work area and move the arrow. Encourage the whole class to blend the phonemes out loud as the arrow is moving along.
- Work through each of the words in sequence.

Spelling
- The children return to their seats.
- Start by selecting the Words tab. Click Say to hear the word and ask the children to repeat it, then ask the children to use their magnetic letters to make the word, saying the word every time they look for a letter. Ask a child to come up to the Work area to make the word. Did everyone get it right?
- Ask a child to use the arrow to push the letters together. Encourage the class to blend the word together out loud.
- Repeat for the remaining word under the Words tab.
- Under the Pictures tab, click Show to display the images and repeat the process for each one. (See pages 8–9.)

Writing
- Ask children to find the letters 'r', 'o', 'p' and 'e' among their magnetic letters and to feel the shape of them. Click Show and ask the children to look and listen as the lowercase letters are formed.
- Ask a child to direct you how to write the letters as you write them on the empty Work area.
- Ask the child to write them on the dashed lines, then ask the children to practise writing "rope" by themselves.
- Select uppercase and repeat.

Follow-up
- Click Say to hear the sentence. Repeat the sentence, then dictate it slowly and deliberately for the children to write it. Then click Show to reveal the correct answer. (See page 13.)

WRAP-UP
- Recap the learning intentions with the children.
- Play the alphabet song and encourage the children to sing along, signifying the end of the session.

Learning intentions are to:
- recap what we know
- say the /oa/ phoneme
- learn different ways to spell the /oa/ phoneme
- read and spell words of one syllable or more
- write a dictated sentence

Focus content: revision

Letters and Sounds
ow (/oa/)
Reading
crow, follow, rainbow, pillow
Writing and Spelling
snow, throw, barrow, shadow

Focus content: lesson

Sounds
/oa/
Visual search
joke, stone, stroke, throne
Reading
Audio: hole, rope, globe, rosebud
No audio: rose, smoke, phone, notebook
Spelling
Words tab: those, spoke
Pictures tab: cone, nose
Writing
rope
Follow-up
Reinforce: 4 steps for reading syllables, using "rosebud" and "notebook" (see page 12) silent 'e' not counting as a vowel sound
Dictation
Will you phone for a taxi?

Next steps
- Play the online pupil games for Unit 16
- Complete the phoneme PCM for Unit 17 (o–e)
- Read the Phonics Bug books that practise /igh/ alternatives: Butterfly Pie, Flying High, I Spy

Unit 17

Target phoneme /oa/ written as 'o' and 'oe'

INTRODUCTION
- Play the alphabet song twice, once with voice accompaniment, children listening and singing along with accompaniment, and once with children singing along to the music without voice accompaniment.
- Discuss with the children the learning intentions for the day.

REVISION
(previously taught grapheme–phoneme correspondences; blending phonemes for reading; segmenting spoken words for spelling)
- Go through the Revision screens at a brisk pace.
- Watch out for any children who have not remembered the phonemes or the graphemes.

LESSON
Sounds
- Choose the relevant lesson session.
- Select and drag the letter 'o' on to the Work area. Click on the letter to hear how to say the phoneme /oa/. Repeat for 'oe'.
- Say the phoneme /oa/, and ask the children to repeat it after you. Make sure you keep the sound pure and encourage the children to do the same.
- Explain that 'o' can sound /oa/, as in "old", "post".
- Explain that 'oe' sounds /oa/ as in "toe", "hoe", but sounds long /oo/ as in "shoe", "canoe". When relevant, mention too that 'ough' sounds /oa/, as in "though" and "dough".

Visual Search
- Bring up the words from the asset bank onto the Work area. Ask the children to highlight the 'o' or 'oe' in each of the words, saying whether it is at the beginning, the middle or the end of the word. Do not pronounce the words.

Reading
- Click the Reading tab to see the word.
- Click Blend to watch and hear the Bug's demonstration of how to blend the word. Click Undo and ask a child to come to the Work area and move the arrow. Encourage the whole class to blend the phonemes out loud as the arrow is moving along.
- Work through each of the words in sequence.

Spelling
- The children return to their seats.
- Start by selecting the Words tab. Click Say to hear the word and ask the children to repeat it, then ask the children to use their magnetic letters to make the word, saying the word every time they look for a letter. Ask a child to come up to the Work area to make the word. Did everyone get it right?
- Ask a child to use the arrow to push the letters together. Encourage the class to blend the word together out loud.
- Repeat for the remaining words under the Words tab.
- Under the Pictures tab, click Show to display the images and repeat the process for each word. (See pages 8–9.)

Writing
- Ask the children to find the letter 'o' among their magnetic letters and to feel the shape of it. Click Show and ask the children to look and listen as the lowercase letter is formed.
- Ask a child to direct you how to write the letter as you write it on the empty Work area.
- Ask the child to write it on the dashed lines, then ask the children to practise writing 'o' themselves.
- Select uppercase and repeat.
- Repeat for 'oe'.

Follow-up
- Click Say to hear the sentence. Repeat the sentence, then dictate it slowly and deliberately for the children to write it. Then click Show to reveal the correct answer. (See page 13.)

WRAP-UP
- Recap the learning intentions with the children.
- Play the alphabet song and encourage the children to sing along, signifying the end of the session.

Learning intentions are to:
- recap what we know
- say the /oa/ phoneme
- learn different ways to spell the /oa/ phoneme
- read and spell words of one syllable or more
- write a dictated sentence

Focus content: revision

Letters and Sounds
o–e

Reading
those, spoke, cone, nose

Writing and Spelling
rose, smoke, phone, notebook

Focus content: lesson

Sounds
/oa/

Visual search
hoe, fold, bolt, ghost

Reading
Audio: cold, both, post, tiptoe

No audio: scold, foe, oboe, old

Spelling
Words tab: most, Joe

Pictures tab: toe, gold

Writing
o, oe

Follow-up
Reinforce:
5 steps for spelling syllables (see page 12)

Dictation

Joe told me he had a cold.

Next steps
- Play the online pupil games for Unit 16
- Complete the phoneme PCM for Unit 17 (o, oe)
- Read the Phonics Bug books that practise /igh/ alternatives: Butterfly Pie, Flying High, I Spy

Unit 17

Language session

After: ow, o-e, o/oe

INTRODUCTION
- Play the alphabet song twice, once with voice accompaniment, children listening and singing along with accompaniment, and once with children singing along to the music without voice accompaniment.
- Discuss with the children the learning intentions for the day.

IRREGULAR

Reading
- Select the Irregular part of the session.
- Click Show to display the words, and ask the children to read them.
- Click Answer to listen to the word being read.

Spelling
- Click Say to hear the words, and ask the children to repeat each word. Put the word into a sentence so that the children understand its meaning, for example, "Who is having packed lunch today?" "We are going to play football again".
- Point out that in "who", 'w' is silent but is needed for spelling. 'o' sounds long /oo/.
- "again" – 'ai' usually sounds /e/, but in some geographical regions sounds /ai/.
- Say the target word, and ask the children to repeat it again. Ask the class to give each letter, and ask a child to come up to the Work area and drag up the correct letters into the spaces provided.
- Ask the class to read the word and click Say for them to hear it again.
- Repeat for the remaining word.

LESSON

Reading
- Click Show to display the sentences, and ask the children to read them.
- Click Answer to reveal whether they are right.

Spelling and Writing
- The children return to their seats.
- Remind the children about the dictation procedure.
- Click Say to hear the caption and ask the children to repeat it.
- Slowly and distinctly dictate the caption, while the children write it using pencil and paper or their magnetic boards.
- Click Answer to reveal the caption. Did the children write it correctly?
- Repeat for the second caption.
- Repeat for the sentence. This time, as you slowly and distinctly dictate the sentence, ask the children to tell you how to write the words. Click Answer to reveal the sentence. Did the children tell you what to write correctly?
- Ask the children to add one or two more items they could play with in the snow. (See page 13.)

Follow-up
- Display the picture and ask the children questions relating to it, to promote discussion and stimulate their thinking skills. You might ask, "How do you know that it's a cold day outside? Why does it snow? What is snow? What kind of snow is needed for sledging and snowboarding? What happens if the sun comes out?"
- Encourage the children to come up with sentences using words they have learnt in the programme – perhaps asking their own question about the picture.
- Write up on the Work area one or more good sentences or questions suggested by the children to further the discussion.

WRAP-UP
- Recap the learning intentions with the children.
- Play the alphabet song again and encourage the children to sing along, signifying the end of the session.

Learning intentions are to:
- learn to read and spell irregular words "who" and "again"
- write sentences from dictation including two-syllable and compound words
- contribute to discussion, learning to ask their own questions

Focus content: irregular

Reading
who, again

Spelling
who, again

Focus content: lesson

Reading
It is cold again today. We woke up to snow, snow and more snow! Who will make the best snowman?

Spelling and Writing
playing in the snow a snowman Both Joe and I can throw snowballs.

Follow-up
Picture shows: children playing in the snow with snowballs and a snowman.

Next steps
- Play the online language pupil games for Unit 17
- Complete the language PCM for Unit 17
- Read the Phonics Bug books that practise /oa/ alternatives: Animal Skeletons, Fun in the Snow, The Snow Monster

Unit 18

Target phoneme long /oo/ written as 'ew'

INTRODUCTION
- Play the alphabet song twice, once with voice accompaniment, children listening and singing along with accompaniment, and once with children singing along to the music without voice accompaniment.
- Discuss with the children the learning intentions for the day.

REVISION
[previously taught grapheme–phoneme correspondences; blending phonemes for reading; segmenting spoken words for spelling]
- Go through the Revision screens at a brisk pace.
- Watch out for any children who have not remembered the phonemes or the graphemes.

LESSON
Sounds
- Choose the relevant lesson session.
- Select and drag the digraph 'ew' on to the Work area. Click on the digraph to hear how to say the long /oo/ phoneme.
- Say the long /oo/ phoneme, and ask the children to repeat it after you. Make sure you keep the sound pure and encourage the children to do the same.
- Explain that 'ew' is used at the end of a word or syllable, and that 'ew' may also sound /oa/, as in "sew".

Visual Search
- Bring up the words from the asset bank onto the Work area. Ask the children to highlight the 'ew' in each of the words, saying whether it is at the beginning, the middle or the end of the word. Do not pronounce the words.

Reading
- Click the Reading tab to see the word.
- Click Blend to watch and hear the Bug's demonstration of how to blend the word. Click Undo and ask a child to come to the Work area and move the arrow. Encourage the whole class to blend the phonemes out loud as the arrow is moving along.
- Work through each of the words in sequence. Note that "Andrew" has uppercase 'A'.

Spelling
- The children return to their seats.
- Start by selecting the Words tab. Click Say to hear the word and ask the children to repeat it, then ask the children to use their magnetic letters to make the word, saying the word every time they look for a letter. Ask a child to come up to the Work area to make the word. Did everyone get it right?
- Ask a child to use the arrow to push the letters together. Encourage the class to blend the word together out loud.
- Repeat for the remaining word under the Words tab.
- Under the Pictures tab, click Show to display the images and repeat the process for each one. (See pages 8–9.)

Writing
- Ask the children to find the letters 'e' and 'w' among their magnetic letters and to feel the shape of them. Click Show and ask the children to look and listen as the lowercase letters are formed.
- Ask a child to direct you how to write the letters as you write them on the empty Work area.
- Ask the child to write them on the dashed lines, then ask the children to practise writing 'ew' themselves.
- Select uppercase and repeat.

Follow-up
- Click Say to hear the sentence. Repeat the sentence. Point out that Andrew and Stewart need uppercase letters at the start. Then dictate the sentence slowly and deliberately for the children to write it. Then click Show to reveal the correct answer. (See page 13.)

WRAP-UP
- Recap the learning intentions with the children.
- Play the alphabet song and encourage the children to sing along, signifying the end of the session.

Learning intentions are to:
- recap what we know
- say the long /oo/ phoneme
- learn different ways to spell the long /oo/ phoneme
- read and spell words of one syllable or more
- write from dictation

Focus content: revision

Letters and Sounds
oo Unit 9
Reading
fool, stool, spoon, roof
Writing and Spelling
too, moon, cool, pool

Focus content: lesson

Sounds
long /oo/
Visual search
grew, chew, stew, threw
Reading
Audio: screw, drew, flew, Andrew
No audio: brew, chew, threw, blew
Spelling
Words tab: grew, flew
Pictures tab: screw, stew
Writing
ew
Follow-up
Reinforce: 5 steps for spelling syllables (see page 12)
Dictation
Andrew and Stewart had sweets to chew.

Next steps
- Play the online pupil games for Unit 17
- Complete the phoneme PCM for Unit 18 (ew)
- Read the Phonics Bug books that practise /oa/ alternatives: Animal Skeletons, Fun in the Snow, The Snow Monster

Unit 18

Target phoneme long /oo/ written as 'ue'

INTRODUCTION
- Play the alphabet song twice, once with voice accompaniment, children listening and singing along with accompaniment, and once with children singing along to the music without voice accompaniment.
- Discuss with the children the learning intentions for the day.

REVISION
[previously taught grapheme–phoneme correspondences; blending phonemes for reading; segmenting spoken words for spelling]
- Go through the Revision screens at a brisk pace.
- Watch out for any children who have not remembered the phonemes or the graphemes.

LESSON
Sounds
- Choose the relevant lesson session.
- Select and drag the digraph 'ue' on to the Work area. Click on the digraph to hear how to say the long /oo/ phoneme.
- Say the long /oo/ phoneme, and ask the children to repeat it after you. Make sure you keep the sound pure and encourage the children to do the same.
- Explain that words do not end in 'u'; instead we use 'ue' as in "blue" and "glue".

Visual Search
- Bring up the words from the asset bank on to the Work area. Ask the children to highlight the 'ue' in each of the words, saying whether it is at the beginning, the middle or the end of the word. Do not pronounce the words.

Reading
- Click the Reading tab to see the word.
- Click Blend to watch and hear the Bug's demonstration of how to blend the word. Click Undo and ask a child to come to the Work area and move the arrow. Encourage the whole class to blend the phonemes out loud as the arrow is moving along.
- Work through each of the words in sequence.

Spelling
- The children return to their seats.
- Start by selecting the Words tab. Click Say to hear the word and ask the children to repeat it, then ask the children to use their magnetic letters to make the word, saying the word every time they look for a letter. Ask a child to come up to the Work area to make the word. Did everyone get it right?
- Ask a child to use the arrow to push the letters together. Encourage the class to blend the word together out loud.
- Repeat for the remaining words under the Words tab.
- Under the Pictures tab, click Show to display the images and repeat the process for each word. (See pages 8–9.)

Writing
- Ask the children to find the letters 'u' and 'e' among their magnetic letters and to feel the shape of them. Click Show and ask the children to look and listen as the lowercase letters are formed.
- Ask a child to direct you how to write the letters as you write them on the empty Work area.
- Ask the child to write them on the dashed lines, then ask the children to practise writing 'ue' themselves.
- Select uppercase and repeat.

Follow-up
- Click Say to hear the sentence. Repeat the sentence, then dictate it slowly and deliberately for the children to write it. Then click Show to reveal the correct answer. (See page 13.)

WRAP-UP
- Recap the learning intentions with the children.
- Play the alphabet song and encourage the children to sing along, signifying the end of the session.

Learning intentions are to:
- recap what we know
- say the long /oo/ phoneme
- learn different ways to spell the long /oo/ phoneme
- read and spell words of one syllable or more
- write from dictation

Focus content: revision

Letters and Sounds
ew
Reading
grew, flew, screw, stew
Writing and Spelling
brew, chew, threw, blew

Focus content: lesson

Sounds
long /oo/
Visual search
blue, true, glue, Sue
Reading
Audio: clue, rescue, due, true
No audio: cue, flue, avenue, hue
Spelling
Words tab: true, Sue
Pictures tab: blue, glue
Writing
ue
Follow-up
Dictation
Sue did not get the clue.

Next steps
- Play the online pupil games for Unit 17
- Complete the phoneme PCM for Unit 18 (ue)
- Read the Phonics Bug books that practise /oa/ alternatives: Animal Skeletons, Fun in the Snow, The Snow Monster

Unit 18

Target phoneme long /oo/ written as 'u–e'

INTRODUCTION
- Play the alphabet song twice, once with voice accompaniment, children listening and singing along with accompaniment, and once with children singing along to the music without voice accompaniment.
- Discuss with the children the learning intentions for the day.

REVISION
[previously taught grapheme–phoneme correspondences; blending phonemes for reading; segmenting spoken words for spelling]
- Go through the Revision screens at a brisk pace.
- Watch out for any children who have not remembered the phonemes or the graphemes.

LESSON
Sounds
- Choose the relevant lesson session.
- Say the phoneme /oo/, and ask the children to repeat it after you. Make sure you keep the sound pure and encourage the children to do the same.
- Explain to the children that 'u–e' is called a 'split digraph'. The silent 'e' changes /u/ to long /oo/.

Visual Search
- Bring up the words from the asset bank onto the Work area. Ask the children to highlight the 'u–e' in each of the words. Do not pronounce the words.

Reading
- Click the Reading tab to see the word.
- Click Blend to watch and hear the Bug's demonstration of how to blend the word. Click Undo and ask a child to come to the Work area and move the arrow. Encourage the whole class to blend the phonemes out loud as the arrow is moving along.
- Work through each of the words in sequence.

Spelling
- The children return to their seats.
- Start by selecting the Words tab. Click Say to hear the word and ask the children to repeat it, then ask the children to use their magnetic letters to make the word, saying the word every time they look for a letter. Ask a child to come up to the Work area to make the word. Did everyone get it right?
- Ask a child to use the arrow to push the letters together. Encourage the class to blend the word together out loud.
- Repeat for the remaining word under the Words tab.
- Under the Pictures tab, click Show to display the images and repeat the process for each one. (See pages 8–9.)
- Select the Spelling video and play it once through.

Writing
- Ask the children to find the letters 'u' and 'e' among their magnetic letters and to feel the shape of them. Click Show and ask children to look and listen as the lowercase letters are formed.
- Ask a child to direct you how to write the letters as you write them on the empty Work area.
- Ask the child to write them on the dashed lines. Then ask the children to practise writing 'u–e' themselves.
- Select uppercase and repeat.

Follow-up
- Click Say to hear the sentence. Repeat the sentence, then dictate it slowly and deliberately for the children to write it. Then click Show to reveal the correct answer. (See page 13.)

WRAP-UP
- Recap the learning intentions with the children.
- Play the alphabet song and encourage the children to sing along, signifying the end of the session.

Learning intentions are to:
- recap what we know
- say the long /oo/ phoneme
- learn different ways to spell the long /oo/ phoneme
- read and spell words of one syllable or more
- write a dictated sentence

Focus content: revision

Letters and Sounds
u–e

Reading
Sue, true, blue, glue

Writing and Spelling
cue, flue, avenue, hue

Focus content: lesson

Sounds
long /oo/

Visual search
tube, yule, June, computer

Reading
Audio: tune, fume, cute, pollute

No audio: mule, dunes, fuse, June

Spelling
Words tab: rule, flute

Pictures tab: tube, cube

Video: moon, blew, glue, flute

Writing
u–e

Follow-up
Dictation

June had to play her flute for the class.

Next steps
- Play the online pupil games for Unit 17
- Complete the phoneme PCM for Unit 18 (u–e)
- Read the Phonics Bug books that practise /oa/ alternatives: Animal Skeletons, Fun in the Snow, The Snow Monster

Unit 18

Target phoneme short /oo/ written as 'u' and 'oul'

INTRODUCTION
- Play the alphabet song twice, once with voice accompaniment, children listening and singing along with accompaniment, and once with children singing along to the music without voice accompaniment.
- Discuss with the children the learning intentions for the day.

REVISION
[previously taught grapheme–phoneme correspondences; blending phonemes for reading; segmenting spoken words for spelling]
- Go through the Revision screens at a brisk pace.
- Watch out for any children who have not remembered the phonemes or the graphemes.

LESSON
Sounds
- Choose the relevant lesson session.
- Select and drag the letter 'u' on to the Work area. Click on the letter to hear how to say the short /oo/ phoneme. Repeat for 'oul'.
- Say the short /oo/ phoneme, and ask the children to repeat it after you. Make sure you keep the sound pure and encourage the children to do the same.
- Explain that 'u' sounds short /oo/ in words such as "push" and "pull".
- Explain that in "could" and "would", 'oul' sounds short /oo/. In "you" and "youth", 'ou' takes the long sound /oo/. When relevant, mention too that another way to spell 'oo' is with 'ui' as in "suit", "fruit", "juice".

Visual Search
- Bring up the words from the asset bank onto the Work area. Ask the children to highlight the 'u' or 'oul' in each of the words, saying whether it is at the beginning, the middle or the end of the word. Do not pronounce the words.

Reading
- Click the Reading tab to see the word.
- Click Blend to watch and hear the Bug's demonstration of how to blend the word. Click Undo and ask a child to come to the Work area and move the arrow. Encourage the whole class to blend the phonemes out loud as the arrow is moving along.
- Work through each of the words in sequence.

Spelling
- The children return to their seats.
- Start by selecting the Words tab. Click Say to hear the word and ask the children to repeat it, then ask the children to use their magnetic letters to make the word, saying the word every time they look for a letter. Ask a child to come up to the Work area to make the word. Did everyone get it right?
- Ask a child to use the arrow to push the letters together. Encourage the class to blend the word together out loud.
- Repeat for the remaining words under the Words tab.
- Under the Pictures tab, click Show to display the images and repeat the process for each one. (See pages 8–9.)
- Select the Spelling video and play it once through.

Writing
- Ask children to find the letter 'u' among their magnetic letters and to feel the shape of it. Click Show and ask children to look and listen as the lowercase letter is formed.
- Ask a child to direct you how to write the letter as you write it on the empty Work area.
- Ask the child to write it on the dashed lines, then ask the children to practise writing 'u' themselves.
- Repeat for 'oul'.

Follow-up
- Use the arrow to select the sentence. Click Say to hear the sentence. What kind of sentence is it? (A question) Repeat the sentence, then dictate it slowly and deliberately for the children to write it. Then click Show to reveal the correct answer. (See page 13.)

WRAP-UP
- Recap the learning intentions with the children.
- Play the alphabet song and encourage the children to sing along, signifying the end of the session.

Learning intentions are to:
- recap what we know
- say the short /oo/ phoneme
- learn different ways to spell the short /oo/ phoneme
- read and spell words of one syllable or more
- write a dictated sentence

Focus content: revision

Letters and Sounds
oo Unit 9
Reading
took, wool, book, wood
Writing and Spelling
look, foot, stood, shook

Focus content: lesson

Sounds
short /oo/
Visual search
put, pudding, would, cushion
Reading
Audio: push, should, full, put
No audio: pull, would, could, bush
Spelling
Words tab: could, put
Pictures tab: bull, bush
Video: book, put, could
Writing
u, oul
Follow-up
Dictation
Could you put it on the blue chair?

Next steps
- Play the online pupil games for Unit 17
- Complete the phoneme PCM for Unit 18 (u/oul)
- Read the Phonics Bug books that practise /oa/ alternatives: Animal Skeletons, Fun in the Snow, The Snow Monster

Unit 18

Language session

After long /oo/: ew, ue, u-e; and short /oo/: u/oul

INTRODUCTION
- Play the alphabet song twice, once with voice accompaniment, children listening and singing along with accompaniment, and once with children singing along to the music without voice accompaniment.
- Discuss with the children the learning intentions for the day.

IRREGULAR

Reading
- Select the Irregular part of the session.
- Click Show to display the words, and ask the children to read them.
- Click Answer to listen to the word being read.

Spelling
- Click Say to hear the words, and ask the children to repeat each word. Put the word into a sentence so that the children understand its meaning, for example, "I thought it was playtime!" "Max stepped through the doorway into the room".
- Point out that 'ough' sounds /aw/ in "thought", but 'ough' sounds long /oo/ in "through".
- Say the target word, and ask the children to repeat it again. Ask the class to give each letter, and ask a child to come up to the Work area and drag up the correct letters into the spaces provided.
- Ask the class to read the word and click Say for them to hear it again.
- Repeat for the remaining word.

LESSON

Reading
- Click Show to display the sentences, and ask the children to read them.
- Click Answer to reveal whether they are right.

Spelling and Writing
- The children return to their seats.
- Remind the children about the dictation procedure.
- Click Say to hear the first sentence and ask the children to repeat it.
- Slowly and distinctly dictate the sentence, asking the children to tell you how to write the words.
- Click Answer to reveal the sentence. Did the children tell you what to write correctly?
- Repeat for the second list sentence, asking the children to write it using pencil and paper or their magnetic letters. Ask the children to add to the list of items that Andrew and Stewart might take with them. (See page 13.)

Follow-up
- Display the picture and ask the children questions relating to it, to promote discussion and stimulate their thinking skills. You might ask, "How do you know what the boys are going to do? Why do you think they chose to camp in the garden? What time of the year do you think is best for this?"
- Encourage the children to come up with sentences using words they have learnt in the programme – perhaps asking their own question about the picture.
- Write up on the Work area one or more good sentences or questions suggested by the children to further the discussion.

WRAP-UP
- Recap the learning intentions with the children.
- Play the alphabet song again and encourage the children to sing along, signifying the end of the session.

Learning intentions are to:
- learn to read and spell irregular words "thought" and "through"
- write linked sentences from dictation including a list sentence
- contribute to discussion learning to ask own questions

Focus content: irregular

Reading
thought, through

Spelling
thought, through

Focus content: lesson

Reading
On a June day, Andrew put on his coat. He went down the avenue to see Stewart. He thought Stewart would camp overnight in the garden with him.

Spelling and Writing
They put up their tent near a big bush. Then they got a torch, juice, food and [ask children to add to the list].

Follow-up
Picture shows: two boys with a tent, camping in the garden.

Next steps
- Play the online language pupil games for Unit 18
- Complete the language PCM for Unit 18
- Read the Phonics Bug books that practise long and short /oo/alternatives: Bullfrog is Best, Follow the Clues, Unlucky!

Unit 19

Target phoneme /or/ written as 'aw'

INTRODUCTION
- Play the alphabet song twice, once with voice accompaniment, children listening and singing along with accompaniment, and once with children singing along to the music without voice accompaniment.
- Discuss with the children the learning intentions for the day.

REVISION
[previously taught grapheme–phoneme correspondences; blending phonemes for reading; segmenting spoken words for spelling]
- Go through the Revision screens at a brisk pace.
- Watch out for any children who have not remembered the phonemes or the graphemes.

LESSON

Sounds
- Choose the relevant lesson session.
- Select and drag the digraph 'aw' on to the Work area. Click on the digraph to hear how to say the phoneme /or/.
- Say the phoneme /or/, and ask the children to repeat it after you. Make sure you keep the sound pure and encourage the children to do the same.
- Explain that we use 'aw' at the end of a word or syllable and before final 'n', 'l', 'k', as in "saw", "yawn".

Visual Search
- Bring up the words from the asset bank onto the Work area. Ask the children to highlight the 'aw' in each of the words, saying whether it is at the beginning, the middle or the end of the word. Do not pronounce the words.

Reading
- Click the Reading tab to see the word.
- Click Blend to watch and hear the Bug's demonstration of how to blend the word. Click Undo and ask a child to come to the Work area and move the arrow. Encourage the whole class to blend the phonemes out loud as the arrow is moving along.
- Work through each of the words in sequence.

Spelling
- The children return to their seats.
- Start by selecting the Words tab. Click Say to hear the word and ask the children to repeat it, then ask the children to use their magnetic letters to make the word, saying the word every time they look for a letter. Ask a child to come up to the Work area to make the word. Did everyone get it right?
- Ask a child to use the arrow to push the letters together. Encourage the class to blend the word together out loud.
- Repeat for the remaining word under the Words tab.
- Under the Pictures tab, click Show to display the images and repeat the process for each word. (See pages 8–9 and 12.)

Writing
- Ask the children to find the letters 'a' and 'w' among their magnetic letters and to feel the shape of them. Click Show and ask the children to look and listen as the lowercase letters are formed.
- Ask a child to direct you how to write the letters as you write them on the empty Work area.
- Ask the child to write them on the dashed lines, then ask the children to practise writing 'aw' themselves.
- Select uppercase and repeat.

Follow-up
- Click Say to hear the sentence. Repeat the sentence, then dictate it slowly and deliberately for the children to write it. Then click Show to reveal the correct answer. (See page 13.)

WRAP-UP
- Recap the learning intentions with the children.
- Play the alphabet song and encourage the children to sing along, signifying the end of the session.

Learning intentions are to:
- recap what we know
- say the /or/ phoneme
- learn different ways to spell the /or/ phoneme
- read and spell words of one syllable or more
- write a dictated sentence

Focus content: revision

Letters and Sounds
or ⟲ Unit 10
Reading
cork, fort, torch, fork
Writing and Spelling
born, stork, orbit, storm

Focus content: lesson

Sounds
/or/
Visual search
raw, straw, draw, yawn
Reading
Audio: paw, claw, jaw
No audio: saw, thaw, hawk, jigsaw
Spelling
Words tab: draw, prawns
Pictures tab: straw, seesaw
Writing
aw
Follow-up
Dictation
Mum asked Dawn to draw the curtains.

Next steps
- Play the online pupil games for Unit 18
- Complete the phoneme PCM for Unit 19 (aw)
- Read the Phonics Bug books that practise long and short /oo/alternatives: Bullfrog is Best, Follow the Clues, Unlucky!

Unit 19

Target phoneme /or/ written as 'au'

INTRODUCTION
- Play the alphabet song twice, once with voice accompaniment, children listening and singing along with accompaniment, and once with children singing along to the music without voice accompaniment.
- Discuss with the children the learning intentions for the day.

REVISION
(previously taught grapheme–phoneme correspondences; blending phonemes for reading; segmenting spoken words for spelling)
- Go through the Revision screens at a brisk pace.
- Watch out for any children who have not remembered the phonemes or the graphemes.

LESSON
Sounds
- Choose the relevant lesson session.
- Select and drag the digraph 'au' on to the Work area. Click on the digraph to hear how to say the phoneme /or/.
- Say the phoneme /or/, and ask the children to repeat it after you. Make sure you keep the sound pure and encourage the children to do the same.

Visual Search
- Bring up the words from the asset bank onto the Work area. Ask the children to highlight the 'au' in each of the words, saying whether it is at the beginning, the middle or the end of the word. Do not pronounce the words.

Reading
- Click the Reading tab to see the word.
- Click Blend to watch and hear the Bug's demonstration of how to blend the word. Click Undo and ask a child to come to the Work area and move the arrow. Encourage the whole class to blend the phonemes out loud as the arrow is moving along.
- Work through each of the words in sequence.

Spelling
- The children return to their seats.
- Start by selecting the Words tab. Click Say to hear the word and ask the children to repeat it, then ask the children to use their magnetic letters to make the word, saying the word every time they look for a letter. Ask a child to come up to the Work area to make the word. Did everyone get it right?
- Ask a child to use the arrow to push the letters together. Encourage the class to blend the word together out loud.
- Repeat for the remaining word under the Words tab.
- Under the Pictures tab, click Show to display the images and repeat the process for each one. (See pages 8–9 and 12.)
- Select the Spelling video and play it once through.

Writing
- Ask the children to find the letters 'a' and 'u' among their magnetic letters and to feel the shape of them. Click Show and ask the children to look and listen as the lowercase letters are formed.
- Ask a child to direct you how to write the letters as you write them on the empty Work area.
- Ask the child to write them on the dashed lines, then ask the children to practise writing 'au' themselves.
- Select uppercase and repeat.

Follow-up
- Click Say to hear the sentence. Repeat the sentence, then dictate it slowly and deliberately for the children to write it. Then click Show to reveal the correct answer. (See page 13.)

WRAP-UP
- Recap the learning intentions with the children.
- Play the alphabet song and encourage the children to sing along, signifying the end of the session.

Learning intentions are to:
- recap what we know
- say the /or/ phoneme
- learn different ways to spell the /or/ phoneme
- read and spell words of one syllable or more
- write a dictated sentence

Focus content: revision

Letters and Sounds
aw

Reading
draw, prawns, straw, seesaw

Writing and Spelling
paw, claw, jaw, saw

Focus content: lesson

Sounds
/or/

Visual search
haul, haunt, fault, taught

Reading
Audio: vault, laundry, applaud, caught
No audio: launch, haul, fraud, author

Spelling
Words tab: haunt, Paul
Pictures tab: vault, astronaut
Video: port, saw, haunt

Writing
au

Follow-up
Dictation
Paul and Shaun like the same author.

Next steps
- Play the online pupil games for Unit 18
- Complete the phoneme PCM for Unit 19 (au)
- Read the Phonics Bug books that practise long and short /oo/ alternatives: Bullfrog is Best, Follow the Clues, Unlucky!

Unit 19

Target phoneme /or/ written as 'al'

INTRODUCTION
- Play the alphabet song twice, once with voice accompaniment, children listening and singing along with accompaniment, and once with children singing along to the music without voice accompaniment.
- Discuss with the children the learning intentions for the day.

REVISION
[previously taught grapheme–phoneme correspondences; blending phonemes for reading; segmenting spoken words for spelling]
- Go through the Revision screens at a brisk pace.
- Watch out for any children who have not remembered the phonemes or the graphemes.

LESSON

Sounds
- Choose the relevant lesson session.
- Select and drag the digraph 'al' on to the Work area. Click on the digraph to hear how to say the phoneme /or/.
- Say the phoneme /or/, and ask the children to repeat it after you. Make sure you keep the sound pure and encourage the children to do the same.
- Explain that 'al' can sound /or/ in words like "ball" or "walk".
- If appropriate, explain to children that there are other ways to spell the /or/ sound:
  - 'augh' sounds /or/ as in "caught"
  - 'our' sounds /or/ as in "four", "pour", but 'our' sounds /ure/ in "your" and "tour". Note that in some geographical regions, 'our' sounds /oa/ as in "four", "pour", "court".

Visual Search
- Bring up the words from the asset bank onto the Work area. Ask the children to highlight the 'al' in each of the words, saying whether it is at the beginning, the middle or the end of the word. Do not pronounce the words.

Reading
- Click the Reading tab to see the word.
- Click Blend to watch and hear the Bug's demonstration of how to blend the word. Click Undo and ask a child to come to the Work area and move the arrow. Encourage the whole class to blend the phonemes out loud as the arrow is moving along.
- Work through each of the words in sequence.

Spelling
- The children return to their seats.
- Start by selecting the Words tab. Click Say to hear the word and ask the children to repeat it, then ask the children to use their magnetic letters to make the word, saying the word every time they look for a letter. Ask a child to come up to the Work area to make the word. Did everyone get it right?
- Ask a child to use the arrow to push the letters together. Encourage the class to blend the word together out loud.
- Repeat for the remaining word under the Words tab.
- Under the Pictures tab, click Show to display the images and repeat the process. (See pages 8–9 and 12.)

Writing
- Ask the children to find the letters 'a' and 'l' among their magnetic letters and to feel the shape of them. Click Show and ask the children to look and listen as the lowercase letters are formed.
- Ask a child to direct you how to write the letters as you write them on the empty Work area.
- Ask the child to write them on the dashed lines, then ask the children to practise writing 'al' themselves.
- Select uppercase and repeat.

Follow-up
- Click Say to hear the sentence. Repeat the sentence, then dictate it slowly and deliberately for the children to write it. Then click Show to reveal the correct answer. (See page 13.)

WRAP-UP
- Recap the learning intentions with the children.
- Play the alphabet song and encourage the children to sing along, signifying the end of the session.

Learning intentions are to:
- recap what we know
- say the /or/ phoneme
- learn different ways to spell the /or/ phoneme
- read and spell words of one syllable or more
- write a dictated sentence

Focus content: revision

Letters and Sounds
au
Reading
haunt, launch, vault, laundry
Writing and Spelling
taught, vault, Paul, applaud

Focus content: lesson

Sounds
/or/
Visual search
all, ball, stall, walk
Reading
Audio: call, small, fall, snowball
No audio: ball, hall, rainfall, talk
Spelling
Words tab: all, tall
Pictures tab: football, wall
Writing
al
Follow-up
Dictation
The ball went over the wall.

Next steps
- Play the online pupil games for Unit 18
- Complete the phoneme PCM for Unit 19 (al)
- Read the Phonics Bug books that practise long and short /oo/ alternatives: Bullfrog is Best, Follow the Clues, Unlucky!

Unit 19

Language session

After: aw, au, al

INTRODUCTION
- Play the alphabet song twice, once with voice accompaniment, children listening and singing along with accompaniment, and once with children singing along to the music without voice accompaniment.
- Discuss with the children the learning intentions for the day.

IRREGULAR

Reading
- Select the Irregular part of the session.
- Click Show to display the words, and ask the children to read them.
- Click Answer to listen to the word being read.

Spelling
- Click Say to hear the words, and ask the children to repeat each word. Put the word into a sentence so that the children understand its meaning, for example, "Some people work in a hospital", "Jenny laughed because the joke was really funny", "I like apples because they are tasty".
- Point out that 'augh' sounds /af/ in "laughed".
- "because" (a conjunction) joins two sentences together.
- Say the target word, and ask the children to repeat it again. Ask the class to give each letter, and ask a child to come up to the Work area and drag up the correct letters into the spaces provided.
- Ask the class to read the word and click Say for them to hear it again.
- Repeat for the remaining words.

LESSON

Reading
- Click Show to display the sentences, and ask the children to read them.
- Click Answer to reveal whether they are right.
- Point out that 'au' in "Aunt" can sound /or/ or /a/, depending on regional variations.
- Point out the use of direct speech in the second sentence.

Spelling and Writing
- The children return to their seats.
- Remind the children about the dictation procedure.
- Click Say to hear the first sentence, and ask the children to repeat it.
- Slowly and distinctly dictate the sentence, asking the children to tell you how to write the words.
- Click Answer to reveal the sentence. Did the children tell you how to write it correctly?
- Repeat for the second sentence, asking the children to write it using pencil and paper or their magnetic letters. (See page 13.)

Follow-up
- Display the picture and ask the children questions relating to it, to promote discussion and stimulate their thinking skills. You might ask, "What is happening to the boys? Do you think they will be able to stop the dog? What do you think will happen next?"
- Encourage the children to come up with sentences using words they have learnt in the programme – perhaps asking their own question about the picture.
- Write up on the Work area one or more good sentences or questions suggested by the children to further the discussion.

WRAP-UP
- Recap the learning intentions with the children.
- Play the alphabet song again and encourage the children to sing along, signifying the end of the session.

Learning intentions are to:
- learn to read and spell irregular words "work", "laughed" and "because"
- write linked related sentences from dictation, including a two-syllable word
- contribute to discussion, learning to ask their own questions

Focus content: irregular

Reading
work, laughed, because

Spelling
work, laughed, because

Focus content: lesson

Reading
Shaun and Paul were going to Aunt Maud's because their mum was going into hospital. 'We can play ball with her dog,' they laughed.

Spelling and Writing
Paul and Shaun took the dog for a walk. The dog saw a small cat and ran after it.

Follow-up
Picture shows: two boys walking a dog in the park.

Next steps
- Play the online language pupil games for Unit 19
- Complete the language PCM for Unit 19
- Read the Phonics Bug books that practise /or/ alternatives: Boring, Boring!, Creepy-Crawly Hunt

Unit 20

Target phoneme /ur/ written as 'ir'

INTRODUCTION
- Play the alphabet song twice, once with voice accompaniment, children listening and singing along with accompaniment, and once with children singing along to the music without voice accompaniment.
- Discuss with the children the learning intentions for the day.

REVISION
[previously taught grapheme–phoneme correspondences; blending phonemes for reading; segmenting spoken words for spelling]
- Go through the Revision screens at a brisk pace.
- Watch out for any children who have not remembered the phonemes or the graphemes.

LESSON
Sounds
- Choose the relevant lesson session.
- Select and drag the digraph 'ir' on to the Work area. Click on the digraph to hear how to say the phoneme /ur/.
- Say the phoneme /ur/, and ask the children to repeat it after you. Make sure you keep the sound pure and encourage the children to do the same.

Visual Search
- Bring up the words from the asset bank onto the Work area. Ask the children to highlight the 'ir' in each of the words, saying whether it is at the beginning, the middle or the end of the word. Do not pronounce the words.

Reading
- Click the Reading tab to see the word.
- Click Blend to watch and hear the Bug's demonstration of how to blend the word. Click Undo and ask a child to come to the Work area and move the arrow. Encourage the whole class to blend the phonemes out loud as the arrow is moving along.
- Work through each of the words in sequence.

Spelling
- The children return to their seats.
- Start by selecting the Words tab. Click Say to hear the word and ask the children to repeat it, then ask the children to use their magnetic letters to make the word, saying the word every time they look for a letter. Ask a child to come up to the Work area to make the word. Did everyone get it right?
- Ask a child to use the arrow to push the letters together. Encourage the class to blend the word together out loud.
- Repeat for the remaining word under the Words tab.
- Under the Pictures tab, click Show to display the images and repeat the process for each word. (See pages 8–9 and 12.)

Writing
- Ask the children to find the letters 'i' and 'r' among their magnetic letters and to feel the shape of them. Click Show and ask the children to look and listen as the lowercase letters are formed.
- Ask a child to direct you how to write the letters as you write them on the empty Work area.
- Ask the child to write them on the dashed lines, then ask the children to practise writing 'ir' themselves.
- Select uppercase and repeat.

Follow-up
- Use the arrows to select one sentence. Click Say to hear the sentence. Repeat the sentence, then dictate it slowly and deliberately for the children to write it. Then click Show to reveal the correct answer. Repeat the procedure for the second sentence. (See page 13.)

WRAP-UP
- Recap the learning intentions with the children.
- Play the alphabet song and encourage the children to sing along, signifying the end of the session.

Learning intentions are to:
- recap what we know
- say the /ur/ phoneme
- learn different ways to spell the /ur/ phoneme
- read and spell words of one syllable or more
- write a dictated sentence

Focus content: revision

Letters and Sounds
ur ➔ Unit 10
Reading
curl, turf, surf, church
Writing and Spelling
burp, turn, churn, murmur

Focus content: lesson

Sounds
/ur/
Visual search
fir, first, birth, third, chirp
Reading
Audio: sir, first, girl, twirl
No audio: bird, stir, third, swirl
Spelling
Words tab: thirty, thirsty
Pictures tab: bird, shirt
Writing
ir
Follow-up
Dictation
Dad will be thirty on his birthday.
The third letter of the alphabet is C.

Next steps
- Play the online pupil games for Unit 19
- Complete the phoneme PCM for Unit 20 (ur)
- Read the Phonics Bug books that practise /or/ alternatives: Boring, Boring!, Creepy-Crawly Hunt

Unit 20

Target phoneme /ur/ written as 'er'

INTRODUCTION
- Play the alphabet song twice, once with voice accompaniment, children listening and singing along with accompaniment, and once with children singing along to the music without voice accompaniment.
- Discuss with the children the learning intentions for the day.

REVISION
[previously taught grapheme–phoneme correspondences; blending phonemes for reading; segmenting spoken words for spelling]
- Go through the Revision screens at a brisk pace.
- Watch out for any children who have not remembered the phonemes or the graphemes.

LESSON

Sounds
- Choose the relevant lesson session.
- Select and drag the digraph 'er' on to the Work area. Click on the digraph to hear how to say the phoneme /ur/.
- Say the phoneme /ur/, and ask the children to repeat it after you. Make sure you keep the sound pure and encourage the children to do the same.

Visual Search
- Bring up the words from the asset bank onto the Work area. Ask the children to highlight the 'er' in each of the words, saying whether it is at the beginning, the middle or the end of the word. Do not pronounce the words.

Reading
- Click the Reading tab to see the word.
- Click Blend to watch and hear the Bug's demonstration of how to blend the word. Click Undo and ask a child to come to the Work area and move the arrow. Encourage the whole class to blend the phonemes out loud as the arrow is moving along.
- Work through each of the words in sequence.

Spelling
- The children return to their seats.
- Start by selecting the Words tab. Click Say to hear the word and ask the children to repeat it, then ask the children to use their magnetic letters to make the word, saying the word every time they look for a letter. Ask a child to come up to the Work area to make the word. Did everyone get it right?
- Ask a child to use the arrow to push the letters together. Encourage the class to blend the word together out loud.
- Repeat for the remaining word under the Words tab.
- Under the Pictures tab, click Show to display the images and repeat the process for each word. (See pages 8–9 and 12.)
- Select the Spelling video and play it once through.

Writing
- Ask the children to find the letters 'e' and 'r' among their magnetic letters and to feel the shape of them. Click Show and ask the children to look and listen as the lowercase letters are formed.
- Ask a child to direct you how to write the letters as you write them on the empty Work area.
- Ask the child to write them on the dashed lines, then ask the children to practise writing 'er' themselves.
- Select uppercase and repeat.

Follow-up
- Click Say to hear the sentence. Repeat the sentence, then dictate it slowly and deliberately for the children to write it. Click Show to reveal the correct answer. (See page 13.)

WRAP-UP
- Recap the learning intentions with the children.
- Play the alphabet song and encourage the children to sing along, signifying the end of the session.

Learning intentions are to:
- recap what we know
- say the /ur/ phoneme
- learn different ways to spell the /ur/ phoneme
- read and spell words of one syllable or more
- write a dictated sentence

Focus content: revision

Letters and Sounds
ir

Reading
thirty, thirsty, bird, shirt

Writing and Spelling
girl, stir, third, swirl

Focus content: lesson

Sounds
/ur/

Visual search
stern, serve, verb, berth

Reading
Audio: herb, perk, servant, berth
No audio: serve, stern, superb, expert

Spelling
Words tab: verb, perky
Pictures tab: fern, desert
Video: number, bird, burn

Writing
er

Follow-up
Dictation
Do ferns grow in the desert?

Next steps
- Play the online pupil games for Unit 19
- Complete the phoneme PCM for Unit 20 (er)
- Read the Phonics Bug books that practise /or/ alternatives: Boring, Boring!, Creepy-Crawly Hunt

Unit 20

Target phoneme /ur/ written as 'ear'

INTRODUCTION
- Play the alphabet song twice, once with voice accompaniment, children listening and singing along with accompaniment, and once with children singing along to the music without voice accompaniment.
- Discuss with the children the learning intentions for the day.

REVISION
[previously taught grapheme–phoneme correspondences; blending phonemes for reading; segmenting spoken words for spelling]
- Go through the Revision screens at a brisk pace.
- Watch out for any children who have not remembered the phonemes or the graphemes.

LESSON

Sounds
- Choose the relevant lesson session.
- Select and drag the trigraph 'ear' on to the Work area. Click on the trigraph to hear how to say the phoneme /ur/.
- Say the phoneme /ur/, and ask the children to repeat it after you. Make sure you keep the sound pure and encourage the children to do the same.

Visual Search
- Bring up the words from the asset bank onto the Work area. Ask the children to highlight the 'ear' in each of the words, saying whether it is at the beginning, the middle or the end of the word. Do not pronounce the words.

Reading
- Click the Reading tab to see the word.
- Click Blend to watch and hear the Bug's demonstration of how to blend the word. Click Undo and ask a child to come to the Work area and move the arrow. Encourage the whole class to blend the phonemes out loud as the arrow is moving along.
- Work through each of the words in sequence.

Spelling
- The children return to their seats.
- Start by selecting the Words tab. Click Say to hear the word and ask the children to repeat it, then ask the children to use their magnetic letters to make the word, saying the word every time they look for a letter. Ask a child to come up to the Work area to make the word. Did everyone get it right?
- Ask a child to use the arrow to push the letters together. Encourage the class to blend the word together out loud.
- Repeat for the remaining word under the Words tab.
- Under the Pictures tab, click Show to display the images and repeat the process for each one. (See pages 8–9 and 12.)

Writing
- Ask the children to find the letters 'e', 'a' and 'r' among their magnetic letters and to feel the shape of them. Click Show and ask the children to look and listen as the lowercase letters are formed.
- Ask a child to direct you how to write the letters as you write them on the empty Work area.
- Ask the child to write them on the dashed lines, then ask the children to practise writing 'ear' themselves.
- Select uppercase and repeat.

Follow-up
- Click Say to hear the sentence. Repeat the sentence, then dictate it slowly and deliberately for the children to write it. Then click Show to reveal the correct answer. (See page 13.)

WRAP-UP
- Recap the learning intentions with the children.
- Play the alphabet song. Encourage children to sing along, signifying the session's end.

Learning intentions are to:
- recap what we know
- say the /ur/ phoneme
- learn different ways to spell the /ur/ phoneme
- read and spell words of one syllable or more
- write a dictated sentence

Focus content: revision

Letters and Sounds
er

Reading
verb, perky, fern, desert

Writing and Spelling
serve, stern, superb, expert

Focus content: lesson

Sounds
/ur/

Visual search
earl, pearl, earth, research

Reading
Audio: learn, search, earth, rehearsal
No audio: earn, heard, earnest, pearly

Spelling
Words tab: learn, early
Pictures tab: pearl, earth

Writing
ear

Follow-up
Dictation
I heard the birds early in the day.

Next steps
- Play the online pupil games for Unit 19
- Complete the phoneme PCM for Unit 20 (ear)
- Read the Phonics Bug books that practise /or/ alternatives: Boring, Boring!, Creepy-Crawly Hunt

Unit 20

Language session

After: ir, er, ear

INTRODUCTION

- Play the alphabet song twice, once with voice accompaniment, children listening and singing along with accompaniment, and once with children singing along to the music without voice accompaniment.
- Discuss with the children the learning intentions for the day.

HIGH-FREQUENCY WORDS

Reading
- Select the H-F words part of the session.
- Click Show to display the words, and ask the children to read them.
- Click Answer to listen to the word being read.

Spelling
- Click Say to hear the words, and ask the children to repeat each word. Put the word into a sentence so that the children understand its meaning, for example, "On Thursday and Saturday I play football", "Some people think that thirteen is an unlucky number", "The number thirty is made from three times ten".
- Point out that numbers are spelt with 'ir' and days are spelt with 'ur'.
- Say the target word, and ask the children to repeat it again. Ask the class to give each letter, and ask a child to come up to the Work area and drag up the correct letters into the spaces provided.
- Ask the class to read the word and click Say for them to hear it again.
- Repeat for the remaining words.

LESSON

Reading
- Click Show to display the sentences, and ask the children to read them.
- Click Answer to reveal whether they are right.

Spelling and Writing
- The children return to their seats.
- Remind the children about the dictation procedure.
- Click Say to hear the first sentence, and ask the children to repeat it.
- Slowly and distinctly dictate the sentence, asking the children to tell you how to write the words.
- Click Answer to reveal the sentence. Did the children tell you how to write it correctly?
- Repeat for the second sentence, asking the children to write it using pencil and paper or their magnetic letters. (See page 13.)

Follow-up
- Display the picture and ask the children questions relating to it, to promote discussion and stimulate their thinking skills. You might ask, "How did you know that Gran has hurt her foot? Why do you think Gran hurt her foot? What does Gran think happened to her? What if you hadn't visited Gran in her flat? How is Gran going to manage when you go home?"
- Encourage the children to come up with sentences using words they have learnt in the programme – perhaps asking their own question about the picture.
- Write up on the Work area one or more good sentences or questions suggested by the children to further the discussion.

WRAP-UP

- Recap the learning intentions with the children.
- Play the alphabet song again and encourage the children to sing along, signifying the end of the session.

Learning intentions are to:
- learn to read and spell high-frequency words "Thursday", "Saturday", "thirteen" and "thirty"
- write related sentences from dictation, including a two-syllable word
- contribute to discussion, learning to ask their own questions

Focus content: h-f words

Reading
Thursday, Saturday, thirteen, thirty

Spelling
Thursday, Saturday, thirteen, thirty

Focus content: lesson

Reading
On Saturday, we are going to visit Gran. I heard she hurt her foot and cannot get up the thirteen steps to her flat.

Spelling and Writing
We will go early and shop for Gran. She will give us a list of things to get for her.

Follow-up
Picture shows: Gran in her flat with a hurt foot.

Next steps
- Play the online language pupil games for Unit 20
- Complete the language PCM for Unit 20
- Read the Phonics Bug books that practise /ur/ alternatives: Sunflowers, The Third Whirligig

Unit 21

Target phoneme /ow/ written as 'ou'

INTRODUCTION
- Play the alphabet song twice, once with voice accompaniment, children listening and singing along with accompaniment, and once with children singing along to the music without voice accompaniment.
- Discuss with the children the learning intentions for the day.

REVISION
- Go through the Revision screens at a brisk pace.
- Watch out for any children who have not remembered the phonemes or the graphemes.
- Explain that 'ow' is used at the end of a word or syllable and before final 'n' and 'l'.

LESSON

Sounds
- Choose the relevant lesson session. Select and drag the digraph 'ou' on to the Work area. Click on the digraph to hear how to say the phoneme /ow/.
- Say the phoneme /ow/, and ask the children to repeat it after you. Make sure you keep the sound pure and encourage the children to do the same.
- Explain that 'ou' is used at the beginning and middle of a word or syllable, never at the end. We use 'ou' before 'nd', 'nt', 't', 'd' as in "round", "count".
- Minor correspondences: Point out that sometimes 'ou' sounds long /oo/ as in "coupon" and /oa/ as in "shoulder", "soul" and "mouldy".

Visual Search
- Bring up the words from the asset bank onto the Work area. Ask the children to highlight the 'ou' in each of the words, saying whether it is at the beginning, the middle or the end of the word. Do not pronounce the words.

Reading
- Click the Reading tab to see the word.
- Click Blend for the Bug's demonstration. Click Undo and ask a child to come to the Work area and move the arrow. Encourage the whole class to blend the phonemes out loud as the arrow is moving along.
- Work through each of the words in sequence.

Spelling
- The children return to their seats.
- Start by selecting the Words tab. Click Say to hear the word and ask the children to repeat it, then ask the children to use their magnetic letters to make the word, saying the word every time they look for a letter. Ask a child to come up to the Work area to make the word. Did everyone get it right?
- Ask a child to use the arrow to push the letters together. Encourage the class to blend the word together out loud.
- Repeat for the remaining word under the Words tab.
- Under the Pictures tab, click Show to display the images and repeat the process for each word. (See pages 8–9.)
- Select the Spelling video and play it once through.

Writing
- Ask children to find the letters 'o' and 'u' among their magnetic letters and to feel the shape of them. Click Show and ask the children to look and listen as the lowercase letters are formed.
- Ask a child to direct you how to write the letters as you write them on the Work area.
- Ask the child to write them on the dashed lines. Then ask the children to practise writing 'ou' themselves.
- Select uppercase and repeat.

Follow-up
- Use the arrows to select one sentence. Click Say to hear the sentence. Repeat the sentence, then dictate it slowly and deliberately for the children to write it. Then click Show to reveal the correct answer. Point out and explain the exclamation mark. Repeat the procedure for the second sentence. (See page 13.)

WRAP-UP
- Recap the learning intentions with the children.
- Play the alphabet song and encourage the children to sing along, signifying the end of the session.

Learning intentions are to:
- recap what we know
- say the /ow/ phoneme
- learn different ways to spell the /ow/ phoneme
- read and spell words of one syllable or more
- write a dictated sentence

Focus content: revision

Letters and Sounds
ow ⟶ Unit 10
Reading
now, drown, owl, clown
Writing and Spelling
gown, howl, crown, downtown

Focus content: lesson

Sounds
/ow/
Visual search
out, loud, mouth, found
Reading
Audio: out, about, proud, pound
No audio: round, count, shout, trousers
Spelling
Words tab: sound, pouch
Pictures tab: cloud, mouth
Video: loud, cow
Writing
ou
Follow-up
Dictation
Shout for help!
The cows are out on the road.

Next steps
- Play the online pupil games for Unit 20
- Complete the phoneme PCM for Unit 21 (ou)
- Read the Phonics Bug books that practise /ur/ alternatives: Sunflowers, The Third Whirligig

Unit 21

Target phoneme /oi/ written as 'oy'

INTRODUCTION
- Play the alphabet song twice, once with voice accompaniment, children listening and singing along with accompaniment, and once with children singing along to the music without voice accompaniment.
- Discuss with the children the learning intentions for the day.

REVISION
[previously taught grapheme–phoneme correspondences; blending phonemes for reading; segmenting spoken words for spelling]
- Go through the Revision screens at a brisk pace.
- Watch out for any children who have not remembered the phonemes or the graphemes.

LESSON
Sounds
- Choose the relevant lesson session.
- Select and drag the digraph 'oy' on to the Work area. Click on the digraph to hear how to say the phoneme /oi/.
- Say the phoneme /oi/, and ask the children to repeat it after you. Make sure you keep the sound pure and encourage the children to do the same.
- Explain that 'oi' is used at the beginning and middle of words. 'oy' is used at the end of a word or syllable.

Visual Search
- Bring up the words from the asset bank onto the Work area. Ask the children to highlight the 'oy' in each of the words, saying whether it is at the beginning, the middle or the end of the word. Do not pronounce the words.

Reading
- Click the Reading tab to see the word and syllables.
- Click Blend to watch and hear the Bug's demonstration of how to blend the syllables and the word. Click Undo and ask a child to come to the Work area and move the arrow. Encourage the whole class to blend the phonemes of the syllables and then the sounds of the word out loud as the arrow is moving along.
- Work through each of the words in sequence.

Spelling
- The children return to their seats.
- Start by selecting the Words tab. Click Say to hear the word and ask the children to repeat it, then ask the children to use their magnetic letters to make the word, saying the word every time they look for a letter. Ask a child to come up to the Work area to make the word. Did everyone get it right?
- Ask a child to use the arrow to push the letters together. Encourage the class to blend the word together out loud.
- Repeat for the remaining word under the Words tab.
- Under the Pictures tab, click Show to display the images and repeat the process for each word. (See pages 8–9 and 12.)
- Select the Spelling video and play it once through.

Writing
- Ask the children to find the letters 'o' and 'y' among their magnetic letters and to feel the shape of them. Click Show and ask the children to look and listen as the lowercase letters are formed.
- Ask a child to direct you how to write the letters as you write them on the empty Work area.
- Ask the child to write them on the dashed lines, then ask the children to practise writing 'oy' themselves.
- Select uppercase and repeat.

Follow-up
- Use the arrows to select one sentence. Click Say to hear the sentence. Repeat the sentence, then dictate it slowly and deliberately for the children to write it. Then click Show to reveal the correct answer. Repeat the procedure for the second sentence. (See page 13.)

WRAP-UP
- Recap the learning intentions with the children.
- Play the alphabet song and encourage the children to sing along, signifying the end of the session.

Learning intentions are to:
- recap what we know
- say the /oi/ phoneme
- learn different ways to spell the /oi/ phoneme
- read and spell words of one syllable or more
- write from dictation

Focus content: revision

Letters and Sounds
oi ↩ Unit 10
Reading
oil, joint, soil, coins
Writing and Spelling
coil, boil, spoil, join

Focus content: lesson

Sounds
/oi/
Visual search
toy, employ, annoy, Joy
Reading
Audio: oyster, destroy, enjoy, loyal
No audio: Roy, ahoy, annoy, royal
Spelling
Words tab: tomboy, enjoy
Pictures tab: boy, toys
Video: boil, joy
Writing
oy
Follow-up
Dictation
Joy and Roy are twins. They enjoy going to the play park.

Next steps
- Play the online pupil games for Unit 20
- Complete the phoneme PCM for Unit 21 (oy)
- Read the Phonics Bug books that practise /ur/ alternatives: Sunflowers, The Third Whirligig

Unit 21

Language session

After: ou, oy

INTRODUCTION
- Play the alphabet song twice, once with voice accompaniment, children listening and singing along with accompaniment, and once with children singing along to the music without voice accompaniment.
- Discuss with the children the learning intentions for the day.

IRREGULAR

Reading
- Select the Irregular part of the session.
- Click Show to display the words, and ask the children to read them.
- Click Answer to listen to the word being read.

Spelling
- Click Say to hear the words, and ask the children to repeat each word. Put the word into a sentence so that the children understand its meaning, for example, "We all like different foods", "The supermarket didn't have any carrots", "Fourteen chocolate bars is too many to eat at once!".
- "different" is a three-syllable word usually pronounced as a two-syllable one. The 'e' in the middle has the schwa sound /ə/.
- In "any" and "many, 'a' sounds /e/.
- Say the target word, and ask the children to repeat it again. Ask the class to give each letter, and ask a child to come up to the Work area and drag up the correct letters into the spaces provided.
- Ask the class to read the word and click Say for them to hear it again.
- Repeat for the remaining words.

LESSON

Reading
- Click Show to display the sentences, and ask the children to read them.
- Click Answer to reveal whether they are right.
- Draw the children's attention to the three-syllable word "roundabout".

Spelling and Writing
- The children return to their seats.
- Remind the children about the dictation procedure. (See page 13.)
- Click Say to hear the first sentence, and ask the children to repeat it.
- Slowly and distinctly dictate the sentence, asking the children to tell you how to write the words.
- Click Answer to reveal the sentence. Did the children tell you how to write it correctly?
- Repeat for the second and third sentences, asking the children to write them using pencil and paper or their magnetic letters. (See page 12.)

Follow-up
- Ask the children questions about the dictation sentences, to promote discussion and stimulate their thinking skills. Discuss what kind of help Roy would need to get for Joy. Why do children think that?
- Encourage the children to come up with sentences using words they have learnt in the programme, including asking their own questions about what happened.
- Write up on the Work area one or more good sentences or questions suggested by the children to further the discussion.

WRAP-UP
- Recap the learning intentions with the children.
- Play the alphabet song again and encourage the children to sing along, signifying the end of the session.

Learning intentions are to:
- learn to read and spell irregular words "different", "any" and "many"
- write related sentences from dictation, including a two-syllable word
- contribute to discussion, learning to ask their own questions

Focus content: irregular

Reading
different, any, many
Spelling
different, any, many

Focus content: lesson

Reading
Roy has lots of different toys but Joy has not got many. They both like going to the theme park near the roundabout.
Spelling and Writing
The ground was wet at the theme park. Joy fell and hurt her elbow. Roy had to get help.
Follow-up
Discuss what kind of help Roy would need to get for Joy.

Next steps
- Play the online language pupil games for Unit 21
- Complete the language PCM for Unit 21
- Read the Phonics Bug books that practise /ow/ and /oi/ alternatives: At the Toy Shop, The Trout Fishing Song

Unit 22

Target phoneme /ear/ written as 'ere' and 'eer'

INTRODUCTION
- Play the alphabet song twice, once with voice accompaniment, children listening and singing along with accompaniment, and once with children singing along to the music without voice accompaniment.
- Discuss with the children the learning intentions for the day.

REVISION
[previously taught grapheme–phoneme correspondences; blending phonemes for reading; segmenting spoken words for spelling]
- Go through the Revision screens at a brisk pace.
- Watch out for any children who have not remembered the phonemes or the graphemes.

LESSON
Sounds
- Choose the relevant lesson session.
- Select and drag the trigraph 'ere' on to the Work area. Click on the trigraph to hear how to say the phoneme /ear/. Repeat for 'eer'.
- Say the phoneme /ear/, and ask the children to repeat it after you. Make sure you keep the sound pure and encourage the children to do the same.

Visual Search
- Bring up the words from the asset bank onto the Work area. Ask the children to highlight the letters for /ear/ in each of the words. Do not pronounce the words.

Reading
- Click the Reading tab to see the word.
- Click Blend to watch and hear the Bug's demonstration of how to blend the word. Click Undo and ask a child to come to the Work area and move the arrow. Encourage the whole class to blend the phonemes out loud as the arrow is moving along.
- Work through each of the words in sequence.

Spelling
- The children return to their seats.
- Start by selecting the Words tab. Click Say to hear the word and ask the children to repeat it, then ask the children to use pencil and paper or their magnetic letters to make the word, saying the word every time they write down or look for a letter. Ask a child to come up to the Work area to make the word. Did everyone get it right?
- Ask a child to use the arrow to push the letters together. Encourage the class to blend the word together out loud.
- Repeat for the remaining word under the Words tab.
- Under the Pictures tab, click Show to display each image and repeat the process for each one. (See pages 8–9.)
- Select the Spelling video and play it once through.

Writing
- Ask the children to find the letters 'e', 'r' and 'e' among their magnetic letters and to feel the shape of them. Click Show and ask the children to look and listen as the lowercase letters are formed.
- Ask a child to direct you how to write the letters as you write them on the empty Work area.
- Ask the child to write them on the dashed lines, then ask the children to practise writing 'ere' themselves.
- Repeat for 'eer'.

Follow-up
- Use the arrows to select the sentence. Click Say to hear the sentence. Repeat the sentence, then dictate it slowly and deliberately for the children to write it. Then click Show to reveal the correct answer.
- Repeat the procedure for the second sentence. (See page 13.)

WRAP-UP
- Recap the learning intentions with the children.
- Play the alphabet song and encourage the children to sing along, signifying the end of the session.

Learning intentions are to:
- recap what we know
- say the /ear/ phoneme
- learn different ways to spell the /ear/ phoneme
- read and spell words of one syllable or more
- write a dictated sentence

Focus content: revision

Letters and Sounds
ear ➔ Unit 11

Reading
year, clear, ear, earring

Writing and Spelling
gear, spear, smear, earwig

Focus content: lesson

Sounds
/ear/

Visual search

here, sphere, cheer, peer

Reading

Audio: here, sphere, beer, reindeer

No audio: mere, interfere, sheer, sneer

Spelling

Words tab: here, cheer

Pictures tab: sphere, deer

Video: fear, deer, here

Writing
ere, eer

Follow-up
Dictation

The boys and girls cheered when a reindeer was found.
A sphere is the shape of a ball.

Next steps
- Play the online pupil games for Unit 21
- Complete the phoneme PCM for Unit 22 (ere/eer)
- Read the Phonics Bug books that practise /ow/ and /oi/ alternatives: At the Toy Shop, The Trout Fishing Song

Unit 22

Target phoneme /air/ written as 'are' and 'ear'

INTRODUCTION
- Play the alphabet song twice, once with voice accompaniment, children listening and singing along with accompaniment, and once with children singing along to the music without voice accompaniment.
- Discuss with the children the learning intentions for the day.

REVISION
(previously taught grapheme–phoneme correspondences; blending phonemes for reading; segmenting spoken words for spelling)
- Go through the Revision screens at a brisk pace.
- Watch out for any children who have not remembered the phonemes or the graphemes.

LESSON
Sounds
- Choose the relevant lesson session.
- Select and drag the trigraph 'are' on to the Work area. Click on the trigraph to hear how to say the phoneme /air/. Repeat for 'ear'.
- Say the phoneme /air/, and ask the children to repeat it after you. Make sure you keep the sound pure and encourage the children to do the same.

Visual Search
- Bring up the words from the asset bank onto the Work area. Ask the children to highlight the 'are' or 'ear' in each of the words. Do not pronounce the words.

Reading
- Click the Reading tab to see the word.
- Click Blend to watch and hear the Bug's demonstration of how to blend the word. Click Undo and ask a child to come to the Work area and move the arrow. Encourage the whole class to blend the phonemes out loud as the arrow is moving along.
- Work through each of the words in sequence.

Spelling
- The children return to their seats.
- Start by selecting the Words tab. Click Say to hear the word and ask the children to repeat it, then ask the children to use paper and pencil or their magnetic letters to make the word, saying the word every time they write down or look for a letter. Ask a child to come up to the Work area to make the word. Did everyone get it right?
- Ask a child to use the arrow to push the letters together. Encourage the class to blend the word together out loud.
- Repeat for the remaining word under the Words tab.
- Under the Pictures tab, click Show to display each image and repeat the process for each one. (See pages 8–9.)
- Select the Spelling video and play it once through.

Writing
- Ask the children to find the letters 'a', 'r' and 'e' among their magnetic letters and to feel the shape of them. Click Show and ask the children to look and listen as the lowercase letters are formed.
- Ask a child to direct you how to write the letters as you write them on the empty Work area.
- Ask the child to write them on the dashed lines, then ask the children to practise writing the letters 'are' themselves.
- Repeat for 'ear'.

Follow-up
- Use the arrows to select the sentence. Click Say to hear the sentence. Repeat the sentence, then dictate it slowly and deliberately for the children to write it. Then click Show to reveal the correct answer. Repeat the procedure for the second sentence. (See page 13.)

WRAP-UP
- Recap the learning intentions with the children.
- Play the alphabet song and encourage the children to sing along, signifying the end of the session.

Learning intentions are to:
- recap what we know
- say the /air/ phoneme
- learn different ways to spell the /air/ phoneme
- read and spell words of one syllable or more
- write sentences from dictation

Focus content: revision

Letters and Sounds
air ↩ Unit 11
Reading
fair, airport, chair, stairs
Writing and Spelling
air, hair, flair, airport

Focus content: lesson

Sounds
/air/
Visual search
dare, hare, bear, pear
Reading
Audio: share, glare, swear
No Audio: rare, scare, wear, pear
Spelling
Words tab: flare, tear
Pictures tab: square, bear
Video: chair, care, bear
Writing
are, ear
Follow-up
Dictation
We sat in the market square to share our lunch.
A bear ate the pears from a tree in the zoo.

Next steps
- Play the online pupil games for Unit 21
- Complete the phoneme PCM for Unit 22 (are, ear)
- Read the Phonics Bug books that practise /ow/ and /oi/ alternatives: At the Toy Shop, The Trout Fishing Song

Unit 22

Language session

After: ere/eer, are/ear

INTRODUCTION
- Play the alphabet song twice, once with voice accompaniment, children listening and singing along with accompaniment, and once with children singing along to the music without voice accompaniment.
- Discuss with the children the learning intentions for the day.

IRREGULAR

Reading
- Select the Irregular part of the session.
- Click Show to display the words, and ask the children to read them.
- Click Answer to listen to the word being read.

Spelling
- Click Say to hear the words, and ask the children to repeat each word. Put the word into a sentence so that the children understand its meaning, for example, "I have blue eyes", "We have always been friends".
- Explain that 'ey' sounds /igh/ in "eye", and 'ie' sounds /e/ in "friends".
- Say the target word, and ask the children to repeat it again. Ask the class to give each letter, and ask a child to come up to the Work area and drag up the correct letters into the spaces provided.
- Ask the class to read the word and click Say for them to hear it again.
- Repeat for the remaining words.

LESSON

Reading
- Click Show to display the sentences, and ask the children to read them.
- Click Answer to reveal whether they are right.

Spelling and Writing
- The children return to their seats.
- Remind the children about the dictation procedure.
- Click Say to hear the first sentence, and ask the children to repeat it.
- Slowly and distinctly dictate the sentence, asking the children to tell you how to write the words.
- Click Answer to reveal the sentence. Did the children tell you how to write it correctly?
- Repeat for the second sentence, asking the children to write it using pencil and paper or their magnetic letters. (See page 13.)

Follow-up
- Display the picture and ask the children questions relating to it, to promote discussion and stimulate their thinking skills. You might ask, "What kind of a picture is this? Who do you think took the photo? How do you think the girls are feeling? How can you tell? Do you and your friends like to wear the same things? Why?"
- Encourage the children to come up with sentences using words they have learnt in the programme – perhaps asking their own question about the picture.
- Write up on the Work area one or more good sentences or questions suggested by the children to further the discussion.

WRAP-UP
- Recap the learning intentions with the children.
- Play the alphabet song again and encourage the children to sing along, signifying the end of the session.

Learning intentions are to:
- learn to read and spell irregular words "eyes" and "friends"
- write related sentences from dictation including a two-syllable word
- contribute to discussion, learning to ask their own questions

Focus content: irregular

Reading
eyes, friends
Spelling
eyes, friends

Focus content: lesson

Reading
I have three best friends and we all have brown eyes. We cheer each other up.
Spelling and Writing
Here is a photo of my friends and me. We like to wear the same things.
Follow-up
Picture shows: a 'photo' of four happy friends.

Next steps
- Play the online language pupil games for Unit 22
- Complete the language PCM for Unit 22
- Read the Phonics Bug books that practise /ear/ and /air/ alternatives: Meerkats, Sid and the Scarecrow Dare

Unit 23

Target phoneme /c/ written as 'c'

INTRODUCTION
- Play the alphabet song twice, once with voice accompaniment, children listening and singing along with accompaniment, and once with children singing along to the music without voice accompaniment.
- Discuss with the children the learning intentions for the day.

REVISION
[previously taught grapheme–phoneme correspondences; blending phonemes for reading; segmenting spoken words for spelling]
- Go through the Revision screens at a brisk pace.
- Watch out for any children who have not remembered the phonemes or the graphemes.

LESSON
Sounds
- Choose the relevant lesson session.
- Select and drag the letter 'c' on to the Work area. Click on the letter to hear how to say the phoneme /c/.
- Say the phoneme /c/, and ask the children to repeat it after you. Make sure you keep the sound pure and encourage the children to do the same.
- Explain that we use 'c' for /c/ before vowels 'a', 'o' and 'u' (it is known as the "hard 'c'"), as in "card", "cod", "cuff".

Visual Search
- Bring up the words from the asset bank onto the Work area. Ask the children to highlight the 'c' in each of the words, saying whether it is at the beginning, the middle or the end of the word. Do not pronounce the words.

Reading
- Click the Reading tab to see the word.
- Click Blend to watch and hear the Bug's demonstration of how to blend the word. Click Undo and ask a child to come to the Work area and move the arrow. Encourage the whole class to blend the phonemes out loud as the arrow is moving along.
- Work through each of the words in sequence.

Spelling
- The children return to their seats.
- Start by selecting the Words tab. Click Say to hear the word and ask the children to repeat it, then ask the children to use pencil and paper or their magnetic letters to make the word, saying the word every time they write down or look for a letter. Ask a child to come up to the Work area to make the word. Did everyone get it right?
- Ask a child to use the arrow to push the letters together. Encourage the class to blend the word together out loud.
- Repeat for the remaining word under the Words tab.
- Under the Pictures tab, click Show to display each image and repeat the process for each one. (See pages 8–9.)

Writing
- Ask the children to find the letter 'c' among their magnetic letters and to feel the shape of it. Click Show and ask the children to look and listen as the lowercase letter is formed.
- Ask a child to direct you how to write the letter as you write it on the empty Work area.
- Ask the child to write it on the dashed lines, then ask the children to practise writing the letter 'c' themselves.
- Select uppercase and repeat.

Follow-up
- Click Say to hear the sentence. Repeat the sentence, then dictate it slowly and deliberately for the children to write it. Then click Show to reveal the correct answer. (See page 13.)

WRAP-UP
- Recap the learning intentions with the children.
- Play the alphabet song and encourage the children to sing along, signifying the end of the session.

Learning intentions are to:
- recap what we know
- say the /c/ phoneme
- learn different ways to spell the /c/ phoneme
- read and spell words of one syllable or more
- write a dictated sentence

Focus content: revision

Letters and Sounds
c ➤ Unit 3
Reading
cot, cob, cat, cap
Writing and Spelling
cab, can, car, act

Focus content: lesson

Sounds
/c/
Visual search
card, cobweb, cuff, camp, collar, cub
Reading
Audio: cash, code, cups, cobweb
No audio: curve, camera, custard, cockpit
Spelling
Words tab: carpet, cotton
Pictures tab: cactus, camel
Writing
c
Follow-up
Dictation
At Sports Day, Carl was given a silver cup and a compass.

Next steps
- Play the online pupil games for Unit 22
- Complete the phoneme PCM for Unit 23 (c)
- Read the Phonics Bug books that practise /ear/ and /air/ alternatives: Meerkats, Sid and the Scarecrow Dare

Unit 23

Target phoneme /c/ written as 'k'

INTRODUCTION
- Play the alphabet song twice, once with voice accompaniment, children listening and singing along with accompaniment, and once with children singing along to the music without voice accompaniment.
- Discuss with the children the learning intentions for the day.

REVISION
[previously taught grapheme–phoneme correspondences; blending phonemes for reading; segmenting spoken words for spelling]
- Go through the Revision screens at a brisk pace.
- Watch out for any children who have not remembered the phonemes or the graphemes.

LESSON

Sounds
- Choose the relevant lesson session.
- Select and drag the letter 'k' on to the Work area. Click on the letter to hear how to say the phoneme /c/.
- Say the phoneme /c/, and ask the children to repeat it after you. Make sure you keep the sound pure and encourage the children to do the same.
- Explain that we use 'k' for /c/ before vowels 'e' and 'i', and after a consonant at the end of the word, as in "keep", "kit", "milk", an exception being "go-kart".

Visual Search
- Bring up the words from the asset bank onto the Work area. Ask the children to highlight the 'k' in each of the words, saying whether it is at the beginning, the middle or the end of the word. Do not pronounce the words.

Reading
- Click the Reading tab to see the word.
- Click Blend to watch and hear the Bug's demonstration of how to blend the word. Click Undo and ask a child to come to the Work area and move the arrow. Encourage the whole class to blend the phonemes out loud as the arrow is moving along.
- Work through each of the words in sequence.

Spelling
- The children return to their seats.
- Start by selecting the Words tab. Click Say to hear the word and ask the children to repeat it, then ask the children to use pencil and paper or their magnetic letters to make the word, saying the word every time they write down or look for a letter. Ask a child to come up to the Work area to make the word. Did everyone get it right?
- Ask a child to use the arrow to push the letters together. Encourage the class to blend the word together out loud.
- Repeat for the remaining word under the Words tab.
- Under the Pictures tab, click Show to display each image and repeat the process for each one. (See pages 8–9 and 12–13.)

Writing
- Ask the children to find the letter 'k' among their magnetic letters and to feel the shape of it. Click Show and ask the children to look and listen as the lowercase letter is formed.
- Ask a child to direct you how to write the letter as you write it on the empty Work area.
- Ask the child to write it on the dashed lines, then ask the children to practise writing the letter 'k' themselves.
- Select uppercase and repeat.

Follow-up
- Click Say to hear the sentence. Repeat the sentence, then dictate it slowly and deliberately for the children to write it. Then click Show to reveal the correct answer. (See page 13.)

WRAP-UP
- Recap the learning intentions with the children.
- Play the alphabet song and encourage the children to sing along, signifying the end of the session.

Learning intentions are to:
- recap what we know
- say the /c/ phoneme
- learn different ways to spell the /c/ phoneme
- read and spell words of one syllable or more
- write a dictated sentence

Focus content: revision

Letters and Sounds
k Unit 3
Reading
Ken, kin, kids, kit
Writing and Spelling
kid, kits, Kim, kept

Focus content: lesson

Sounds
/c/
Visual search
kennel, kettle, kiss, skin, ask, think
Reading
Audio: keep, kilt, thank, Kenny
No audio: kerb, bank, kitten, kingdom
Spelling
Words tab: bark, kipper
Pictures tab: king, kennel
Writing
k
Follow-up
Dictation
Kenny's kitten fell into a sink of water.

Next steps
- Play the online pupil games for Unit 22
- Complete the phoneme PCM for Unit 23 (k)
- Read the Phonics Bug books that practise /ear/ and /air/ alternatives: Meerkats, Sid and the Scarecrow Dare

Unit 23

Target phoneme /c/ written as 'ck'

INTRODUCTION
- Play the alphabet song twice, once with voice accompaniment, children listening and singing along with accompaniment, and once with children singing along to the music without voice accompaniment.
- Discuss with the children the learning intentions for the day.

REVISION
[previously taught grapheme–phoneme correspondences; blending phonemes for reading; segmenting spoken words for spelling]
- Go through the Revision screens at a brisk pace.
- Watch out for any children who have not remembered the phonemes or the graphemes.

LESSON
Sounds
- Choose the relevant lesson session.
- Select and drag the digraph 'ck' on to the Work area. Click on the digraph to hear how to say the phoneme /c/.
- Say the phoneme /c/, and ask the children to repeat it after you. Make sure you keep the sound pure and encourage the children to do the same.
- Explain that we use 'ck' for /c/ after a short vowel at the end of a word or syllable, as in "duck", "rocket".

Visual Search
- Bring up the words from the asset bank onto the Work area. Ask the children to highlight the 'ck' in each of the words, saying whether it is at the beginning, the middle or the end of the word. Do not pronounce the words.

Reading
- Click the Reading tab to see the word.
- Click Blend to watch and hear the Bug's demonstration of how to blend the word. Click Undo and ask a child to come to the Work area and move the arrow. Encourage the whole class to blend the phonemes out loud as the arrow is moving along.
- Work through each of the words in sequence.

Spelling
- The children return to their seats.
- Start by selecting the Words tab. Click Say to hear the word and ask the children to repeat it, then ask the children to use pencil and paper or their magnetic letters to make the word, saying the word every time they write down or look for a letter. Ask a child to come up to the Work area to make the word. Did everyone get it right?
- Ask a child to use the arrow to push the letters together. Encourage the class to blend the word together out loud.
- Repeat for the remaining word under the Words tab.
- Under the Pictures tab, click Show to display each image and repeat the process for each one. (See pages 8–9 and 12–13.)
- Select the Spelling video and play it once through.

Writing
- Ask the children to find the letters 'c' and 'k' among their magnetic letters and to feel the shape of them. Click Show and ask the children to look and listen as the lowercase letters are formed.
- Ask a child to direct you how to write the letters as you write them on the empty Work area.
- Ask the child to write them on the dashed lines, then ask the children to practise writing the letters 'c' and 'k' themselves.
- Select uppercase and repeat.

Follow-up
- Use the arrows to select the sentence. Click Say to hear the sentence. Repeat the sentence, then dictate it slowly and deliberately for the children to write it. Then click Show to reveal the correct answer. (See page 13.)

WRAP-UP
- Recap the learning intentions with the children.
- Play the alphabet song and encourage the children to sing along, signifying the end of the session.

Learning intentions are to:
- recap what we know
- say the /c/ phoneme
- learn different ways to spell the /c/ phoneme
- read and spell words of one syllable or more
- write a dictated sentence

Focus content: revision

Letters and Sounds
ck ⬭ Unit 4
Reading
kick, neck, pack, pick
Writing and Spelling
tick, deck, sack, sock

Focus content: lesson

Sounds
/c/
Visual search
black, brick, peck, sock
Reading
Audio: duck, track, flock, pocket
No audio: black, quick, luck, rocket
Spelling
Words tab: duck, packet
Pictures tab: clock, rocket
Video: can, kit, lock
Writing
ck
Follow-up
Dictation
At the Air Show, Jack had a ticket to go into the cockpit.

Next steps
- Play the online pupil games for Unit 22
- Complete the phoneme PCM for Unit 23 (ck)
- Read the Phonics Bug books that practise /ear/ and /air/ alternatives: Meerkats, Sid and the Scarecrow Dare

Unit 23

Target phoneme /c/ written as 'ch'

INTRODUCTION
- Play the alphabet song twice, once with voice accompaniment, children listening and singing along with accompaniment, and once with children singing along to the music without voice accompaniment.
- Discuss with the children the learning intentions for the day.

REVISION
[previously taught grapheme–phoneme correspondences; blending phonemes for reading; segmenting spoken words for spelling]
- Go through the Revision screens at a brisk pace.
- Watch out for any children who have not remembered the phonemes or the graphemes.

LESSON
Sounds
- Choose the relevant lesson session.
- Select and drag the digraph 'ch' on to the Work area. Click on the digraph to hear how to say the phoneme /c/.
- Say the phoneme /c/, and ask the children to repeat it after you. Make sure you keep the sound pure and encourage the children to do the same.
- Explain that 'ch' can sound /c/, as in "chemist", "ache".
- Explain that 'qu' can also sound /c/, as in "quoits".

Visual Search
- Bring up the words from the asset bank onto the Work area. Ask the children to highlight the 'ch' in each of the words, saying whether it is at the beginning, the middle or the end of the word. Do not pronounce the words.

Reading
- Click the Reading tab to see the word and syllables.
- Click Blend to watch and hear the Bug's demonstration of how to blend the syllables and the word. Click Undo and ask a child to come to the Work area and move the arrow. Encourage the whole class to blend the phonemes of the syllables and then the sounds of the word out loud as the arrow is moving along.
- Work through each of the words in sequence.

Spelling
- The children return to their seats.
- Start by selecting the Words tab. Click Say to hear the word and ask the children to repeat it, then ask the children to use pencil and paper or their magnetic letters to make the word, saying the word every time they write down or look for a letter. Ask a child to come up to the Work area to make the word. Did everyone get it right?
- Ask a child to use the arrow to push the letters together. Encourage the class to blend the word together out loud.
- Repeat for the remaining words under the Words tab.
- Under the Pictures tab, click Show to display each image and repeat the process for each one. (See pages 8–9 and 12–13.)

Writing
- Ask the children to find the letters 'c' and 'h' among their magnetic letters and to feel the shape of them. Click Show and ask the children to look and listen as the lowercase letters are formed.
- Ask a child to direct you how to write the letters as you write them on the empty Work area.
- Ask the child to write them on the dashed lines, then ask the children to practise writing 'ch' themselves.
- Select uppercase and repeat.

Follow-up
- Use the arrows to select the sentence. Click Say to hear the sentence. Repeat the sentence, then dictate it slowly and deliberately for the children to write it. Then click Show to reveal the correct answer. (See page 13.)

WRAP-UP
- Recap the learning intentions with the children.
- Play the alphabet song and encourage the children to sing along, signifying the end of the session.

Learning intentions are to:
- recap what we know
- say the /c/ phoneme
- learn different ways to spell the /c/ phoneme
- read and spell words of one syllable or more
- write a dictated sentence

Focus content: revision

Letters and Sounds
/ch/ ⊃ Unit 8
Reading
chum, much, chop, chug
Writing and Spelling
check, such, chill, chicken

Focus content: lesson

Sounds
/c/
Visual search
choir, anchor, ache, Christmas
Reading
Audio: chemist, chorus, school, Chris
No audio: chrome, anchor, chaos, ache
Spelling
Words tab: chord, chaos
Pictures tab: toothache, anchor
Writing
ch
Follow-up
Dictation
Chris sang in the choir at school.

Next steps
- Play the online pupil games for Unit 22
- Complete the phoneme PCM for Unit 23 (ck)
- Read the Phonics Bug books that practise /ear/ and /air/ alternatives: Meerkats, Sid and the Scarecrow Dare

Language session

After: c, k, ck, ch

INTRODUCTION
- Play the alphabet song twice, once with voice accompaniment, children listening and singing along with accompaniment, and once with children singing along to the music without voice accompaniment.
- Discuss with the children the learning intentions for the day.

IRREGULAR
Reading
- Select the Irregular part of the session.
- Click Show to display the words, and ask the children to read them.
- Click Answer to listen to the word being read.

Spelling
- Click Say to hear the words, and ask the children to repeat each word. Put the word into a sentence so that the children understand its meaning, for example, "I have one nose and two eyes", "I will say this only once".
- Point out that in "one" and "once", the 'o' is pronounced as /wu/.
- Explain that "to", "too" and "two" all sound /t/ /oo/ (long /oo/ sound).
- Say the target word, and ask the children to repeat it again. Ask the class to give each letter, and ask a child to come up to the Work area and drag up the correct letters into the spaces provided.
- Ask the class to read the word and click Say for them to hear it again.
- Repeat for the remaining words.

LESSON
Reading
- Click Show to display the sentences, and ask the children to read them.
- Click Answer to reveal whether they are right.
- Explain to the children that "as" can be used as a conjunction, to join two sentences into one.

Spelling and Writing
- The children return to their seats.
- Remind the children about the dictation procedure.
- Click Say to hear the first sentence, and ask the children to repeat it.
- Slowly and distinctly dictate the sentence, asking the children to tell you how to write the words.
- Click Answer to reveal the sentence. Did the children tell you how to write it correctly?
- Draw the children's attention to "said Mark". Remind the children about direct speech and demonstrate the use of speech marks (see Unit 19).
- Repeat for the second sentence, asking the children to write it using pencil and paper or their magnetic letters. (See page 13.)

Follow-up
- Display the picture and ask the children questions relating to it, to promote discussion and stimulate their thinking skills. You might ask, "What do you think the boy holding the rocket is feeling? How can you tell? What will the boys do with the photo?"
- Encourage the children to come up with sentences using words they have learnt in the programme – perhaps asking their own question about the picture.
- Write up on the Work area one or more good sentences or questions suggested by the children to further the discussion.

WRAP-UP
- Recap the learning intentions with the children.
- Play the alphabet song again and encourage the children to sing along, signifying the end of the session.

Unit 23

Learning intentions are to:
- learn to read and spell irregular words "two" and "once"
- write related sentences from dictation, including a two-syllable word and direct speech
- contribute to discussion, learning to ask their own questions

Focus content: irregular

Reading
two, once

Spelling
two, once

Focus content: lesson

Reading
Once, two boys, Chris and Mark, made a rocket from card. Mark took a photo of it, as he had a camera.

Spelling and Writing
'You can keep the rocket,' said Mark. 'Thank you,' said Chris.

Follow-up
Picture shows: a boy holding a rocket made from card and his friend taking a photo.

Next steps
- Play the online language pupil games for Unit 23
- Complete the language PCM for Unit 23
- Read the Phonics Bug books that practise /c/ alternatives: Go-Kart, Go!, Hungry Birds

Unit 24

Target phoneme /s/ written as 'c(e)', 'c(i)', 'c(y)'

INTRODUCTION
- Play the alphabet song twice, once with voice accompaniment, children listening and singing along with accompaniment, and once with children singing along to the music without voice accompaniment.
- Discuss with the children the learning intentions for the day.

REVISION
[previously taught grapheme–phoneme correspondences; blending phonemes for reading; segmenting spoken words for spelling]
- Go through the Revision screens at a brisk pace.
- Watch out for any children who have not remembered the phonemes or the graphemes.

LESSON

Sounds
- Choose the relevant lesson session.
- Say the phoneme /s/, and ask the children to repeat it after you. Make sure you keep the sound pure and encourage the children to do the same.
- Explain that 'c' followed by 'e' sounds /s/ (known as "soft 'c'"), as in "cent", "grocer", "slice". 'ce' sounding /s/ is used more often at the end of words than 'se'. Exceptions include "horse", "house". 'c' followed by 'i', and 'c' followed by 'y', also sound /s/ ("soft 'c'") as in "cinema"; "cymbal".

Visual Search
- Bring up the words from the asset bank onto the Work area. Ask the children to highlight the 'ce', 'ci' or 'cy' in each of the words, saying whether it is at the beginning, the middle or the end of the word. Do not pronounce the words.

Reading
- Click the Reading tab to see the word.
- Click Blend to watch and hear the Bug's demonstration of how to blend the word. Click Undo and ask a child to come to the Work area and move the arrow. Encourage the whole class to blend the phonemes out loud as the arrow is moving along.
- Work through each of the words in sequence.

Spelling
- The children return to their seats.
- Start by selecting the Words tab. Click Say to hear the word and ask the children to repeat it, then ask the children to use pencil and paper or their magnetic letters to make the word, saying the word every time they write down or look for a letter. Ask a child to come up to the Work area to make the word. Did everyone get it right?
- Ask a child to use the arrow to push the letters together. Encourage the class to blend the word together out loud.
- Repeat for the remaining words under the Words tab.
- Under the Pictures tab, click Show to display each image and repeat the process for each one. (See pages 8–9 and 12–13.)

Writing
- Ask the children to find the letters 'c' and 'e' among their magnetic letters and to feel the shape of them. Click Show and ask the children to look and listen as the lowercase letters are formed.
- Ask a child to direct you how to write the letters as you write them on the empty Work area.
- Ask the child to write them on the dashed lines, then ask the children to practise writing 'ce' themselves.
- Repeat for 'c' and 'i', and 'c' and 'y'.

Follow-up
- Click Say to hear the sentence. Repeat the sentence, then dictate it slowly and deliberately for the children to write it. Then click Show to reveal the correct answer. (See page 13.)

WRAP-UP
- Recap the learning intentions with the children.
- Play the alphabet song and encourage the children to sing along, signifying the end of the session.

Learning intentions are to:
- recap what we know
- say the /s/ phoneme
- learn different ways to spell the /s/ phoneme
- read and spell words of one syllable or more
- write a dictated sentence

Focus content: revision

Letters and Sounds
s ➲ Unit 1
Reading
pants, Stan, past, spins
Writing and Spelling
set, mats, stamp, slug

Focus content: lesson

Sounds
/s/
Visual search
cent, grocer, circle, council, bicycle, cylinder
Reading
Audio: force, celery, circus, excite, fancy, cyclone
No audio: ice, cement, city, decide, cymbal, Lucy
Spelling
Words tab: price, cinema, fancy
Pictures tab: face, pencil, cyclist
Writing
ce, ci, cy
Follow-up
Dictation
Grace gave me her pencil to draw a circle.

Next steps
- Play the online pupil games for Unit 23
- Complete the phoneme PCM for Unit 24 (ce, ci, cy)
- Read the Phonics Bug books that practise /c/ alternatives: Go-Kart, Go!, Hungry Birds

Unit 24

Target phoneme /s/ written as 'sc' and 'st(l)'

INTRODUCTION
- Play the alphabet song twice, once with voice accompaniment, children listening and singing along with accompaniment, and once with children singing along to the music without voice accompaniment.
- Discuss with the children the learning intentions for the day.

REVISION
[previously taught grapheme–phoneme correspondences; blending phonemes for reading; segmenting spoken words for spelling]
- Go through the Revision screens at a brisk pace.
- Watch out for any children who have not remembered the phonemes or the graphemes.

LESSON

Sounds
- Choose the relevant lesson session.
- Say the phoneme /s/, and ask the children to repeat it after you. Make sure you keep the sound pure and encourage the children to do the same.
- Explain that 'sc' followed by 'e' at the beginning of the word sounds /s/ ("soft 'c'"), as in "scene", "scent".
- 'st' followed by 'le' at the end of words sounds /s/. E.g. in '"castle", the 's' at the end of the first syllable sounds /s/ and in the second syllable 't' is silent and 'le' sounds /ul/ to make /c/ /a/ /s/ /ul/.

Visual Search
- Bring up the words from the asset bank onto the Work area. Ask the children to highlight the 'sc' or 'stl' in each of the words, saying whether it is at the beginning, the middle or the end of the word. Do not pronounce the words.

Reading
- Click the Reading tab to see the word.
- Click Blend to watch and hear the Bug's demonstration of how to blend the word. Click Undo and ask a child to come to the Work area and move the arrow. Encourage the whole class to blend the phonemes out loud as the arrow is moving along.
- Work through each of the words in sequence.

Spelling
- The children return to their seats.
- Start by selecting the Words tab. Click Say to hear the word and ask the children to repeat it, then ask the children to use pencil and paper or their magnetic letters to make the word, saying the word every time they write down or look for a letter. Ask a child to come up to the Work area to make the word. Did everyone get it right?
- Ask a child to use the arrow to push the letters together. Encourage the class to blend the word together out loud.
- Repeat for the remaining words under the Words tab.
- Under the Pictures tab, click Show to display each image and repeat the process for each one. (See pages 8–9 and 12–13.)

Writing
- Ask the children to find the letters 's' and 'c' among their magnetic letters and to feel the shape of them. Click Show and ask the children to look and listen as the lowercase letters are formed.
- Ask a child to direct you how to write the letters as you write them on the empty Work area.
- Ask the child to write them on the dashed lines, then ask the children to practise writing 'sc' themselves.
- Repeat for 'st(l)'.

Follow-up
- Click Say to hear the sentence. Repeat the sentence, then dictate it slowly and deliberately for the children to write it. Then click Show to reveal the correct answer. (See page 13.)

WRAP-UP
- Recap the learning intentions with the children.
- Play the alphabet song and encourage the children to sing along, signifying the end of the session.

Learning intentions are to:
- recap what we know
- say the /s/ phoneme
- learn different ways to spell the /s/ phoneme
- read and spell words of more than one syllable
- write a dictated sentence

Focus content: revision

Letters and Sounds
c(e), c(i), c(y)

Reading
price, cinema, fancy, face, pencil, cyclist

Writing and Spelling
ice, cement, city, decide, cymbal, Lucy

Focus content: lesson

Sounds
/s/

Visual search
scene, muscle, nestle, rustle

Reading
Audio: scent, science, castle, whistle
No audio: descend, scenic, muscle, jostle

Spelling
Words tab: scene, bustle
Pictures tab: scissors, castle

Writing
sc, stl

Follow-up
Dictation
The scene inside the castle was all hustle and bustle.

Next steps
- Play the online pupil games for Unit 23
- Complete the phoneme PCM for Unit 24 (sc/stl)
- Read the Phonics Bug books that practise /c/ alternatives: Go-Kart, Go!, Hungry Birds

Unit 24

Target phonemes /s/ and /z/ written as 's'

INTRODUCTION
- Play the alphabet song twice, once with voice accompaniment, children listening and singing along with accompaniment, and once with children singing along to the music without voice accompaniment.
- Discuss with the children the learning intentions for the day.

REVISION
[previously taught grapheme–phoneme correspondences; blending phonemes for reading; segmenting spoken words for spelling]
- Go through the Revision screens at a brisk pace.
- Watch out for any children who have not remembered the phonemes or the graphemes.

LESSON

Sounds
- Choose the relevant lesson session.
- Say the phoneme /s/, and ask the children to repeat it after you. Make sure you keep the sound pure and encourage the children to do the same.
- Explain that 'se' at the end of a word sometimes sounds /s/ and sometimes sounds /z/.

Visual Search
- Bring up the words from the asset bank onto the Work area. Ask the children to highlight the 'se' in each of the words. Do not pronounce the words.

Reading
- Click the Reading tab to see the word.
- Click Blend to watch and hear the Bug's demonstration of how to blend the word. Click Undo and ask a child to come to the Work area and move the arrow. Encourage the whole class to blend the phonemes out loud as the arrow is moving along.
- Work through each of the words in sequence.

Spelling
- The children return to their seats.
- Start by selecting the Words tab. Click Say to hear the word and ask the children to repeat it, then ask the children to use pencil and paper or their magnetic letters to make the word, saying the word every time they write down or look for a letter. Ask a child to come up to the Work area to make the word. Did everyone get it right?
- Ask a child to use the arrow to push the letters together. Encourage the class to blend the word together out loud.
- Repeat for the remaining words under the Words tab.
- Under the Pictures tab, click Show to display each image and repeat the process for each one. (See pages 8–9.)
- Select the Spelling video and play it once through.

Writing
- Ask the children to find the letters 's' and 'e' among their magnetic letters and to feel the shape of them. Click Show and ask the children to look and listen as the lowercase letters are formed.
- Ask a child to direct you how to write the letters as you write them on the empty Work area.
- Ask the child to write them on the dashed lines, then ask the children to practise writing 'se' themselves.
- Select uppercase and repeat.

Follow-up
- Use the arrows to select the sentence. Click Say to hear the sentence. Repeat the sentence, then dictate it slowly and deliberately for the children to write it. Then click Show to reveal the correct answer. (See page 13.)

WRAP-UP
- Recap the learning intentions with the children.
- Play the alphabet song and encourage the children to sing along, signifying the end of the session.

Learning intentions are to:
- recap what we know
- say the /s/ phoneme
- learn different ways to spell the /s/ phoneme
- read and spell words of one syllable or more
- write a dictated sentence

Focus content: revision

Letters and Sounds
sc, st(l)

Reading
scene, bustle, scissors, castle

Writing and Spelling
descend, scenic, muscle, jostle

Focus content: lesson

Sounds
/s/

Visual search
house, purse, please, cheese

Reading
Audio: use, horse, noise, pause
No audio: purse, tease, amuse, applause

Spelling
Words tab: mouse, please
Pictures tab: house, cheese
Video: sit, cent, house

Writing
se

Follow-up
Dictation
There was no noise in the house as the mouse ate the cheese.

Next steps
- Play the online pupil games for Unit 23
- Complete the phoneme PCM for Unit 24 (se)
- Read the Phonics Bug books that practise /c/ alternatives: Go-Kart, Go!, Hungry Birds

Unit 24

Language session
After: alternatives for /s/

INTRODUCTION
- Play the alphabet song twice, once with voice accompaniment, children listening and singing along with accompaniment, and once with children singing along to the music without voice accompaniment.
- Discuss with the children the learning intentions for the day.

IRREGULAR
Reading
- Select the H-F words part of the session.
- Click Show to display the words, and ask the children to read them.
- Click Answer to listen to the word being read.

Spelling
- Click Say to hear the words, and ask the children to repeat each word. Put the word into a sentence so that the children understand its meaning, for example, "Jess scored a great goal", "Wear your old clothes for painting".
- Point out that in "great", the 'ea' sounds /ā/. In "clothes", 'o' sounds /ō/, but in "cloth" 'o' sounds /o/. Note also that the 'es' in "clothes" sounds /z/.
- Say the target word, and ask the children to repeat it again. Ask the class to give each letter, and ask a child to come up to the Work area and drag up the correct letters into the spaces provided.
- Ask the class to read the word and click Say for them to hear it again.
- Repeat for the remaining words.

LESSON
Reading
- Click Show to display the sentences, and ask the children to read them.
- Click Answer to reveal whether they are right.
- Point out that in "water", 'a' sounds /o/.
- Point out the use of an exclamation mark in "You should have seen my face!"

Spelling and Writing
- The children return to their seats.
- Remind the children about the dictation procedure. (See page 13.)
- Click Say to hear the first sentence, and ask the children to repeat it.
- Slowly and distinctly dictate the sentence, asking the children to tell you how to write the words.
- Click Answer to reveal the sentence. Did the children tell you how to write it correctly?
- Repeat for the second sentence, asking the children to write it using pencil and paper or their magnetic letters. (See page 12.)

Follow-up
- Display the picture and ask the children questions relating to it, to promote discussion and stimulate their thinking skills. You might ask, "What sort of celebration is this? How can you tell?"
- Encourage the children to come up with sentences using words they have learnt in the programme – perhaps asking their own question about the picture.
- Write up on the Work area one or more good sentences or questions suggested by the children to further the discussion.

WRAP-UP
- Recap the learning intentions with the children.
- Play the alphabet song again and encourage the children to sing along, signifying the end of the session.

Learning intentions are to:
- learn to read and spell irregular words "great" and "clothes"
- write related sentences from dictation including two- and three-syllable words
- contribute to discussion, framing and using own sentences or questions to stimulate thinking skills

Focus content: irregular words

Reading
great, clothes

Spelling
great, clothes

Focus content: lesson

Reading
My great aunt sent me some fancy clothes for my birthday. The first time I wore them, I spilt water on the blouse. You should have seen my face!

Spelling and Writing
We went to the cinema for my birthday. Then we came back to my house for cake.

Follow-up
Picture shows: children at a birthday party.

Next steps
- Play the online language pupil games for Unit 24
- Complete the language PCM for Unit 24
- Read the Phonics Bug books that practise /s/ alternatives: Dressed for the Job, Kat's Great Act

Unit 25

Target phoneme /j/ written as 'g(e)', 'g(i)', 'g(y)'

INTRODUCTION
- Play the alphabet song twice, once with voice accompaniment, children listening and singing along with accompaniment, and once with children singing along to the music without voice accompaniment.
- Discuss with the children the learning intentions for the day.

REVISION
[previously taught grapheme–phoneme correspondences; blending phonemes for reading; segmenting spoken words for spelling]
- Go through the Revision screens at a brisk pace.
- Watch out for any children who have not remembered the phonemes or the graphemes.

LESSON

Sounds
- Choose the relevant lesson session.
- Say the phoneme /j/, and ask the children to repeat it after you. Make sure you keep the sound pure and encourage the children to do the same.
- Explain to the children that 'g' followed by 'e', 'c' or 'y' sounds /j/ (known as "soft 'g'") as in "gems", "rage", "magic", "gym". Exceptions include "get", "girl", "begin".

Visual Search
- Bring up the words from the asset bank onto the Work area. Ask the children to highlight the 'ge', 'gi' or 'gy' in each of the words, saying whether it is at the the beginning, the middle or the end of the word. Do not pronounce the words.

Reading
- Click the Reading tab to see the word.
- Click Blend to watch and hear the Bug's demonstration of how to blend the word. Click Undo and ask a child to come to the Work area and move the arrow. Encourage the whole class to blend the phonemes out loud as the arrow is moving along.
- Work through each of the words in sequence.

Spelling
- Start by selecting the Words tab. Click Say to hear the word and ask the children to repeat it, then ask the children to use pencil and paper or their magnetic letters to make the word, saying the word every time they write down or look for a letter. Ask a child to come up to the Work area to make the word. Did everyone get it right?
- Ask a child to use the arrow to push the letters together. Encourage the class to blend the word together out loud.
- Repeat for the remaining words under the Words tab.
- Under the Pictures tab, click Show to display each image and repeat the process for each one. (See pages 8–9 and 12–13.)
- Select the Spelling video and play it once through.

Writing
- Ask the children to find the letters 'g' and 'e' among their magnetic letters and to feel the shape of them. Click Show and ask the children to look and listen as the lowercase letters are formed.
- Ask a child to direct you how to write the letters as you write them on the empty Work area.
- Ask the child to write them on the dashed lines, then ask the children to practise writing 'ge' themselves.
- Repeat for 'g' and 'i', and 'g' and 'y'.

Follow-up
- Click Say to hear the sentence. Repeat the sentence, then dictate it slowly and deliberately for the children to write it. Then click Show to reveal the correct answer. (See page 13.)

WRAP-UP
- Recap the learning intentions with the children.
- Play the alphabet song and encourage the children to sing along, signifying the end of the session.

Learning intentions are to:
- recap what we know
- say the /j/ phoneme
- learn different ways to spell the /j/ phoneme
- read and spell words of one syllable or more
- write a dictated sentence.

Focus content: revision

Letters and Sounds
j ⊃ Unit 6
Reading
Jim, jug, jet, jam
Writing and Spelling
Jill, jog, jut, jacket

Focus content: lesson

Sounds
/j/
Visual search
gems, rage, giblet, tragic, Egypt, gym
Reading
Audio: age, ginger, margin, gym, energy
No audio: large, fringe, tragic, giblet, gypsy
Spelling
Words tab: danger, magic, gypsy
Pictures tab: angel, giraffe, giant
Video: jam, giant
Writing
ge, gi, gy
Follow-up
Dictation
The girl cut one slice of gingerbread.

Next steps
- Play the online pupil games for Unit 24
- Complete the phoneme PCM for Unit 25 (ge/gi/gy)
- Read the Phonics Bug books that practise /s/ alternatives: Dressed for the Job, Kat's Great Act

Unit 25

Target phoneme /j/ written as 'dge'

INTRODUCTION
- Play the alphabet song twice, once with voice accompaniment, children listening and singing along with accompaniment, and once with children singing along to the music without voice accompaniment.
- Discuss with the children the learning intentions for the day.

REVISION
[previously taught grapheme–phoneme correspondences; blending phonemes for reading; segmenting spoken words for spelling]
- Go through the Revision screens at a brisk pace.
- Watch out for any children who have not remembered the phonemes or the graphemes.

LESSON

Sounds
- Choose the relevant lesson session.
- Say the phoneme /j/, and ask the children to repeat it after you. Make sure you keep the sound pure and encourage the children to do the same.
- Explain that when 'dge' appears at the end of a word, it sounds /j/, as in "edge".

Visual Search
- Bring up the words from the asset bank onto the Work area. Ask the children to highlight the 'dge' in each of the words. Do not pronounce the words.

Reading
- Click the Reading tab to see the word.
- Click Blend to watch and hear the Bug's demonstration of how to blend the word. Click Undo and ask a child to come to the Work area and move the arrow. Encourage the whole class to blend the phonemes out loud as the arrow is moving along.
- Work through each of the words in sequence.

Spelling
- The children return to their seats.
- Start by selecting the Words tab. Click Say to hear the word and ask the children to repeat it, then ask the children to use pencil and paper or their magnetic letters to make the word, saying the word every time they write down or look for a letter. Ask a child to come up to the Work area to make the word. Did everyone get it right?
- Ask a child to use the arrow to push the letters together. Encourage the class to blend the word together out loud.
- Repeat for the remaining word under the Words tab.
- Under the Pictures tab, click Show to display each image and repeat the process for each one. (See pages 8–9 and 12–13.)

Writing
- Ask the children to find the letters 'd', 'g' and 'e' among their magnetic letters and to feel the shape of them. Click Show and ask the children to look and listen as the lowercase letters are formed.
- Ask a child to direct you how to write the letters as you write them on the empty Work area.
- Ask the child to write them on the dashed lines, then ask the children to practise writing 'dge' themselves.
- Select uppercase and repeat.

Follow-up
- Click Say to hear the sentence. Repeat the sentence, then dictate it slowly and deliberately for the children to write it. Then click Show to reveal the correct answer. (See page 13.)

WRAP-UP
- Recap the learning intentions with the children.
- Play the alphabet song and encourage the children to sing along, signifying the end of the session.

Learning intentions are to:
- recap what we know
- say the /j/ phoneme
- learn different ways to spell the /j/ phoneme
- read and spell words of one syllable or more
- write a dictated sentence

Focus content: revision

Letters and Sounds
g(e), g(i), g(y)

Reading
danger, magic, gypsy, angel, giraffe, giant

Writing and Spelling
large, fringe, tragic, giblet, gypsy, gigantic

Focus content: lesson

Sounds
/j/

Visual search
edge, fridge, budget, lodge

Reading
Audio: bridge, judge, ledge, smudge
No audio: badge, dodge, pledge, hedgerow

Spelling
Words tab: fudge, gadget
Pictures tab: sledge, badger

Writing
dge

Follow-up
Dictation
Madge put the fudge in the fridge.

Next steps
- Play the online pupil games for Unit 24
- Complete the phoneme PCM for Unit 25 (dge)
- Read the Phonics Bug books that practise /s/ alternatives: Dressed for the Job, Kat's Great Act

Unit 25

Language session

After: alternatives for /j/

INTRODUCTION
- Play the alphabet song twice, once with voice accompaniment, children listening and singing along with accompaniment, and once with children singing along to the music without voice accompaniment.
- Discuss with the children the learning intentions for the day.

HIGH-FREQUENCY WORDS

Reading
- Select the H-F words part of the session.
- Click Show to display the words, and ask the children to read them.
- Click Answer to listen to the word being read.
- Point out the punctuation mark in each word which takes the place of a letter(s).

Spelling
- Click Say to hear the words, and ask the children to repeat each word. Put the word into a sentence so that the children understand its meaning, for example, "It's time for lunch", "I'm the oldest in my family", "I'll go and see Grandpa at the weekend", "I've got seven stickers".
- (i) You may want to explain to the children when appropriate that:
  - "it's" stands for "it is" – the apostrophe replaces the 'i' of "is".
  - "its" (without an apostrophe) is a possessive pronoun.
  - "I'm" stands for "I am" – the apostrophe replaces the 'a' of "am".
  - "I'll" stands for "I will" – the apostrophe replaces the 'wi' of "will".
  - "I've" stands for "I have"; the apostrophe replaces the 'ha' of "have".
- Say the target word, and ask the children to repeat it again. Ask the class to give each letter, and ask a child to come up to the Work area and drag up the correct letters into the spaces provided. Point out that the apostrophe is already on the screen.
- Ask the class to read the word and click Say for them to hear it again.
- Repeat for the remaining words.

LESSON

Reading
- Click Show to display the sentences, and ask the children to read them.
- Click Answer to reveal whether they are right.
- Point out another example of an exclamation mark (see Unit 24).

Spelling and Writing
- The children return to their seats.
- Remind the children about the dictation procedure.
- Click Say to hear the first sentence and ask the children to repeat it.
- Slowly and distinctly dictate the sentence, asking the children to tell you how to write the words.
- Click Answer to reveal the sentence. Did the children tell you how to write it correctly?
- Repeat for the second sentence asking the children to write it using pencil and paper or their magnetic letters. (See page 13.)

Follow-up
- Write "it is", "I am", "I will" and "I have" on the Work area.
- Ask the children to write the short version (contraction) with an apostrophe.
- Then reverse the procedure: write the shortened version on the Work area and ask the children to write the full version.
- Ask the children to write their own sentence containing any of it's, I'm, I'll, or I've.

WRAP-UP
- Recap the learning intentions with the children.
- Play the alphabet song again and encourage the children to sing along, signifying the end of the session.

Learning intentions are to:
- learn about the punctuation mark used instead of a letter or letters, known as an "apostrophe"
- learn to read and spell irregular words with an apostrophe – "it's", "I'm", "I'll" and "I've"
- write sentences from dictation which include an apostrophe

Focus content: h-f words

Reading
it's, I'm, I'll, I've

Spelling
it's, I'm, I'll, I've

Focus content: lesson

Reading
I've put the fudge in the fridge. I'll have it later when I need some energy!

Spelling and Writing
I'm going to the gym. It's down the road by the bridge.

Follow-up
Children write their own sentence containing any of it's, I'm, I'll or I've.

Next steps
- Play the online language pupil games for Unit 25
- Complete the language PCM for Unit 25
- Read the Phonics Bug books that practise /j/ alternatives: Different Homes, Giant George and the Robin

Unit 26

Target phoneme /l/ written as 'le'

INTRODUCTION
- Play the alphabet song twice, once with voice accompaniment, children listening and singing along with accompaniment, and once with children singing along to the music without voice accompaniment.
- Discuss with the children the learning intentions for the day.

REVISION
[previously taught grapheme–phoneme correspondences; blending phonemes for reading; segmenting spoken words for spelling]
- Go through the Revision screens at a brisk pace.
- Watch out for any children who have not remembered the phonemes or the graphemes.

LESSON
Sounds
- Choose the relevant lesson session.
- Say the phoneme /l/, and ask the children to repeat it after you. Make sure you keep the sound pure and encourage the children to do the same.
- Explain that 'le' at the end of a word can sound /ul/ as in "saddle", "puddle" and "castle" (see Unit 24).

Visual Search
- Bring up the words from the asset bank onto the Work area. Ask the children to highlight the 'le' in each of the words. Do not pronounce the words.

Reading
- Click the Reading tab to see the word and syllables.
- Click Blend to watch and hear the Bug's demonstration of how to blend the syllables and the word. Click Undo and ask a child to come to the Work area and move the arrow. Encourage the whole class to blend the phonemes of the syllables and then the sounds of the word out loud as the arrow is moving along.
- Work through each of the words in sequence.

Spelling
- The children return to their seats.
- Start by selecting the Words tab. Click Say to hear the word and ask the children to repeat it, then ask the children to use pencil and paper or their magnetic letters to make the word, saying the word every time they write down or look for a letter. Ask a child to come up to the Work area to make the word. Did everyone get it right?
- Ask a child to use the arrow to push the letters together. Encourage the class to blend the word together out loud.
- Repeat for the remaining word under the Words tab.
- Under the Pictures tab, click Show to display each image and repeat the process for each one. (See pages 8–9 and 12–13.)

Writing
- Ask the children to find the letters 'l' and 'e' among their magnetic letters and to feel the shape of them. Click Show and ask the children to look and listen as the lowercase letters are formed.
- Ask a child to direct you how to write the letters as you write them on the empty Work area.
- Ask the child to write them on the dashed lines themselves.
- Select uppercase and repeat.

Follow-up
- Click Say to hear the sentence. Repeat the sentence, then dictate it slowly and deliberately for the children to write it. Then click Show to reveal the correct answer. (See page 13.)

WRAP-UP
- Recap the learning intentions with the children.
- Play the alphabet song and encourage the children to sing along, signifying the end of the session.

Learning intentions are to:
- recap what we know
- say the /l/ phoneme
- learn different ways to spell the /l/ phoneme
- read and spell words of one syllable or more
- write a dictated sentence

Focus content: revision

Letters and Sounds
l ⟳ Unit 5
Reading
let, tell, leg, doll
Writing and Spelling
lock, sell, dull, laptop

Focus content: lesson

Sounds
/l/
Visual search
table, eagle, puddle, uncle
Reading
Audio: purple, ankle, circle, table
No audio: stable, needle, pebble, saddle
Spelling
Words tab: simple, sparkle
Pictures tab: apple, candle
Writing
le
Follow-up
Dictation
Apple, purple and candle all end with the same sound.

Next steps
- Play the online pupil games for Unit 25
- Complete the phoneme PCM for Unit 26 (le)
- Read the Phonics Bug books that practise /j/ alternatives: Different Homes, Giant George and the Robin

Unit 26

Target phoneme /m/ written as 'mb'

INTRODUCTION
- Play the alphabet song twice, once with voice accompaniment, children listening and singing along with accompaniment, and once with children singing along to the music without voice accompaniment.
- Discuss with the children the learning intentions for the day.

REVISION
[previously taught grapheme–phoneme correspondences; blending phonemes for reading; segmenting spoken words for spelling]
- Go through the Revision screens at a brisk pace.
- Watch out for any children who have not remembered the phonemes or the graphemes.

LESSON
Sounds
- Choose the relevant lesson session.
- Say the phoneme /m/, and ask the children to repeat it after you. Make sure you keep the sound pure and encourage the children to do the same.
- Explain that 'mb' sounds /m/ as in "crumb" ("silent 'b'").

Visual Search
- Bring up the words from the asset bank onto the Work area. Ask the children to highlight the 'mb' in each of the words, saying whether it is at the beginning, the middle or the end of the word. Do not pronounce the words.

Reading
- Click the Reading tab to see the word.
- Click Blend to watch and hear the Bug's demonstration of how to blend the word. Click Undo and ask a child to come to the Work area and move the arrow. Encourage the whole class to blend the phonemes out loud as the arrow is moving along.
- Work through each of the words in sequence.

Spelling
- The children return to their seats.
- Start by selecting the Words tab. Click Say to hear the word and ask the children to repeat it, then ask the children to use pencil and paper or their magnetic letters to make the word, saying the word every time they write down or look for a letter. Ask a child to come up to the Work area to make the word. Did everyone get it right?
- Ask a child to use the arrow to push the letters together. Encourage the class to blend the word together out loud.
- Repeat for the remaining word under the Words tab.
- Under the Pictures tab, click Show to display each image and repeat the process for each one. (See pages 8–9 and 12–13.)
- Select the Spelling video and play it once through.

Writing
- Ask the children to find the letters 'm' and 'b' among their magnetic letters and to feel the shape of them. Click Show and ask the children to look and listen as the lowercase letters are formed.
- Ask a child to direct you how to write the letters as you write them on the empty Work area.
- Ask the child to write them on the dashed lines, then ask the children to practise writing 'mb' themselves.
- Select uppercase and repeat.

Follow-up
- Click Say to hear the sentence. Repeat the exclamation word "Look!", then dictate the sentence slowly and deliberately for the children to write it. Then click Show to reveal the correct answer. (See page 13.)

WRAP-UP
- Recap the learning intentions with the children.
- Play the alphabet song and encourage the children to sing along, signifying the end of the session.

Learning intentions are to:
- recap what we know
- say the /m/ phoneme
- learn different ways to spell the /m/ phoneme
- read and spell words of one syllable or more
- write a dictated sentence with an exclamation mark

Focus content: revision

Letters and Sounds
m ➰ Unit 2
Reading
Tim, man, mat, map
Writing and Spelling
Sam, pram, stamp, mint

Focus content: lesson

Sounds
/m/
Visual search
climb, dumb, crumb, bomb
Reading
Audio: climb, crumb, thumb, plumber
No audio: limb, numb, tomb, bomber
Spelling
Words tab: thumb, plunber
Pictures tab: lamb, comb
Video: man, lamb
Writing
mb
Follow-up
Dictation
Look! The little lamb is sucking my thumb.

Next steps
- Play the online pupil games for Unit 25
- Complete the phoneme PCM for Unit 26 (mb)
- Read the Phonics Bug books that practise /j/ alternatives: Different Homes, Giant George and the Robin

Unit 26

Target phoneme /n/ written as 'kn' and 'gn'

INTRODUCTION
- Play the alphabet song twice, once with voice accompaniment, children listening and singing along with accompaniment, and once with children singing along to the music without voice accompaniment.
- Discuss with the children the learning intentions for the day.

REVISION
[previously taught grapheme–phoneme correspondences; blending phonemes for reading; segmenting spoken words for spelling]
- Go through the Revision screens at a brisk pace.
- Watch out for any children who have not remembered the phonemes or the graphemes.

LESSON
Sounds
- Choose the relevant lesson session.
- Say the phoneme /n/, and ask the children to repeat it after you. Make sure you keep the sound pure and encourage the children to do the same.
- Explain that 'kn' sounds /n/ as in "knock" ("silent 'k'") and 'gn' sounds /n/ as in "gnome" ("silent 'g'").

Visual Search
- Bring up the words from the asset bank onto the Work area. Ask the children to highlight the 'kn' or 'gn' in each of the words, saying whether it is at the beginning, the middle or the end of the word. Do not pronounce the words.

Reading
- Click the Reading tab to see the word.
- Click Blend to watch and hear the Bug's demonstration of how to blend the word. Click Undo and ask a child to come to the Work area and move the arrow. Encourage the whole class to blend the phonemes out loud as the arrow is moving along.
- Work through each of the words in sequence.

Spelling
- The children return to their seats.
- Start by selecting the Words tab. Click Say to hear the word and ask the children to repeat it, then ask the children to use pencil and paper or their magnetic letters to make the word, saying the word every time they write down or look for a letter. Ask a child to come up to the Work area to make the word. Did everyone get it right?
- Ask a child to use the arrow to push the letters together. Encourage the class to blend the word together out loud.
- Repeat for the remaining words under the Words tab.
- Under the Pictures tab, click Show to display each image and repeat the process for each one. (See pages 8–9.)
- Select the Spelling video and play it once through.

Writing
- Ask the children to find the letters 'k' and 'n' among their magnetic letters and to feel the shape of them. Click Show and ask the children to look and listen as the lowercase letters are formed.
- Ask a child to direct you how to write the letters as you write them on the empty Work area.
- Ask the child to write them on the dashed lines, then ask the children to practise writing 'kn' themselves.
- Repeat for 'g' and 'n'.

Follow-up
- Use the arrows to select the 'kn' sentence. Click Say to hear the sentence. Repeat the sentence, then dictate it slowly and deliberately for the children to write it. Then click Show to reveal the correct answer.
- Repeat the procedure for the 'gn' sentence. (See page 13.)

WRAP-UP
- Recap the learning intentions with the children.
- Play the alphabet song and encourage the children to sing along, signifying the end of the session.

Learning intentions are to:
- recap what we know
- say the /n/ phoneme
- learn different ways to spell the /n/ phoneme
- read and spell words of one syllable or more
- write a dictated sentence

Focus content: revision

Letters and Sounds
n ➲ Unit 2

Reading
nap, pins, pan, in

Writing and Spelling
ant, tins, an, nip

Focus content: lesson

Sounds
/n/

Visual search
knife, knew, gnome, sign

Reading
Audio: knit, knapsack, gnome, reign
No audio: knob, knock, design, campaign

Spelling
Words tab: knife, kneel, gnaw, gnat
Pictures tab: knob, knot
Video: net, knot, gnat

Writing
kn, gn

Follow-up
Dictation
Knock at the door and turn the knob to enter.
We put a sign next to the gnome in the garden.

Next steps
- Play the online pupil games for Unit 25
- Complete the phoneme PCM for Unit 26 (kn, gn)
- Read the Phonics Bug books that practise /j/ alternatives: Different Homes, Giant George and the Robin

Unit 26

Target phoneme /r/ written as 'wr'

INTRODUCTION
- Play the alphabet song twice, once with voice accompaniment, children listening and singing along with accompaniment, and once with children singing along to the music without voice accompaniment.
- Discuss with the children the learning intentions for the day.

REVISION
[previously taught grapheme–phoneme correspondences; blending phonemes for reading; segmenting spoken words for spelling]
- Go through the Revision screens at a brisk pace.
- Watch out for any children who have not remembered the phonemes or the graphemes.

LESSON

Sounds
- Choose the relevant lesson session.
- Say the phoneme /r/, and ask the children to repeat it after you. Make sure you keep the sound pure and encourage the children to do the same.
- Explain that 'wr' at the beginning of words sounds /r/ as in "write" ("silent 'w'").

Visual Search
- Bring up the words from the asset bank onto the Work area. Ask the children to highlight the 'wr' in each of the words. Do not pronounce the words.

Reading
- Click the Reading tab to see the word.
- Click Blend to watch and hear the Bug's demonstration of how to blend the word. Click Undo and ask a child to come to the Work area and move the arrow. Encourage the whole class to blend the phonemes out loud as the arrow is moving along.
- Work through each of the words in sequence.

Spelling
- The children return to their seats.
- Start by selecting the Words tab. Click Say to hear the word and ask the children to repeat it, then ask the children to use pencil and paper or their magnetic letters to make the word, saying the word every time they write down or look for a letter. Ask a child to come up to the Work area to make the word. Did everyone get it right?
- Ask a child to use the arrow to push the letters together. Encourage the class to blend the word together out loud.
- Repeat for the remaining word under the Words tab.
- Under the Pictures tab, click Show to display each image and repeat the process for each one. (See pages 8–9 and 12–13.)

Writing
- Ask the children to find the letters 'w' and 'r' among their magnetic letters and to feel the shape of them. Click Show and ask the children to look and listen as the lowercase letters are formed.
- Ask a child to direct you how to write the letters as you write them on the empty Work area.
- Ask the child to write them on the dashed lines, then ask the children to practise writing 'wr' themselves.
- Select uppercase and repeat.

Follow-up
- Click Say to hear the sentence. Repeat the sentence, then dictate it slowly and deliberately for the children to write it. Then click Show to reveal the correct answer. (See page 13.)

WRAP-UP
- Recap the learning intentions with the children.
- Play the alphabet song and encourage the children to sing along, signifying the end of the session.

Learning intentions are to:
- recap what we know
- say the /r/ phoneme
- learn different ways to spell the /r/ phoneme
- read and spell words of more than one syllable
- write a dictated sentence

Focus content: revision

Letters and Sounds
r ➲ Unit 4
Reading
print, rock, rag, rim
Writing and Spelling
red, ran, rug, rid

Focus content: lesson

Sounds
/r/
Visual search
wrinkled, wring, wriggle, wrong
Reading
Audio: wrist, write, wrestle, wreck
No audio: wrong, wrote, wriggle, wrinkle
Spelling
Words tab: wrap, write
Pictures tab: wren, wrapper
Writing
wr
Follow-up
Dictation
Wrap the present and write your name on the card.

Next steps
- Play the online pupil games for Unit 25
- Complete the phoneme PCM for Unit 26 (wr)
- Read the Phonics Bug books that practise /j/ alternatives: Different Homes, Giant George and the Robin

Unit 26

Language session

After: alternatives for /l/, /m/, /n/, /r/

INTRODUCTION
- Play the alphabet song twice, once with voice accompaniment, children listening and singing along with accompaniment, and once with children singing along to the music without voice accompaniment.
- Discuss with the children the learning intentions for the day.

HIGH-FREQUENCY WORDS

Reading
- Select the H-F words part of the session.
- Click Show to display the words, and ask the children to read them.
- Click Answer to listen to the word being read.
- Ask the children about the punctuation mark. Did the children remember it is called an "apostrophe"?

Spelling
- Click Say to hear the words, and ask the children to repeat each word. Put the word into a sentence so that the children understand its meaning, for example, "I don't like pickle", "We can't play outdoors because it's raining", "Mary didn't eat all of her lunch".
- ⓘ You may want to explain to the children when appropriate that:
  - "don't" stands for "do not" – the apostrophe replaces the 'o' of "not".
  - "can't" stands for "cannot" – the apostrophe replaces the 'no' of "not".
  - "didn't" stands for "did not" – the apostrophe replaces the 'o' of "not".
- Say the target word, and ask the children to repeat it again. Ask the class to give each letter, and ask a child to come up to the Work area and drag up the correct letters into the spaces provided. Point out that the apostrophe is already on the screen.
- Ask the class to read the word, and click Say for them to hear it again.
- Repeat for the remaining words.

LESSON

Reading
- Click Show to display the sentences, and ask the children to read them.
- Click Answer to reveal whether they are right.
- Point out the use of direct speech again and the use of speech marks (see Unit 23).

Spelling and Writing
- The children return to their seats.
- Remind the children about the dictation procedure.
- Click Say to hear the first sentence, and ask the children to repeat it.
- Slowly and distinctly dictate the sentence, asking the children to tell you how to write the words.
- Click Answer to reveal the sentence. Did the children tell you how to write it correctly?
- Repeat for the second sentence asking the children to write it using pencil and paper or their magnetic letters. (See page 13.)

Follow-up
- Write "do not", "cannot" and "did not" on the Work area.
- Ask the children to write the short version (contraction) with an apostrophe.
- Then reverse the procedure: write the shortened version on the Work area and ask the children to write the full version.
- Ask the children to write their own sentence containing any of don't, can't or didn't.

WRAP-UP
- Recap the learning intentions with the children.
- Play the alphabet song again and encourage the children to sing along, signifying the end of the session.

Learning intentions are to:
- learn to read and spell irregular words with an apostrophe – "don't", "can't" and "didn't"
- write sentences from dictation which include "don't", "can't" and "didn't"

Focus content: h-f words

Reading
don't, can't, didn't

Spelling
don't, can't, didn't

Focus content: lesson

Reading
The sign said: 'Don't climb this apple tree', but I did. I fell and hurt my wrist. Now I can't write.

Spelling and Writing
I knew I was wrong, but I didn't think. It was a hard but simple lesson.

Follow-up
Children write their own sentence containing any of don't, can't or didn't.

Next steps
- Play the online language pupil games for Unit 26
- Complete the language PCM for Unit 26
- Read the Phonics Bug books that practise /l/, /m/, /n/, /r/ alternatives: Dinosaurs, The Purple Muncher

Unit 27

Target phoneme /ch/ written as 'tch'

INTRODUCTION
- Play the alphabet song twice, once with voice accompaniment, children listening and singing along with accompaniment, and once with children singing along to the music without voice accompaniment.
- Discuss with the children the learning intentions for the day.

REVISION
[previously taught grapheme–phoneme correspondences; blending phonemes for reading; segmenting spoken words for spelling]
- Go through the Revision screens at a brisk pace.
- Watch out for any children who have not remembered the phonemes or the graphemes.

LESSON
Sounds
- Choose the relevant lesson session.
- Say the phoneme /ch/, and ask the children to repeat it after you. Make sure you keep the sound pure and encourage the children to do the same.

Visual Search
- Bring up the words from the asset bank onto the Work area. Ask the children to highlight the 'tch' in each of the words, saying whether it is at the beginning, the middle or the end of the word. Do not pronounce the words.

Reading
- Click the Reading tab to see the word.
- Click Blend to watch and hear the Bug's demonstration of how to blend the word. Click Undo and ask a child to come to the Work area and move the arrow. Encourage the whole class to blend the phonemes out loud as the arrow is moving along.
- Work through each of the words in sequence.

Spelling
- The children return to their seats.
- Start by selecting the Words tab. Click Say to hear the word and ask the children to repeat it, then ask the children to use pencil and paper or their magnetic letters to make the word, saying the word every time they write down or look for a letter. Ask a child to come up to the Work area to make the word. Did everyone get it right?
- Ask a child to use the arrow to push the letters together. Encourage the class to blend the word together out loud.
- Repeat for the remaining word under the Words tab.
- Under the Pictures tab, click Show to display each image and repeat the process for each one. (See pages 8–9.)
- Select the Spelling video and play it once through.

Writing
- Ask the children to find the letters 't', 'c' and 'h' among their magnetic letters and to feel the shape of them. Click Show and ask the children to look and listen as the lowercase letters are formed.
- Ask a child to direct you how to write the letters as you write them on the empty Work area.
- Ask the child to write them on the dashed lines, then ask the children to practise writing 'tch' themselves.
- Select uppercase and repeat.

Follow-up
- Click Say to hear the sentence. Repeat the sentence, then dictate it slowly and deliberately for the children to write it. Then click Show to reveal the correct answer. (See page 13.)

WRAP-UP
- Recap the learning intentions with the children.
- Play the alphabet song and encourage the children to sing along, signifying the end of the session.

Learning intentions are to:
- recap what we know
- say the /ch/ phoneme
- learn different ways to spell the /ch/ phoneme
- read and spell words of one syllable or more
- write a dictated sentence

Focus content: revision

Letters and Sounds
ch ⤺ Unit 8
Reading
chat, chin, chest, chips
Writing and Spelling
check, such, chill, chicken

Focus content: lesson

Sounds
/ch/
Visual search
catch, fetch, ditch, clutch
Reading
Audio: batch, pitch, kitchen, scratch
No audio: patch, stitch, witch, switch
Spelling
Words tab: catch, hutch
Pictures tab: match, crutch
Video: chip, catch
Writing
tch
Follow-up
Dictation
Please fetch a dish from the kitchen.

Next steps
- Play the online pupil games for Unit 26
- Complete the phoneme PCM for Unit 27 (tch)
- Read the Phonics Bug books that practise /l/, /m/, /n/, /r/ alternatives: Dinosaurs, The Purple Muncher

Unit 27

Target phoneme /sh/ alternatives

INTRODUCTION
- Play the alphabet song twice, once with voice accompaniment, children listening and singing along with accompaniment, and once with children singing along to the music without voice accompaniment.
- Discuss with the children the learning intentions for the day.

REVISION
[previously taught grapheme–phoneme correspondences; blending phonemes for reading; segmenting spoken words for spelling]
- Go through the Revision screens at a brisk pace.
- Watch out for any children who have not remembered the phonemes or the graphemes.

LESSON

Sounds
- Choose the relevant lesson session.
- Say the phoneme /sh/, and ask the children to repeat it after you. Make sure you keep the sound pure and encourage the children to do the same.
- Explain that there are different ways to make the /sh/ sound:
  – 'ch' sounds /sh/ in "chef".
  – 'c(ious)' sounds /sh/ in "precious".
  – 'c(ion)' sounds /sh/ in "suspicion".

Visual Search
- Bring up the words from the asset bank onto the Work area. Ask the children to highlight the letters that make the /sh/ sound in each of the words. Do not pronounce the words.

Reading
- Click the Reading tab to see the word and syllables.
- Click Blend to watch and hear the Bug's demonstration of how to blend the syllables and the word. Click Undo and ask a child to come to the Work area and move the arrow. Encourage the whole class to blend the phonemes of the syllables and then the sounds of the word out loud as the arrow is moving along.
- Work through each of the words in sequence.

Spelling
- The children return to their seats.
- Start by selecting the Words tab. Click Say to hear the word and ask the children to repeat it, then ask the children to use pencil and paper or their magnetic letters to make the word, saying the word every time they write down or look for a letter. Ask a child to come up to the Work area to make the word. Did everyone get it right?
- Ask a child to use the arrow to push the letters together. Encourage the class to blend the word together out loud.
- Repeat for the remaining word under the Words tab.
- Under the Pictures tab, click Show to display each image and repeat the process for each one. (See pages 8–9 and 12–13.)

Writing
- Ask the children to find the letters 't,' 'i,' 'o' and 'n' among their magnetic letters and to feel the shape of them. Click Show and ask the children to look and listen as the lowercase letters are formed.
- Ask a child to direct you how to write the letters as you write them on the empty Work area.
- Ask the child to write them on the dashed lines, then ask the children to practise writing 'tion' themselves.
- Repeat for ss(ion), s(ian), c(ial), c(ian).

Follow-up
- Click Say to hear the sentence. Repeat the sentence, then dictate it slowly and deliberately for the children to write it. Then click Show to reveal the correct answer. (See page 13.)

WRAP-UP
- Recap the learning intentions with the children.
- Play the alphabet song and encourage the children to sing along, signifying the end of the session.

Learning intentions are to:
- recap what we know
- say the /sh/ phoneme
- learn different ways to spell the /sh/ phoneme
- read and spell words of one syllable or more
- write a dictated sentence with sh alternatives in it

Focus content: revision

Letters and Sounds
sh ⟳ Unit 8
Reading
ship, flash, fish, shell
Writing and Spelling
shop, cash, rush, shed

Focus content: lesson

Sounds
/sh/
Visual search
education, mission, special, magician
Reading
Audio: action, potion, Asian, special
No audio: motion, lotion, social, nation
Spelling
Words tab: potion, mission
Pictures tab: station, lotion
Writing
t(ion), ss(ion), s(ian), c(ial), c(ian)
Follow-up
Dictation
We got on a special train at the station.

Next steps
- Play the online pupil games for Unit 26
- Complete the phoneme PCM for Unit 27 (sh alternatives)
- Read the Phonics Bug books that practise /l/, /m/, /n/, /r/ alternatives: Dinosaurs, The Purple Muncher

Unit 27

Target phoneme /e/ written as 'ea'

INTRODUCTION
- Play the alphabet song twice, once with voice accompaniment, children listening and singing along with accompaniment, and once with children singing along to the music without voice accompaniment.
- Discuss with the children the learning intentions for the day.

REVISION
[previously taught grapheme–phoneme correspondences; blending phonemes for reading; segmenting spoken words for spelling]
- Go through the Revision screens at a brisk pace.
- Watch out for any children who have not remembered the phonemes or the graphemes.

LESSON
Sounds
- Choose the relevant lesson session.
- Select and drag the digraph 'ea' on to the Work area. Click on the digraph to hear how to say the phoneme /e/.
- Say the phoneme /e/, and ask the children to repeat it after you. Make sure you keep the sound pure and encourage the children to do the same.
- Explain that 'ea' can sound /e/ in some words, as in "head", "breath", "heavy".

Visual Search
- Bring up the words from the asset bank onto the Work area. Ask the children to highlight the 'ea' in each of the words, saying whether it is at the beginning, the middle or the end of the word. Do not pronounce the words.

Reading
- Click the Reading tab to see the word.
- Click Blend to watch and hear the Bug's demonstration of how to blend the word. Click Undo and ask a child to come to the Work area and move the arrow. Encourage the whole class to blend the phonemes out loud as the arrow is moving along.
- Work through each of the words in sequence.

Spelling
- The children return to their seats.
- Start by selecting the Words tab. Click Say to hear the word and ask the children to repeat it, then ask the children to use pencil and paper or their magnetic letters to make the word, saying the word every time they write down or look for a letter. Ask a child to come up to the Work area to make the word. Did everyone get it right?
- Ask a child to use the arrow to push the letters together. Encourage the class to blend the word together out loud.
- Repeat for the remaining word under the Words tab.
- Under the Pictures tab, click Show to display each image and repeat the process for each one. (See pages 8–9 and 12–13.)

Writing
- Ask the children to find the letters 'e' and 'a' among their magnetic letters and to feel the shape of them. Click Show and ask the children to look and listen as the lowercase letters are formed.
- Ask a child to direct you how to write the letters as you write them on the empty Work area.
- Ask the child to write them on the dashed lines, then ask the children to practise writing 'ea' themselves.
- Select uppercase and repeat.

Follow-up
- Click Say to hear the sentence. Repeat the sentence, then dictate it slowly and deliberately for the children to write it. Then click Show to reveal the correct answer. (See page 13.)

WRAP-UP
- Recap the learning intentions with the children.
- Play the alphabet song and encourage the children to sing along, signifying the end of the session.

Learning intentions are to:
- recap what we know
- say the /e/ phoneme
- learn different ways to spell the /e/ phoneme
- read and spell words of one syllable or more
- write a dictated sentence

Focus content: revision

Letters and Sounds
e ➔ Unit 4
Reading
den, met, pen, peg
Writing and Spelling
men, set, deck, peck

Focus content: lesson

Sounds
/e/
Visual search
head, spread, ready, tread
Reading
Audio: deaf, bread, breath, instead
No audio: head, thread, ahead, feather
Spelling
Words tab: deaf, heavy
Pictures tab: head, feather
Writing
ea
Follow-up
Dictation
Mum wore a hat with feathers on it.

Next steps
- Play the online pupil games for Unit 26
- Complete the phoneme PCM for Unit 27 (ea)
- Read the Phonics Bug books that practise /l/, /m/, /n/, /r/ alternatives: Dinosaurs, The Purple Muncher

Unit 27

Target phonemes /w/ /o/ written as 'wa'

INTRODUCTION
- Play the alphabet song twice, once with voice accompaniment, children listening and singing along with accompaniment, and once with children singing along to the music without voice accompaniment.
- Discuss with the children the learning intentions for the day.

REVISION
[previously taught grapheme–phoneme correspondences; blending phonemes for reading; segmenting spoken words for spelling]
- Go through the Revision screens at a brisk pace.
- Watch out for any children who have not remembered the phonemes or the graphemes.

LESSON
Sounds
- Choose the relevant lesson session.
- Blend aloud the phonemes /w/ /o/, and ask the children to repeat them after you. Make sure you keep the sound pure and encourage the children to do the same.
- Explain that 'a' after 'w' sounds /o/, as in "was", "want". Exceptions: "wag", "wax".

Visual Search
- Bring up the words from the asset bank onto the Work area. Ask the children to highlight the 'wa' in each of the words, saying whether it is at the beginning, the middle or the end of the word. Do not pronounce the words.

Reading
- Click the Reading tab to see the word.
- Click Blend to watch and hear the Bug's demonstration of how to blend the word. Click Undo and ask a child to come to the Work area and move the arrow. Encourage the whole class to blend the phonemes out loud as the arrow is moving along.
- Work through each of the words in sequence.

Spelling
- The children return to their seats.
- Start by selecting the Words tab. Click Say to hear the word and ask the children to repeat it, then ask the children to use pencil and paper or their magnetic letters to make the word, saying the word every time they write down or look for a letter. Ask a child to come up to the Work area to make the word. Did everyone get it right?
- Ask a child to use the arrow to push the letters together. Encourage the class to blend the word together out loud.
- Repeat for the remaining word under the Words tab.
- Under the Pictures tab, click Show to display each image and repeat the process for each one. (See pages 8–9 and 12–13.)
- Select the Spelling video and play it once through.

Writing
- Ask the children to find the letters 'w' and 'a' among their magnetic letters and to feel the shape of them. Click Show and ask the children to look and listen as the lowercase letters are formed.
- Ask a child to direct you how to write the letters as you write them on the empty Work area.
- Ask the child to write them on the dashed lines, then ask the children to practise writing 'wa' themselves.
- Select uppercase and repeat.

Follow-up
- Click Say to hear the sentence. Repeat the sentence, then dictate it slowly and deliberately for the children to write it. Then click Show to reveal the correct answer. (See page 13.)

WRAP-UP
- Recap the learning intentions with the children.
- Play the alphabet song and encourage the children to sing along, signifying the end of the session.

Learning intentions are to:
- recap what we know
- blend the /w/ /o/ phonemes
- learn different ways to spell the blended /w/ /o/ phonemes
- read and spell words of one syllable or more
- write a dictated sentence

Focus content: revision

Letters and Sounds
o ⟶ Unit 3
Reading
top, dot, dog, mop
Writing and Spelling
pots, nod, got, lock

Focus content: lesson

Sounds
blended /w/ /o/
Visual search
want, swamp, ward, wasp
Reading
Audio: was, wash, swamp, wallet
No audio: swallow, waffle, wander, wand
Spelling
Words tab: wasp, wallet
Pictures tab: watch, swan
Video: hot, wasp
Writing
wa
Follow-up
Dictation
Walter wants to swap his stamps for a watch.

Next steps
- Play the online pupil games for Unit 26
- Complete the phoneme PCM for Unit 27 (wa)
- Read the Phonics Bug books that practise /l/, /m/, /n/, /r/ alternatives: Dinosaurs, The Purple Muncher

Unit 27

Target phoneme /u/ written as 'o'

INTRODUCTION
- Play the alphabet song twice, once with voice accompaniment, children listening and singing along with accompaniment, and once with children singing along to the music without voice accompaniment.
- Discuss with the children the learning intentions for the day.

REVISION
[previously taught grapheme–phoneme correspondences; blending phonemes for reading; segmenting spoken words for spelling]
- Go through the Revision screens at a brisk pace.
- Watch out for any children who have not remembered the phonemes or the graphemes.

LESSON
Sounds
- Choose the relevant lesson session.
- Select and drag the letter 'o' on to the Work area. Click on the letter to hear how to say the phoneme /u/.
- Say the phoneme /u/, and ask the children to repeat it after you. Make sure you keep the sound pure and encourage the children to do the same.
- Explain that in "some", "come", 'o' sounds /u/; the 'e' is silent for reading, but is needed for spelling.

Visual Search
- Bring up the words from the asset bank onto the Work area. Ask the children to highlight the 'o' in each of the words, saying whether it is at the beginning, the middle or the end of the word. Do not pronounce the words.

Reading
- Click the Reading tab to see the word.
- Click Blend to watch and hear the Bug's demonstration of how to blend the word. Click Undo and ask a child to come to the Work area and move the arrow. Encourage the whole class to blend the phonemes out loud as the arrow is moving along.
- Work through each of the words in sequence.

Spelling
- The children return to their seats.
- Start by selecting the Words tab. Click Say to hear the word and ask the children to repeat it, then ask the children to use pencil and paper or their magnetic letters to make the word, saying the word every time they write down or look for a letter. Ask a child to come up to the Work area to make the word. Did everyone get it right?
- Ask a child to use the arrow to push the letters together. Encourage the class to blend the word together out loud.
- Repeat for the remaining word under the Words tab.
- Under the Pictures tab, click Show to display each image and repeat the process for each one. (See pages 8–9 and 12–13.)

Writing
- Ask the children to find the letter 'o' among their magnetic letters and to feel the shape of it. Click Show and ask the children to look and listen as the lowercase letter is formed.
- Ask a child to direct you how to write the letter as you write it on the empty Work area.
- Ask the child to write it on the dashed lines, then ask the children to practise writing 'o' themselves.
- Repeat for 'oo'.

Follow-up
- Use the arrows to select the sentence. Click Say to hear the sentence. Repeat the sentence, then dictate it slowly and deliberately for the children to write it. Then click Show to reveal the correct answer. (See page 13.)

WRAP-UP
- Recap the learning intentions with the children.
- Play the alphabet song and encourage the children to sing along, signifying the end of the session.

Learning intentions are to:
- recap what we know
- say the /u/ phoneme
- learn different ways to spell the /u/ phoneme
- read and spell words of one syllable or more
- write a dictated sentence

Focus content: revision

Letters and Sounds
u ▶ Unit 4
Reading
sum, mud, cup, sun
Writing and Spelling
up, cut, mug, duck

Focus content: lesson

Sounds
/u/
Visual search
son, become, worry, blood
Reading
Audio: come, done, flood, skeleton
No audio: won, none, worry, unison
Spelling
Words tab: some, come
Pictures tab: blood, skeleton
Writing
o, oo
Follow-up
Dictation
None of the girls could come to the party.

Next steps
- Play the online pupil games for Unit 26
- Complete the phoneme PCM for Unit 27 (o)
- Read the Phonics Bug books that practise /l/, /m/, /n/, /r/ alternatives: Dinosaurs, The Purple Muncher

Unit 27

Language session

After: tch, sh alternatives, ea, (w)a, o

INTRODUCTION
- Play the alphabet song twice, once with voice accompaniment, children listening and singing along with accompaniment, and once with children singing along to the music without voice accompaniment.
- Discuss with the children the learning intentions for the day.

HIGH-FREQUENCY WORDS

Reading
- Select the H-F words part of the session.
- Click Show to display the words, and ask the children to read them.
- Click Answer to listen to the word being read.

Spelling
- Click Say to hear the words, and ask the children to repeat each word. Put the word into a sentence so that the children understand its meaning, for example, "The blue group tidied their table up first", "Jim came second in the race", "If you get a bronze medal you have come third in the competition".
- Say the target word, and ask the children to repeat it again. Ask the class to give each letter, and ask a child to come up to the Work area and drag up the correct letters into the spaces provided.
- Ask the class to read the word, and click Say for them to hear it again.
- Repeat for the remaining words.

LESSON

Reading
- Click Show to display the sentences, and ask the children to read them.
- Click Answer to reveal whether they are right.

Spelling and Writing
- The children return to their seats.
- Remind the children about the dictation procedure.
- Click Say to hear the sentence, and ask the children to repeat it.
- Slowly and distinctly dictate the sentence, asking the children to tell you how to write the words.
- Click Answer to reveal the sentence. Did the children tell you how to write it correctly?
- Repeat for the second sentence, asking the children to write it using pencil and paper or their magnetic letters. (See page 13.)

Follow-up
- Discuss who was second in the race.
- If Madge came third and she was also last, how many children were in the race?
- Discuss examples in the classroom, demonstrating first, second and third.

WRAP-UP
- Recap the learning intentions with the children.
- Play the alphabet song again and encourage the children to sing along, signifying the end of the session.

Learning intentions are to:
- learn to read and spell high-frequency words "first", "second" and "third"
- write sentences from dictation which include "first", "second" and "third"
- understand the meaning of the ordinal numbers "first", "second" and third"

Focus content: h-f words

Reading
first, second, third

Spelling
first, second, third

Focus content: lesson

Reading
The first one comes before all the others.
Second is the one that comes after the first.
Third is the one that comes after the second.

Spelling and Writing
Lance was the first in the race before Gemma.
Madge came third after Gemma.

Follow-up
Discussion points will help prepare children for working on the PCM for Unit 27: language.

Next steps
- Play the online language pupil games for Unit 27
- Complete the language PCM for Unit 27
- Read the Phonics Bug books that practise /ch/, /sh/, /e/, /w/ /o/, /u/ alternatives: Rabbits, The Itch Factor

Unit 28

Suffix ending: '-ing' (a morpheme)

INTRODUCTION
- Play the alphabet song twice, once with voice accompaniment, children listening and singing along with accompaniment, and once with children singing along to the music without voice accompaniment.
- Discuss with the children the learning intentions for the day.

REVISION
[previously taught grapheme–phoneme correspondences; blending phonemes for reading; segmenting spoken words for spelling]
- Go through the Revision screens at a brisk pace.
- Watch out for any children who have not remembered the phonemes or the graphemes.

LESSON
Sounds
- Choose the relevant lesson session.
- Say the suffix -ing, and ask the children to repeat it after you. It is important that children learn to recognise morphemes as units and say them without blending.
- ⓘ If you want to use the term "morpheme", refer to page 13.

Visual Search
- Bring up the words from the asset bank onto the Work area. Ask the children to highlight the 'ing' in each of the words, saying whether it is at the beginning, the middle or the end of the word. Do not pronounce the words.

Reading
- Click the Reading tab to see the word and syllables.
- Click Blend to watch and hear the Bug's demonstration of how to blend the syllables and the word. Click Undo and ask a child to come to the Work area and move the arrow. Encourage the whole class to blend the phonemes of the syllables and then the sounds of the word out loud as the arrow is moving along.
- Work through each of the words in sequence.

Spelling
- The children return to their seats.
- Explain that some rules apply for spelling:
  – if a word ends in a single vowel and consonant, we double the consonant before adding 'ing', as in "shop/shopping". (We treat 'ck' and 'x' as double consonants as in "pack/packing" and "fix/fixing".)
- Start by selecting the Words tab. Click Say to hear the word and ask the children to repeat it, then ask the children to use pencil and paper or their magnetic letters to make the word, saying the word every time they write down or look for a letter. Ask a child to come up to the Work area to make the word. Did everyone get it right?
- Ask a child to use the arrow to push the letters together. Encourage the class to blend the word together out loud.
- Repeat for the remaining word under the Words tab.
- Under the Pictures tab, click Show to display each image and repeat the process for each one. (See pages 8–9 and 12–13.)

Writing
- Ask the children to find the letters 'i', 'n' and 'g' among their magnetic letters and to feel the shape of them. Click Show and ask the children to look and listen as the lowercase letters are formed.
- Ask a child to direct you how to write the letters as you write them on the empty Work area.
- Ask the child to write them on the dashed lines, then ask the children to practise writing 'ing' themselves.
- Select uppercase and repeat.

Follow-up
- Use the arrows to select the sentence. Click Say to hear the sentence. Repeat the sentence, then dictate it slowly and deliberately for the children to write it. Then click Show to reveal the correct answer. (See page 13.)

WRAP-UP
- Recap the learning intentions with the children.
- Play the alphabet song and encourage the children to sing along, signifying the end of the session.

Learning intentions are to:
- recap what we know
- say the suffix -ing
- learn how to use the suffix '-ing'
- read and spell words of one syllable or more
- write a dictated sentence

Focus content: revision

Letters and Sounds

ng ➤ Unit 8

Reading

rang, song, king, ring

Writing and Spelling

sing, long, rang, bring

Focus content: lesson

Sounds

suffix -ing

Visual search

wedding, shopping, rubbing, knitting

Reading

Audio: batting, swimming, jogging, hugging

No audio: shopping, humming, patting, wagging

Spelling

Words tab: padding, nodding

Pictures tab: wedding, hopping

Writing

ing

Follow-up

Dictation

At the school Sports Day, we had jumping, running and swimming events.

Next steps
- Play the online pupil games for Unit 27
- Complete the phoneme PCM for Unit 28 ('-ing')
- Read the Phonics Bug books that practise /ch/, /sh/, /e/, /w/ /o/, /u/ alternatives: Rabbits, The Itch Factor

Unit 28

Suffix ending: '-ed' (a morpheme)

INTRODUCTION
- Play the alphabet song twice, once with voice accompaniment, children listening and singing along with accompaniment, and once with children singing along to the music without voice accompaniment.
- Discuss with the children the learning intentions for the day.

REVISION
[previously taught suffixes; blending phonemes for reading; segmenting spoken words for spelling]
- Go through the Revision screens at a brisk pace.
- Watch out for any children who have not remembered the phonemes or the graphemes.

LESSON

Sounds
- Choose the relevant lesson session.
- Say the suffix -ed, and ask the children to repeat it after you. It is important that children learn to recognise morphemes as units and say them without blending.
- Explain that 'ed' has different sounds in different words: 'ed' can sound /t/ as in "hopped", "jumped", and also /d/ as in "nodded", "spotted".
- ⓘ If you want to use the term "morpheme", refer to page 13.

Visual Search
- Bring up the words from the asset bank onto the Work area. Ask the children to highlight the 'ed' in each of the words, saying whether it is at the beginning, the middle or the end of the word. Do not pronounce the words.

Reading
- Click the Reading tab to see the word.
- Click Blend to watch and hear the Bug's demonstration of how to blend the word. Click Undo and ask a child to come to the Work area and move the arrow. Encourage the whole class to blend the phonemes out loud as the arrow is moving along.
- Work through each of the words in sequence.

Spelling
- The children return to their seats.
- Explain that some rules apply for spelling:
  - If a word ends in a single vowel and consonant, we double the consonant before adding 'ed' as in "shop/shopped". (We treat 'ck' and 'x' as double consonants as in "pack/packed" and "fix/fixed".)
- Start by selecting the Words tab. Click Say to hear the word and ask the children to repeat it, then ask the children to use pencil and paper or their magnetic letters to make the word, saying the word every time they write down or look for a letter. Ask a child to come up to the Work area to make the word. Did everyone get it right?
- Ask a child to use the arrow to push the letters together. Encourage the class to blend the word together out loud.
- Repeat for the remaining word under the Words tab.
- Under the Pictures tab, click Show to display each image and repeat the process for each one. (See pages 8–9 and 12–13.)

Writing
- Ask children to find the letters 'e' and 'd' among their magnetic letters and to feel the shape of them. Click Show and ask children to look and listen as the lowercase letters are formed.
- Ask a child to direct you how to write the letters as you write them on the empty Work area.
- Ask the child to write them on the dashed lines, then ask the children to practise writing 'ed' themselves.
- Select uppercase and repeat.

Follow-up
- Click Say to hear the sentence. Repeat the sentence, then dictate it slowly and deliberately for the children to write it. Then click Show to reveal the correct answer. (See page 13.)

WRAP-UP
- Recap the learning intentions with the children.
- Play the alphabet song and encourage the children to sing along, signifying the end of the session.

Learning intentions are to:
- recap what we know
- say the suffix -ed and phonemes /t/, /d/
- learn how to use the suffix '-ed'
- read and spell words of one syllable or more
- write a dictated sentence

Focus content: revision

Letters and Sounds
ing

Reading
padding, nodding, wedding, hopping

Writing and Spelling
batting, swimming, jogging, hugging

Focus content: lesson

Sounds
suffix -ed; /t/, /d/

Visual search
shopped, clapped, skipped, chatted

Reading
Audio: rubbed, jogged, dimmed, batted
No Audio: hopped, hummed, wagged, patted

Spelling
Words tab: padded, nodded
Pictures tab: ripped, dotted

Writing
ed

Follow-up
Dictation
Spot wagged his tail as he was patted and hugged.

Next steps
- Play the online pupil games for Unit 27
- Complete the phoneme PCM for Unit 28 ('-ed')
- Read the Phonics Bug books that practise /ch/, /sh/, /e/, /w/ /o/, /u/ alternatives: Rabbits, The Itch Factor

Unit 28

Suffix ending: split digraph silent 'e' + '-ing', '-ed'

INTRODUCTION
- Play the alphabet song twice, once with voice accompaniment, children listening and singing along with accompaniment, and once with children singing along to the music without voice accompaniment.
- Discuss with the children the learning intentions for the day.

REVISION
[previously taught suffixes; blending phonemes for reading; segmenting spoken words for spelling]
- Go through the Revision screens at a brisk pace.
- Watch out for any children who have not remembered the phonemes or the graphemes.

LESSON
Sounds
- Choose the relevant lesson session.
- Say the suffixes -ing and -ed and the phonemes /t/ and /d/, and ask the children to repeat them after you. It is important that children learn to recognise morphemes as units and say them without blending.

Visual Search
- Bring up the words from the asset bank onto the Work area. Ask the children to highlight the 'ing' or 'ed' in each of the words, saying whether it is at the beginning, the middle or the end of the word. Do not pronounce the words.

Reading
- Click the Reading tab to see the word.
- Click Blend to watch and hear the Bug's demonstration of how to blend the word. Click Undo and ask a child to come to the Work area and move the arrow. Encourage the whole class to blend the phonemes out loud as the arrow is moving along.
- Work through each of the words in sequence.

Spelling
- The children return to their seats.
- Explain that we drop the final 'e' of words before adding 'ing' or 'ed', as in "hope/hoping/hoped". If there is a vowel before 'y' at the end of the word, keep the 'y', as in "play/playing".
- Start by selecting the Words tab. Click Say to hear the word and ask the children to repeat it, then ask the children to use pencil and paper or their magnetic letters to make the word, saying the word every time they write down or look for a letter. Ask a child to come up to the Work area to make the word. Did everyone get it right?
- Ask a child to use the arrow to push the letters together. Encourage the class to blend the word together out loud.
- Repeat for the remaining word under the Words tab.
- Under the Pictures tab, click Show to display each image and repeat the process for each one. (See pages 8–9 and 12–13.)

Writing
- Ask the children to find the letters 'i', 'n' and 'g' among their magnetic letters and to feel the shape of them. Click Show and ask the children to look and listen as the lowercase letters are formed.
- Ask a child to direct you how to write the letters as you write them on the empty Work area.
- Ask the child to write them on the dashed lines, then ask the children to practise writing 'ing' themselves.
- Select uppercase and repeat.
- Repeat for 'ed'.

Follow-up
- Click Say to hear the sentence. Repeat the sentence, then dictate it slowly and deliberately for the children to write it. Then click Show to reveal the correct answer. (See page 13.)

WRAP-UP
- Recap the learning intentions with the children.
- Play the alphabet song and encourage the children to sing along, signifying the end of the session.

Learning intentions are to:
- recap what we know
- learn how to use the suffixes '-ing' and '-ed' when the word ends in silent 'e'
- read and spell words of one syllable or more
- write a dictated sentence

Focus content: revision

Letters and Sounds
ed
Reading
padded, nodded, ripped, dotted
Writing and Spelling
batted, rubbed, jogged, hugged

Focus content: lesson

Sounds
suffixes -ing, -ed; /t/, /d/
Visual search
hoping, ruling, grating, hoped, ruled, grated
Reading
Audio: joked, saved, pasted, joking, pasting, saving
No audio: shared, chased, waded, sharing, chasing, wading
Spelling
Words tab: chased, hoped
Pictures tab: skating, dancing
Writing
ing, ed
Follow-up
Dictation
Pete hoped to go skating when the ice was frozen.

Next steps
- Play the online pupil games for Unit 27
- Complete the phoneme PCM for Unit 28 (silent 'e' words + 'ing' and 'ed')
- Read the Phonics Bug books that practise /ch/, /sh/, /e/, /w/ /o/, /u/ alternatives: Rabbits, The Itch Factor

Unit 28

Language session
After: suffix endings '-ing' and '-ed'

INTRODUCTION
- Play the alphabet song twice, once with voice accompaniment, children listening and singing along with accompaniment, and once with children singing along to the music without voice accompaniment.
- Discuss with the children the learning intentions for the day.

HIGH-FREQUENCY WORDS
Reading
- Select the H-F words part of the session.
- Click Show to display the words, and ask the children to read them.
- Click Answer to listen to the word being read.
- Explain that the word endings '-ing' and '-ed' are known as suffix endings.

Spelling
- Click Say to hear the words, and ask the children to repeat each word. Put the word into a sentence so that the children understand its meaning, for example, "Clearing up after dinner is really boring", "Those pearl earrings are gleaming", "On Wednesday it rained all day", "Jane mailed a letter".
- Say the target word, and ask the children to repeat it again. Ask the class to give each letter, and ask a child to come up to the Work area and drag up the correct letters into the spaces provided.
- Ask the class to read the word and click Say for them to hear it again.
- Repeat for the remaining words.

LESSON
Reading
- Click Show to display the sentences, and ask the children to read them.
- Click Answer to reveal whether they are right.

Spelling and Writing
- The children return to their seats.
- Remind the children about the dictation procedure.
- Click Say to hear the first sentence, and ask the children to repeat it.
- Slowly and distinctly dictate the sentence, asking the children to tell you how to write the words.
- Click Answer to reveal the sentence. Did the children tell you how to write it correctly?
- Repeat for the second sentence asking the children to write it using pencil and paper or their magnetic letters. (See page 13.)

Follow-up
- "Peter jumped a personal best". Explain to children that "personal" is a three-syllable word. To spell a three-syllable word, children need to hear the word:
- Say the word "personal".
- Break the word into syllables, pronouncing each syllable: per/son/al.
- ⓘ For guidance with breaking words into syllables, see "Syllable categories" on page 12.
- Segment and spell the successive letters of each syllable: p-e-r, per, s-o-n, son, a-l, al.
- Sound and blend the successive syllables to say the word: per/son/al, personal.
- Spell the word orally using the letter names 'p', 'e', 'r', 's', 'o', 'n', 'a', 'l', and say the word "personal".
- Repeat for other three-syllable words, for example from the Phonics Bug books.
- ⓘ See pages 11 to 13 for further information about reading and spelling words of more than one syllable.

WRAP-UP
- Recap the learning intentions with the children.
- Play the alphabet song again and encourage the children to sing along, signifying the end of the session.

Learning intentions are to:
- learn to read and spell high-frequency words with suffix endings – "clearing", "gleaming", "rained" and "mailed"
- write sentences from dictation which include words with suffix endings '-ing' and '-ed'
- breaking three-syllable words into syllables for reading and spelling

Focus content: h-f words

Reading
clearing, gleaming, rained, mailed

Spelling
clearing, gleaming, rained, mailed

Focus content: lesson

Reading
In the swimming event, Peter shared first place. In the high jump, Peter jumped a personal best.

Spelling and Writing
At the prize giving, Peter won the cup. The silver cup was shiny and gleaming.

Follow-up
Focus on reading and spelling three-syllable words.

Next steps
- Play the online language pupil games for Unit 28
- Complete the language PCM for Unit 28

Unit 29

Suffix ending: '-s' (as plural morpheme)

INTRODUCTION
- Play the alphabet song twice, once with voice accompaniment, children listening and singing along with accompaniment, and once with children singing along to the music without voice accompaniment.
- Discuss with the children the learning intentions for the day.

REVISION
[previously taught suffixes; blending phonemes for reading; segmenting spoken words for spelling]
- Go through the Revision screens at a brisk pace.
- Watch out for any children who have not remembered the phonemes or the graphemes.

LESSON

Sounds
- Choose the relevant lesson session.
- Say the phoneme /s/ corresponding to the suffix -s, and ask the children to repeat it after you. Make sure you keep the sound pure and encourage the children to do the same.

(i) If you want to use the term "morpheme", refer to page 13.

Visual Search
- Bring up the words from the asset bank onto the Work area. Ask the children to highlight the 's' in each of the words. Do not pronounce the words.

Reading
- Click the Reading tab to see the word.
- Click Blend to watch and hear the Bug's demonstration of how to blend the word. Click Undo and ask a child to come to the Work area and move the arrow. Encourage the whole class to blend the phonemes out loud as the arrow is moving along.
- Work through each of the words in sequence.

Spelling
- The children return to their seats.
- Start by selecting the Words tab. Click Say to hear the word and ask the children to repeat it, then ask the children to use pencil and paper or their magnetic letters to make the word, saying the word every time they write down or look for a letter. Ask a child to come up to the Work area to make the word. Did everyone get it right?
- Ask a child to use the arrow to push the letters together. Encourage the class to blend the word together out loud.
- Repeat for the remaining word under the Words tab.
- Under the Pictures tab, click Show to display each image and repeat the process for each one. (See pages 8–9 and 12–13.)

Writing
- Ask the children to find the letter 's' among their magnetic letters and to feel the shape of it. Click Show and ask the children to look and listen as the lowercase letter is formed.
- Ask a child to direct you how to write the letter as you write it on the empty Work area.
- Ask the child to write it on the dashed lines, then ask the children to practise writing the letter 's' themselves.
- Select uppercase and repeat.

Follow-up
- Click Say to hear the sentence. Repeat the sentence, then dictate it slowly and deliberately for the children to write it. Then click Show to reveal the correct answer. (See page 13.)

WRAP-UP
- Recap the learning intentions with the children.
- Play the alphabet song and encourage the children to sing along, signifying the end of the session.

Learning intentions are to:
- recap what we know
- say the /s/ phoneme
- learn how to use the suffix '-s'
- read and spell words of one syllable or more
- write a dictated sentence

Focus content: revision

Letters and Sounds
ing, ed
Reading
chased, dancing, skating, hoped
Writing and Spelling
joked, shared, pasting, saving

Focus content: lesson

Sounds
/s/
Visual search
trains, forks, crumbs, dolphins
Reading
Audio: dogs, stars, chimes, stables
No audio: stones, sweets, apples, circles
Spelling
Words tab: clowns, jigsaws
Pictures tab: oars, rockets
Writing
s
Follow-up
Dictation
At the circus, clowns and dogs were doing tricks.

Next steps
- Play the online pupil games for Unit 28
- Complete the phoneme PCM for Unit 29 ('-s')

Unit 29

Suffix ending: '-es' after 'ss', 'x'

INTRODUCTION
- Play the alphabet song twice, once with voice accompaniment, children listening and singing along with accompaniment, and once with children singing along to the music without voice accompaniment.
- Discuss with the children the learning intentions for the day.

REVISION
[previously taught suffixes; blending phonemes for reading; segmenting spoken words for spelling]
- Go through the Revision screens at a brisk pace.
- Watch out for any children who have not remembered the phonemes or the graphemes.

LESSON

Sounds
- Choose the relevant lesson session.
- Say the suffix -es, and ask the children to repeat it after you. It is important that children learn to recognise morphemes as units and say them without blending.
- If you want to use the term "morpheme", refer to page 13.
- Explain that when 'es' is added to words as a plural suffix, it makes another syllable, as in "dress/dresses", "fox/foxes". We use 'es' after 's' and 'zz' as in 'bus/buses', "gas/gases", "buzz/buzzes".

Visual Search
- Bring up the words from the asset bank onto the Work area. Ask the children to highlight the 'es' in each of the words. Do not pronounce the words.

Reading
- Click the Reading tab to see the word and syllables.
- Click Blend to watch and hear the Bug's demonstration of how to blend the syllables and the word. Click Undo and ask a child to come to the Work area and move the arrow. Encourage the whole class to blend the phonemes of the syllables and then the sounds of the word out loud as the arrow is moving along.
- Work through each of the words in sequence.

Spelling
- The children return to their seats.
- Start by selecting the Words tab. Click Say to hear the word and ask the children to repeat it, then ask the children to use pencil and paper or their magnetic letters to make the word, saying the word every time they write down or look for a letter. Ask a child to come up to the Work area to make the word. Did everyone get it right?
- Ask a child to use the arrow to push the letters together. Encourage the class to blend the word together out loud.
- Repeat for the remaining word under the Words tab.
- Under the Pictures tab, click Show to display each image and repeat the process for each one. (See pages 8–9 and 12–13.)

Writing
- Ask the children to find the letters 'e' and 's' among their magnetic letters and to feel the shape of them. Click Show and ask the children to look and listen as the lowercase letters are formed.
- Ask a child to direct you how to write the letters as you write them on the empty Work area.
- Ask the child to write them on the dashed lines, then ask the children to practise writing 'es' themselves.
- Select uppercase and repeat.

Follow-up
- Click Say to hear the sentence. Repeat the sentence, then dictate it slowly and deliberately for the children to write it. Then click Show to reveal the correct answer. (See page 13.)

WRAP-UP
- Recap the learning intentions with the children.
- Play the alphabet song and encourage the children to sing along, signifying the end of the session.

Learning intentions are to:
- recap what we know
- say the suffix -es
- learn how to use the plural suffix '-es'
- read and spell words of one syllable or more
- write a dictated sentence

Focus content: revision

Letters and Sounds
s

Reading
rockets, clowns, oars, jigsaws

Writing and Spelling
dogs, stars, chimes, stables

Focus content: lesson

Sounds
Suffix -es

Visual search
passes, kisses, foxes, sixes

Reading
Audio: masses, losses, boxes, foxes
No audio: bosses, grasses, dresses, hoaxes

Spelling
Words tab: classes, sixes
Pictures tab: glasses, boxes

Writing
es

Follow-up
Dictation
I counted all the glasses in the boxes.

Next steps
- Play the online pupil games for Unit 28
- Complete the phoneme PCM for Unit 29 (suffix plural '-es' after 'ss' and 'x')

Unit 29

Suffix ending: '-es' after 'ch', 'sh', 'tch'

INTRODUCTION
- Play the alphabet song twice, once with voice accompaniment, children listening and singing along with accompaniment, and once with children singing along to the music without voice accompaniment.
- Discuss with the children the learning intentions for the day.

REVISION
[previously taught suffixes; blending phonemes for reading; segmenting spoken words for spelling]
- Go through the Revision screens at a brisk pace.
- Watch out for any children who have not remembered the phonemes or the graphemes.

LESSON

Sounds
- Choose the relevant lesson session.
- Say the suffix -es and ask the children to repeat it after you. It is important that children learn to recognise morphemes as units and say them without blending.
- (i) If you want to use the term "morpheme", refer to page 13.
- Explain that we use 'es' after 'ch', 'sh' and 'tch', as in "church/churches", "dish/dishes", "ditch/ditches".

Visual Search
- Bring up the words from the asset bank onto the Work area. Ask the children to highlight the 'es' in each of the words. Do not pronounce the words.

Reading
- Click the Reading tab to see the word and syllables.
- Click Blend to watch and hear the Bug's demonstration of how to blend the syllables and the word. Click Undo and ask a child to come to the Work area and move the arrow. Encourage the whole class to blend the phonemes of the syllables and then the sounds of the word out loud as the arrow is moving along.
- Work through each of the words in sequence.

Spelling
- The children return to their seats.
- Start by selecting the Words tab. Click Say to hear the word and ask the children to repeat it, then ask the children to use pencil and paper or their magnetic letters to make the word, saying the word every time they write down or look for a letter. Ask a child to come up to the Work area to make the word. Did everyone get it right?
- Ask a child to use the arrow to push the letters together. Encourage the class to blend the word together out loud.
- Repeat for the remaining word under the Words tab.
- Under the Pictures tab, click Show to display each image and repeat the process for each one.
- Explain that words ending in 'f' or 'fe' usually change the 'f' to 'v' then add 'es' to make the words plural, as in "knife/knives", "loaf/loaves", "shelf/shelves". (See pages 8–9 and 12–13.)

Writing
- Ask the children to find the letters 'e' and 's' among their magnetic letters and to feel the shape of them. Click Show and ask the children to look and listen as the lowercase letters are formed.
- Ask a child to direct you how to write the letters as you write them on the empty Work area.
- Ask the child to write them on the dashed lines, then ask the children to practise writing the letters 'es' themselves.
- Select uppercase and repeat.

Follow-up
- Click Say to hear the sentence. Repeat the sentence, then dictate it slowly and deliberately for the children to write it. Then click Show to reveal the correct answer. (See page 13.)

WRAP-UP
- Recap the learning intentions with the children.
- Play the alphabet song and encourage the children to sing along, signifying the end of the session.

Learning intentions are to:
- recap what we know
- learn how to use the suffix '-es' after 'ch', 'sh' and 'tch'
- read and spell words of one syllable or more
- write a dictated sentence

Focus content: revision

Letters and Sounds
es
Reading
dresses, classes, glasses, crosses
Writing and Spelling
masses, tosses, bosses, grasses

Focus content: lesson

Sounds
Suffix -es

Visual search

churches, branches, dishes, stitches

Reading
Audio: bunches, wishes, arches, ditches
No audio: brushes, splashes, lunches, watches
Spelling
Words tab: crashes, hutches
Pictures tab: arches, brushes
Writing
es
Follow-up
Dictation
She packed two brushes, a toothbrush and a hair brush.

Next steps
- Play the online pupil games for Unit 28
- Complete the phoneme PCM for Unit 29 (Suffix plural '-es' after 'ch', 'sh' and 'tch')

Unit 29

Language session

After: suffix endings '-s' and '-es'

INTRODUCTION
- Play the alphabet song twice, once with voice accompaniment, children listening and singing along with accompaniment, and once with children singing along to the music without voice accompaniment.
- Discuss with the children the learning intentions for the day.

HIGH-FREQUENCY/IRREGULAR WORDS

Reading
- Select the H-F words part of the session.
- Click Show to display the words, and ask the children to read them.
- Click Answer to listen to the word being read.

Spelling
- Check that the children know the meaning of "plural" (more than one).
- Click Say to hear the words, and ask the children to repeat each word.
- Explain to the children that the second word each time is a plural.
- Say the target word, and ask the children to repeat it again. Ask the class to give each letter, and ask a child to come up to the Work area and drag up the correct letters into the spaces provided.
- Ask the class to read the word and click Say for them to hear it again.
- Repeat for the remaining words.

LESSON

Reading
- Click Show to display the sentences, and ask the children to read them.
- Click Answer to reveal whether they are right.

Spelling and Writing
- The children return to their seats.
- Remind the children about the dictation procedure.
- Click Say to hear the first sentence, and ask the children to repeat it.
- Slowly and distinctly dictate the sentence, asking the children to tell you how to write the words.
- Click Answer to reveal the sentence. Did the children tell you how to write it correctly?
- Repeat for the second sentence, asking the children to write it using pencil and paper or their magnetic letters. (See page 13.)

Follow-up
- "The farmer's wife was collecting eggs". Explain to children that "collecting" is a three-syllable word.
- Say the word "collecting".
- Break the word into syllables, pronouncing each syllable: col/lect/ing.
- ⓘ For guidance with breaking words into syllables, see "Syllable categories" on page 12.
- Segment and spell the successive letters of each syllable: c-o-l, col, l-e-c-t, lect, i-n-g, ing.
- Sound and blend the successive syllables to say the word: col/lect/ing, collecting.
- Spell the word orally using the letter names 'c', 'o', 'l', 'l', 'e', 'c', 't', 'i', 'n', 'g', and say the word "collecting".
- Repeat for other three-syllable words, for example from the Phonics Bug books.
- ⓘ See pages 11 to 13 for more information about reading and spelling words of more than one syllable.

WRAP-UP
- Recap the learning intentions with the children.
- Play the alphabet song again and encourage the children to sing along, signifying the end of the session.

Learning intentions are to:
- learn to read and spell high-frequency/irregular plural words
- learn to read and spell words with plural suffix endings 's' and 'es'
- write sentences from dictation which include two- and three-syllable words and suffix endings 's' and 'es'.

Focus content: h-f words

Reading
man/men, mouse/mice, foot/feet, tooth/teeth, sheep/sheep

Spelling
man/men, mouse/mice, foot/feet, tooth/teeth, sheep/sheep

Focus content: lesson

Reading
At the farm shop, we bought apples, carrots and radishes. At the farm we saw cows, sheep, lambs and goats.

Spelling and Writing
The ducks were splashing in the puddles. The farmer's wife was collecting eggs.

Follow-up
Focus on spelling three-syllable words.

Next steps
- Play the online language pupil games for Unit 29
- Complete the language PCM for Unit 29

Unit 30

Prefix 're-'

INTRODUCTION
- Play the alphabet song twice, once with voice accompaniment, children listening and singing along with accompaniment, and once with children singing along to the music without voice accompaniment.
- Discuss with the children the learning intentions for the day.

REVISION
(previously taught grapheme–phoneme correspondences; blending phonemes for reading; segmenting spoken words for spelling)
- Go through the Revision screens at a brisk pace.
- Watch out for any children who have not remembered the phonemes or the graphemes.

LESSON

Sounds
- Choose the relevant lesson session.
- Say the prefix re-, and ask the children to repeat it after you. It is important that children learn to recognise morphemes as units and say them without blending.
- ⓘ If you want to use the term "morpheme", refer to page 13.
- Explain that the prefix 're' can mean "again" or "back" – e.g. "replay" – to play again; "return" – to turn back.

Visual Search
- Bring up the words from the asset bank onto the Work area. Ask the children to highlight the 're' in each of the words. Do not pronounce the words.

Reading
- Click the Reading tab to see the word and syllables.
- Click Blend to watch and hear the Bug's demonstration of how to blend the syllables and the word. Click Undo and ask a child to come to the Work area and move the arrow. Encourage the whole class to blend the phonemes of the syllables and then the sounds of the word out loud as the arrow is moving along.
- Work through each of the words in sequence.

Spelling
- The children return to their seats.
- Start by selecting the Words tab. Click Say to hear the word and ask the children to repeat it, then ask the children to use pencil and paper or their magnetic letters to make the word, saying the word every time they write down or look for a letter. Ask a child to come up to the Work area to make the word. Did everyone get it right?
- Ask a child to use the arrow to push the letters together. Encourage the class to blend the word together out loud.
- Repeat for the remaining word under the Words tab.
- Under the Pictures tab, click Show to display each image and repeat the process for each one. (See pages 8–9 and 12–13.)

Writing
- Ask the children to find the letters 'r' and 'e' among their magnetic letters and to feel the shape of them. Click Show and ask the children to look and listen as the lowercase letters are formed.
- Ask a child to direct you how to write the letters as you write them on the empty Work area.
- Ask the child to write them on the dashed lines, then ask the children to practise writing 're' themselves.
- Select uppercase and repeat.

Follow-up
- Use the arrows to select the sentence. Click Say to hear the sentence. Repeat the sentence, then dictate it slowly and deliberately for the children to write it. Then click Show to reveal the correct answer. (See page 13.)

WRAP-UP
- Recap the learning intentions with the children.
- Play the alphabet song and encourage the children to sing along, signifying the end of the session.

Learning intentions are to:
- recap what we know
- say the prefix re-
- learn how to use the prefix 're-'
- read and spell words of one syllable or more
- write a dictated sentence

Focus content: revision

Letters and Sounds
ee, ea

Reading
peacock, seesaw, teapot

Writing and Spelling
teapot, seaweed

Focus content: lesson

Sounds
prefix re-

Visual search

reform, return, refill, reuse

Reading
Audio: rejoin, reset, replace, retry
No audio: replay, renew, recall, return

Spelling
Words tab: refresh, restart
Pictures tab: refuel, relight

Writing
re

Follow-up
Dictation
To replay the film, please reset the DVD player.

Next steps
- Play the online pupil games for Unit 29
- Complete the phoneme PCM for Unit 30 (Prefix 're-')

Unit 30

Prefix 'un-'

INTRODUCTION
- Play the alphabet song twice, once with voice accompaniment, children listening and singing along with accompaniment, and once with children singing along to the music without voice accompaniment.
- Discuss with the children the learning intentions for the day.

REVISION
[previously taught prefixes; blending phonemes for reading; segmenting spoken words for spelling]
- Go through the Revision screens at a brisk pace.
- Watch out for any children who have not remembered the phonemes or the graphemes.

LESSON

Sounds
- Choose the relevant lesson session.
- Say the prefix un-, and ask the children to repeat it after you. It is important that children learn to recognise morphemes as units and say them without blending.
- ⓘ If you want to use the term "morpheme", refer to page 13.
- The prefix 'un-' denotes a negative action. It can mean "not", e.g. "unlucky" – not lucky.

Visual Search
- Bring up the words from the asset bank onto the Work area. Ask the children to highlight the 'un-' in each of the words. Do not pronounce the words.

Reading
- Click the Reading tab to see the word and syllables.
- Click Blend to watch and hear the Bug's demonstration of how to blend the syllables and the word. Click Undo and ask a child to come to the Work area and move the arrow. Encourage the whole class to blend the phonemes of the syllables and then the sounds of the word out loud as the arrow is moving along.
- Work through each of the words in sequence.

Spelling
- The children return to their seats.
- Start by selecting the Words tab. Click Say to hear the word and ask the children to repeat it, then ask the children to use pencil and paper or their magnetic letters to make the word, saying the word every time they write down or look for a letter. Ask a child to come up to the Work area to make the word. Did everyone get it right?
- Ask a child to use the arrow to push the letters together. Encourage the class to blend the word together out loud.
- Repeat for the remaining word under the Words tab.
- Under the Pictures tab, click Show to display each image and repeat the process for each one. (See pages 8–9 and 12–13.)

Writing
- Ask the children to find the letters 'u' and 'n' among their magnetic letters and to feel the shape of them. Click Show and ask children to look and listen as the lowercase letters are formed.
- Ask a child to direct you how to write the letters as you write them on the empty Work area.
- Ask the child to write them on the dashed lines, then ask the children to practise writing 'un' themselves.
- Select uppercase and repeat.

Follow-up
- Click Say to hear the sentence. Repeat the sentence, then dictate it slowly and deliberately for the children to write it. Then click Show to reveal the correct answer. (See page 13.)

WRAP-UP
- Recap the learning intentions with the children.
- Play the alphabet song and encourage the children to sing along, signifying the end of the session.

Learning intentions are to:
- recap what we know
- say the prefix un-
- learn how to use the prefix 'un-'
- read and spell words of one syllable or more
- write a dictated sentence

Focus content: revision

Letters and Sounds
re-

Reading
reset, refresh, restart, return

Writing and Spelling
rejoin, reset, retry, replay

Focus content: lesson

Sounds
prefix un-

Visual search
unlock, unkind, unwell, unpack

Reading
Audio: unfair, uneven, unhappy, unlucky
No audio: unwell, unsafe, unclean, undress

Spelling
Words tab: unfit, unpack
Pictures tab: uncover, unload

Writing
un

Follow-up
Dictation
Dad went to unload the car and unpack the cases.

Next steps
- Play the online pupil games for Unit 29
- Complete the phoneme PCM for Unit 30 (prefix 'un-')

Unit 30

Prefix, root, suffix

INTRODUCTION
- Play the alphabet song twice, once with voice accompaniment, children listening and singing along with accompaniment, and once with children singing along to the music without voice accompaniment.
- Discuss with the children the learning intentions for the day.

REVISION
[previously taught prefixes; blending phonemes for reading; segmenting spoken words for spelling]
- Go through the Revision screens at a brisk pace.
- Watch out for any children who have not remembered the phonemes or the graphemes.

LESSON

Sounds
- Choose the relevant lesson session.
- Say the blended phonemes /r/ /ee/ and ask children to repeat them after you. It is important that children learn to recognise morphemes as units and say them without blending.
- Repeat for /u/ /n/, /i/ /ng/, /e/ /d/, /d/, /t/, /s/.
- Explain that a "suffix" is added after the root word, and a "prefix" is added before the root word, and counts as another syllable.

Visual Search
- Bring up the words from the asset bank onto the Work area. Ask children to highlight the prefix and suffix in each of the words, saying what the root word is. Do not pronounce the words.

Reading
- Click the Reading tab to see the word and syllables.
- Click Blend to watch and hear the Bug's demonstration of how to blend the syllables and the word. Click Undo and ask a child to come to the Work area and move the arrow. Encourage the whole class to blend the phonemes of the syllables and then the sounds of the word out loud as the arrow is moving along.
- Work through each of the words in sequence.

Spelling
- The children return to their seats.
- Start by selecting the Words tab. Click Say to hear the word and ask the children to repeat it, then ask the children to use pencil and paper or their magnetic letters to make the word, saying the word every time they write down or look for a letter. Ask a child to come up to the Work area to make the word. Did everyone get it right?
- Ask a child to use the arrow to push the letters together. Encourage the class to blend the word together out loud.
- Repeat for the remaining word under the Words tab.
- Under the Pictures tab, click Show to display each image and repeat the process for each one. (See pages 8–9 and 12–13.)

Writing
- Ask the children to find the letters 'r' and 'e' among their magnetic letters and to feel the shape of them. Click Show and ask the children to look and listen as the lowercase letters are formed.
- Ask a child to direct you how to write the letters as you write them on the empty Work area.
- Ask the child to write them on the dashed lines themselves, then ask the children to practise writing 're' themselves.
- Select uppercase and repeat.
- Repeat for 'un', 'ing', 'ed', 's'.

Follow-up
- Use the arrows to select the sentence. Click Say to hear the sentence. Repeat the sentence, then dictate it slowly and deliberately for the children to write it. Then click Show to reveal the correct answer. (See page 13.)

WRAP-UP
- Recap the learning intentions with the children.
- Play the alphabet song and encourage the children to sing along, signifying the end of the session.

Learning intentions are to:
- recap what we know
- learn about prefix, root and suffix
- read and spell words of more than one syllable
- write a dictated sentence

Focus content: revision

Letters and Sounds
un

Reading
unfit, unpack, uncover, unload

Writing and Spelling
unfair, uneven, unhappy, unlucky

Focus content: lesson

Sounds
/r/ /ee/, /u/ /n/, /i/ /ng/, /e/ /d/, /d/, /t/, /s/

Visual search

reformed, unpacks, uncovered, refreshing

Reading
Audio: unloads, replayed, unfolds, retrying
No audio: recalled, unplugs, reusing, renewed

Spelling
Words tab: unrolled, unbolts
Pictures tab: reloading, refilling

Writing
re, un, ing, ed, s

Follow-up
Dictation
I recalled unbolting the door.

Next steps
- Play the online pupil games for Unit 29
- Complete the phoneme PCM for Unit 30 (prefix, root, suffix)

Unit 30

Language session

After: prefix 're-', 'un-', prefix, root, suffix

INTRODUCTION
- Play the alphabet song twice, once with voice accompaniment, children listening and singing along with accompaniment, and once with children singing along to the music without voice accompaniment.
- Discuss with the children the learning intentions for the day.

HIGH-FREQUENCY WORDS

Reading
- Select the H-F words part of the session.
- Click Show to display the words, and ask the children to read them.
- Click Answer to listen to the word being read.

Spelling
- Click Say to hear the words, and ask the children to repeat each word.
- Say the target word, and ask the children to repeat it again. Ask the class to give each letter, and ask a child to come up to the Work area and drag up the correct letters into the spaces provided.
- Ask the class to read the word and click Say for them to hear it again.
- Repeat for the remaining words.

LESSON

Reading
- Click Show to display the sentences, and ask the children to read them.
- Click Answer to reveal whether they are right.

Spelling and Writing
- The children return to their seats.
- Remind the children about the dictation procedure.
- Click Say to hear the first sentence, and ask the children to repeat it.
- Slowly and distinctly dictate the sentence, asking the children to tell you how to write the words.
- Click Answer to reveal the sentence. Did the children tell you how to write it correctly?
- Repeat for the second sentence, asking the children to write it using pencil and paper or their magnetic letters. (See page 12.)

Follow-up
- Explain to children that "syllable" is a three-syllable word.
- Say the word "syllable".
- Break the word into syllables, pronouncing each syllable: syl/la/ble.
- ⓘ For guidance with breaking words into syllables, see "Syllable categories" on page 12.
- Segment and spell the successive letters of each syllable: s-y-l, syl, l-a, la, b-l-e, ble (pronounced /bul/, see Unit 26).
- Sound and blend the successive syllables to say the word: syl/la/ble, syllable.
- Spell the word orally using the letter names 's', 'y', 'l', 'l', 'a', 'b', 'l', 'e', and say the word "syllable".
- Repeat for the word "alphabet".
- ⓘ See pages 11 to 13 for more information about reading and spelling words of more than one syllable.

WRAP-UP
- Recap the learning intentions with the children.
- Play the alphabet song again and encourage the children to sing along, signifying the end of the session.

Learning intentions are to:
- learn to read and spell words of two and three syllables
- write sentences from dictation which include two- and three-syllable words

Focus content: h-f words

Reading
vowel, consonant, prefix, suffix, syllable

Spelling
vowel, consonant, prefix, suffix, syllable

Focus content: lesson

Reading
Vowels are the letters 'a', 'e', 'i', 'o', 'u' and sometimes 'y'. Vowels can be short or long. Consonants are all the letters of the alphabet except 'a', 'e', 'i', 'o', and 'u'.

Spelling and Writing
A prefix is put in front of a root word as in reuse. A suffix is put after a root word as in playing.

Follow-up
Focus on spelling three-syllable words.

Next steps
- Play the online language pupil games for Unit 30
- Complete the language PCM for Unit 30

a	b	c	d	e	f	g	h	i
j	k	l	m	n	o	p	q	r
s	t	u	v	w	x	y	z	

About the Authors

Dr. Joyce Watson An Early Years teacher for a number of years, she was a lecturer in the Northern College of Education, Dundee, for over 20 years (in Primary Development and Early Education, and in the Psychology Department). She was also a postdoctoral fellow, and an Honorary Research Fellow, in the School of Psychology at the University of St. Andrews for over 10 years. Dr. Watson holds the PGCE Open University Diploma in Reading Development, an M.Ed from the University of Dundee (on reading comprehension), and a Ph.D in Psychology from the University of St. Andrews (on the effects of phonics teaching on children's progress in reading and spelling).

Professor Rhona Johnston A Learning Support teacher for two years, she was in the School of Psychology at the University of St Andrews for 20 years. She was a Reader in the School of Psychology at the University of Birmingham and is now a Professor in the Department of Psychology at the University of Hull. Professor Johnston has researched extensively in the areas of reading disorders and reading development. She received an MBE for services to education in the 2012 New Year Honours list.

The authors have together investigated the teaching of reading with beginning readers for the past 18 years. These studies have been reported in Johnston, R.S. and Watson, J. (2004), 'Accelerating the development of reading, spelling and phonemic awareness', Reading and Writing, 17 (4), 327-357; Johnston, R.S. and Watson, J.E. (2006), 'The effectiveness of synthetic phonics teaching in developing reading and spelling skills in English speaking boys and girls', in Joshi, R.M., and Aaron, P.G. (Eds), *Handbook of Orthography and Literacy*, LEA: London; Johnston, R.S., Watson, J.E., and Logan, S. (2009), 'Enhancing word reading, spelling and reading comprehension skills with synthetic phonics teaching: studies in Scotland and England', in Wood, C. and Connelly, V., *Contemporary Perspectives on Reading and Spelling*, Routledge, London.

There are also a number of reports for the Scottish government: 'Accelerating reading attainment: the effectiveness of synthetic phonics', *Interchange 57* (SOEID, 1998), 'Accelerating reading and spelling with synthetic phonics: A five year follow up', *Insight 4* (SEED, 2003), 'A seven year study of the effects of synthetic phonics teaching on reading and spelling attainment', *Insight 17* (SEED, 2005) and 'The effects of synthetic phonics teaching on reading and spelling attainment: a seven year longitudinal study' (The Scottish Executive Central Research Unit, 2005), available at <http://www.scotland.gov.uk/library5/education/sptrs-00.asp>.